Reading
Alice
Munro

Reading Alice Munro
1973-2013

ROBERT THACKER

© 2016 Robert Thacker

University of Calgary Press
2500 University Drive NW
Calgary, Alberta
Canada T2N 1N4
www.uofcpress.com

This book is available as an ebook which is licensed under a Creative Commons license. The publisher should be contacted for any commercial use which falls outside the terms of that license.

LIBRARY AND ARCHIVES CANADA CATALOGUING IN PUBLICATION

Thacker, Robert, author
    Reading Alice Munro : 1973-2013 / Robert Thacker.

Includes bibliographical references and index.
Issued in print and electronic formats.
ISBN 978-1-55238-839-6 (paperback).–ISBN 978-1-55238-842-6 (epub).–
ISBN 978-1-55238-843-3 (mobi).–ISBN 978-1-55238-840-2 (open access pdf).–
ISBN 978-1-55238-841-9 (pdf).

    1. Munro, Alice, 1931- –Criticism and interpretation. I. Title.

PS8576.U57Z8857 2016   C813'.54   C2015-907919-5

                                                                                                     C2015-907920-9

The University of Calgary Press acknowledges the support of the Government of Alberta through the Alberta Media Fund for our publications. We acknowledge the financial support of the Government of Canada through the Canada Book Fund for our publishing activities. We acknowledge the financial support of the Canada Council for the Arts for our publishing program.

Editing by Correy Baldwin
Cover design, page design, and typesetting by Melina Cusano

Once Again for Debbie

Contents

Acknowledgments ix

Introduction: Alice Munro's "Approach and Recognition" 1

Part One: Narrative Techniques, Forms, and Critical Issues: 21
Establishing a Presence

    Clear Jelly: Alice Munro's Narrative Dialectics (1983) 23

    Connection: Alice Munro and Ontario (1984) 45

Critical Interlude: Conferring Munro (1987) 65

    Munro's Progress: A Review of *The Progress of Love* (1987) ... 73

    "So Shocking a Verdict in Real Life": Autobiography in 79
    Alice Munro's Stories" (1988)

Critical Interlude: Go Ask Alice: The Progress of Munro Criticism ... 89
(1991)

Part Two: *What the Archives Reveal: Reading a Deepening Aesthetic* 111
    Alice Munro's Willa Cather (1992) 115
    Alice Munro and the Anxiety of American Influence (1994) 133
    Alice Munro, Writing "Home": "Seeing This Trickle in Time" (1998) 145
Critical Interlude: What's "Material"?: The Progress of Munro Criticism, Part 2 (1998) 167
    Mapping Munro: Reading the "Clues" (1999) 189

Part Three: Understanding the Oeuvre 197
    Alice Munro's Ontario (2007) 201
    A "Booming Tender Sadness": Alice Munro's Irish (2008) 217
    No Problem Here: A Review of *Too Much Happiness* (2009) 227
    "The Way the Skin of the Moment Can Break Open": Reading Alice Munro's "White Dump" (2010) 231
Critical Interlude: Alice Munro: Critical Reception (2013) 243
Afterword: "A Wonderful Stroke of Good Fortune for Me": Reading Alice Munro, 1973–2013 261

Notes 271
Works Cited 285
Index 301

Acknowledgments

"Clear Jelly: Alice Munro's Narrative Dialectics" first appeared in *Probable Fictions: Alice Munro's Narrative Acts*. Ed. Louis K. McKendrick. Downsview: ECW Press, 1983. 37–60. Republished with permission.

"Connection: Alice Munro and Ontario" first appeared in *The American Review of Canadian Studies* 14 (1984): 213–26. Copyright the American Association for Canadian Studies (ACSUS), reprinted with permission of Taylor & Francis Ltd., www.tandfonline.com, on behalf of ACSUS.

"Conferring Munro" first appeared in *Essays on Canadian Writing* 34 (1987): 162–69. Republished with permission.

"Munro's Progress" first appeared in *Canadian Literature* 115 (1987): 239–42.

"So Shocking a Verdict in Real Life" Autobiography in Alice Munro's Stories" first appeared in *Reflections: Autobiography and Canadian Literature*. Ed. K. P. Stich. Ottawa: U of Ottawa P, 1988. 153–61.

"Go Ask Alice: The Progress of Munro Criticism" first appeared in the *Journal of Canadian Studies* 26 (Summer 1991): 156–69. Republished with permission.

"Alice Munro's Willa Cather" first appeared in *Canadian Literature* 134 (1992): 42–57.

"Alice Munro and the Anxiety of American Influence" first appeared in *Context North America: Canadian / U.S. Literary Relations*. Ed. Camille La Bossière. Ottawa: University of Ottawa Press, 1994. 133–44.

"Alice Munro, Writing 'Home': "Seeing This Trickle in Time" first appeared in *Essays on Canadian Writing* 66 (Winter 1998): 1–20. Republished with permission.

"What's 'Material'?: The Progress of Munro Criticism, Part 2" *Journal of Canadian Studies* 33 (Summer 1998): 196–210. Republished with permission.

"Mapping Munro: Reading the 'Clues'" first appeared in *Dominant Impressions: Essays on the Canadian Short Story*. Ed. Gerald Lynch. Ottawa: U Ottawa P, 1999. 127–35. Republished with permission.

"Alice Munro's Ontario" first appeared *Tropes and Territories: Short Fiction, Postcolonial Readings, Canadian Writing in Context*. Ed. Marta Dvorák and W. H. New. Montreal and Kingston: McGill-Queen's UP, 2007. 103–118.

"A 'Booming Tender Sadness': Alice Munro's Irish" first appeared in *Canada: Text and Territory*. Ed. Máire Áine Ní Mhainnín and Elizabeth Tilley. Cambridge: Cambridge Scholars Publishing, 2008. 132–40. Republished with the permission of Cambridge Scholars Publishing.

"No Problem Here" first appeared in the *Literary Review of Canada* 17.7 (September 2009): 19. Republished with the permission of the *Literary Review of Canada*.

"The Way the Skin of the Moment Can Break Open": Reading Alice Munro's "White Dump" first appeared in *Canadian Notes & Queries* 79 (Spring/Summer 2010): 24–29. Republished with permission.

"Alice Munro: Critical Reception" first appeared in *Critical Insights: Alice Munro*. Ed. Charles E. May. Ipswich, MA: Salem Press/EBSCO, 2013. 29–51. Republished with permission of EBSCO Information Services, Ipswich, MA.

Introduction:

Alice Munro's "Approach and Recognition"

This book is an exercise in literary, professional, and personal history. Sometime in the fall or winter of 1973/74, when I was 22 years old and a recent university graduate planning to marry and trying to figure out just what I would try to do in this life, having pretty much decided on graduate school in Canada, I received my first issue of a subscription to the *Tamarack Review*: number 61 (November 1973). It opened with a new story, "Material," by someone unknown to me, a writer named Alice Munro. Seeing that magazine as my first independent foray into Canadian writing, I read the story, was struck hard by it, and found myself hooked: if this was Canadian literature, I thought, then sign me up.

And so I signed up. I moved north from my native Ohio during the summer of 1974 to begin graduate work at the University of Waterloo—my new wife and I entered Canada on that August day when Richard Nixon resigned the presidency, and we listened to his speech as we drove along the 401: we were embarking on a new direction in a new country. By then, "Material" had appeared again, this time as the second story in Munro's third book, *Something I've Been Meaning to Tell You* (1974), published that May by McGraw-Hill Ryerson. The brief biography on its dust jacket noted Munro's beginnings in Wingham, Ontario, her time in university, and her marriage, saying that afterwards she moved to Victoria,

British Columbia, "where she has lived until recently." She was then living in London, Ontario, and during that academic year was the writer-in-residence at the University of Western Ontario, where she had been a student herself. After over 20 years on the West Coast, Munro had come home.

Meanwhile, I began my studies at Waterloo, and although mostly I was doing what newly embarked graduate students did—reading, trying to keep up with my courses, figuring out what directions to go in—I had begun watching Munro and her career closely. I read and studied her first two books, and in my second term I served as teaching assistant in a course on Ontario writing; there I taught my first formal class, a lecture on *Dance of the Happy Shades* (1968), Munro's first book. At the same time, I was thinking about doing my MA thesis on the Ontario small town in fiction, with a consideration of Munro among other writers. As it turned out, I narrowed the focus of my writing, first to just Munro and then, shaping my material in terms of narrative technique, to just the uncollected stories from the 1950s and those in *Dance of the Happy Shades*. I took as my title an apt descriptive phrase from "Material": "A fine and lucky benevolence" (*Something* 43). While this was happening, Munro had finished her residency at Western and had reconnected with Gerald Fremlin, an old attraction from her undergraduate days. By August 1975 she had moved to Clinton, Ontario—back to Huron County, just south of Wingham—to live there with Fremlin. There Munro continued to write another 11 books, and in 2013 the unalloyed excellence of that writing won her the Nobel Prize in Literature—the first Canadian to be so honoured.

These contexts present a first rationale for *Reading Alice Munro, 1973–2013*. I discovered Munro and her writing at a propitious moment in my own career and, as it turned out, at such a moment in hers as well. Because of *Dance of the Happy Shades*—which won the Governor General's Award—and *Lives of Girls and Women* (1971)—which became a feminist *cri de coeur* and also won a major award—Munro's writing was, during the early 1970s, beginning to receive real academic attention. The first published articles date from those years, a time of both deep English-Canadian nationalism and a concurrent demand—both in the universities and in the culture more broadly—for greater attention to Canadian writers and their works. Read Canadian! was an imperative frequently heard, read, and repeated. Margaret Atwood's *Surfacing* and especially her *Survival*—both published in 1972, urtexts each—were indicative of the times. Along with many others, Munro's growing reputation was both noticed and celebrated, seen as further evidence of the emergence of Canadian literature as an academic specialty.

Concurrently, Munro's move back to Ontario in 1973 at the end of her marriage and her eventual return to Huron County in 1975—to her home place, putting her "in the midst of, so to speak, my material," as Munro once wrote (proof *Who* 229)—set the stage for her emergence as a powerful writer. That is, just as her work was beginning to receive significant attention as a part of Canadian literature, Munro, an established writer in her mid-40s, returned home and saw her material anew, with different eyes and a different understanding. In late 1973, too, she wrote a memoir story called "Home" (which she published in a collection of new writing the following year but withheld from including in a book of her own until 2006). Her material became more immediate, no longer recalled through time and memory from far away, off in British Columbia. Once settled in Clinton, Munro turned to the aesthetic struggles that defined, in part, her breakthrough collections *Who Do You Think You Are?* (1978) and *The Moons of Jupiter* (1982), the latter something of a legacy volume from the former. Here the structures of her stories became more complex. It was during this time, too, that Munro hired as her agent Virginia Barber, who successfully brought her stories to the attention of American commercial magazines; by far the most prominent of these—and longstanding in its relationship with Munro—was the *New Yorker*. When the Nobel Prize was announced, that magazine's editors republished her "The Bear Came Over the Mountain" (1999–2000) as a tribute to her accomplishment and for its own special recognition. It was Munro's 63rd appearance in the *New Yorker*.

Once I had submitted my thesis on Munro to the University of Waterloo in 1976, I headed west to begin doctoral studies at the University of Manitoba. Although my focus there was largely on other things, I kept working on Munro, and in 1979 offered "Alice Munro and the Critics: A Paradigm" as my third academic conference paper to the Association for Canadian Studies in the United States (ACSUS). It began with a stern exposé and denunciation of thematic criticism as applied to Munro. That approach was then holding sway in analyses of Canadian writing generally, most especially through the influence of Atwood's *Survival*; thematic articles on Munro's work had linked her to larger "Canadian" themes such as Northrop Frye's idea of the garrison mentality. Some of the early essays on Munro had approached her work through this idea. Asserting the inappropriateness of such analysis for Munro, I suggested rather that the strength of her stories lay in their narrative, in the techniques she used in writing them, and in their mimetic recreation of 1930s and 1940s Ontario, as they were remembered. The polemic portion of the essay—which my editor then called "your kamikaze attack"—was later dropped, and the balance of the essay became "Clear Jelly: Alice Munro's Narrative Dialectics" (1983), the first essay in the first critical book on Munro. It is also the first essay included here.

I followed "Clear Jelly" at regular intervals with other essays and reviews on Munro's fiction, an annotated bibliography in 1984, and a succession of pieces focused on Munro criticism, the most recent appearing in 2013. In 2000 my focus shifted to biography when Munro agreed to cooperate on a book about her literary life; *Alice Munro: Writing Her Lives* was published in 2005 and was revised as an updated paperback in 2011. Once that book was completed I returned to critical writing on Munro, taking up new subjects I had noticed along the way as I researched my book—such as Munro's Irish heritage and her story "White Dump" (1985), which concludes what I consider to be one of Munro's best collections, *The Progress of Love* (1986). Those two essays are included here. I plan to keep doing this, for as long as I can, while keeping an eye on the factual details of Munro's ongoing career.

The intention of *Reading Alice Munro, 1973–2013* is to use a selection of my essays—most of them, actually—to track a perpetually deepening fascination with Munro's writing and, because of that writing and its effects, with her life and the trajectory of her writing career. Although it is not intended as a monograph critical study of Munro's work—her work has long seemed beyond such treatment—my hope is that, when it is read sequentially within a single volume, along with the contextualizations I offer along the way, readers will be able to see and understand the gradual making of an entire, most remarkable career. To this end, the essays are arranged chronologically and, because of separate emphases, divided into three sections. Each of these sections, as well, derives from a single decade. The first deals with techniques, forms, and publishing contexts during the 1980s; the second, made up of pieces that were published during the 1990s, reflects my frequent use during that period of the Alice Munro fonds at the University of Calgary and takes up issues revealed by the archival materials found there, along with gauging the deepened complexities of her fiction. The third section, "Understanding the *Oeuvre*," is made up of essays published after *Alice Munro: Writing Her Lives*. These both derive from and straddle that biographical work: the first, "Alice Munro's Ontario," which extends analyses begun in the 1980s, was written before the biography but revised after it. The others were directly derived from that work: "A 'Booming Tender Sadness': Alice Munro's Irish" owes itself to my study in the Calgary archives of the contexts of Munro's television script, "1847: The Irish" (1978), and of its story version, "A Better Place Than Home" (1979). Similarly, the essay on "White Dump" owes itself to the better understanding I came to of that story's importance through reading its archival contexts.

Also included in that section is my short review of *Too Much Happiness*, one of six reviews I have included here. It, like the other short review, "Munro's Progress," a review of *The Progress of Love*, serves to define a particular moment in Munro's career. With that book, as I think the review makes clear, Munro reached a higher level of accomplishment than readers had seen previously, and with that review I tried to articulate what I then saw, and still see, as her increasing acuity during the 1980s—the results of her return to Huron County, where she lived "in the midst, so to speak, of [her] material." Similarly, the publication of *Too Much Happiness* in 2009 allowed for the same sort of analysis, with—ever innovative, this writer—some consideration of the unique qualities of that volume's title story; in some ways, it is unlike any other Munro story. That review also allowed me to take up, and to attempt to refute, some reviewers of *The View from Castle Rock* (2006) who had made almost no attempt to understand, let alone appreciate, the core significance of that book. This seemed an especially necessary action because, and this is clear, *The View from Castle Rock* will ultimately be seen as utterly crucial to any thorough understanding of Munro's *oeuvre*. Looking back now, Munro appears to have been heading toward *The View from Castle Rock* for much of her writing career.

In the same way, I have interleaved four review essays within the three sections—I have called them "critical interludes," and in various ways they establish the larger contexts the essays explore. Published at intervals—respectively in 1987, 1991, 1998, and 2013—these pieces offer a comprehensive overview of Munro's critical reception from the 1980s on. Read today they are certainly a bit cheeky, and also stern and insistent, but they seem also to still capture some of the energy of their times. Although I had initially thought to place these review essays in a section of their own, I ultimately decided that reading each review essay within the trajectories of the times, the one seen in relation to the other and to the other essays, made more sense. This contextualization also recreates moments in literary history, a feeling for the times—something that I am after. Finally, *Reading Alice Munro* concludes, as a postlude, with an afterword that considers *Dear Life* (2012), its "Finale," and the Nobel Prize as likely conclusions to Munro's career.

* * *

In a recent essay focused on the importance of A. E. Housman to Willa Cather, I drew on Munro and invoked her story "Wenlock Edge" (2005), most especially its differing endings—the ending in the *New Yorker* version versus the final one found in *Too Much Happiness* (Thacker "One"). When she first submitted the story to the *New Yorker* in July 2005, it ended with this statement from the narrator: "I discovered that Uricon was Wroxeter, a Roman camp on the Severn River" (Submitted 29). The reference is to Housman's "On Wenlock Edge the wood's in trouble" (poem 31) from *A Shropshire Lad* (1896), seen by scholars as among the best in that collection. Munro revised this sentence for the final version published in the *New Yorker*, and it came just after the narrator observes other students who were "on a course, as [she] was, of getting to know the ways of their own wickedness" (91). By the time "Wenlock Edge" appeared in *Too Much Happiness*, having been held out of *The View from Castle Rock*, Munro had dropped this particular reference to Uricon, although obviously the reference to the poem remains in the story's title, along with the larger presence of Housman through quotations of his poems. In my essay on Housman and Cather, too, I invoke W. H. Auden's elegiac poem, "A. E. Housman" (1939), which, after a caustic portrait of the other poet ("He timidly attacked the life he led"), concludes that "only geographical divisions / Parted the coarse hanged soldier from the don" (182). "I kept on learning things," Munro's narrator says in the *New Yorker* version, just before she tells us "that Uricon, the Roman camp, is now Wroxeter, a town on the Severn River" (91).

I mention these cruxes here for various reasons. The first is autobiographical. As a Munro scholar, I began focusing in the 1980s on her narratives and evocations of Ontario's Huron County as a fully imagined place. I also attended, more than most others, to the progress of both Munro's own publication and that of critics and reviewers on her work. Although the internet and searchable databases have made published bibliographies largely obsolete, during the 1980s and into the 1990s my annotated Munro bibliography was the place for students to start discovering her critical contexts. Early in the 1980s, too, Munro began donating her papers to the University of Calgary, an archive I first visited in January 1988. Quite literally, its contents transformed the ways I went about my Munro scholarship: they often reveal the exact extent of her activity as a writer, they provide biographical nuance wherever one looks, and they define a trajectory for her career.

My first visit to the Alice Munro fonds in Calgary coincided with the period when I was concluding revisions to my doctoral thesis and transforming it into a book, *The Great Prairie Fact and Literary Imagination* (New Mexico, 1989). While doing that work, I discovered my other writer, Willa Cather. Simply put, Cather was the first writer to really contend with the imaginative effects of the prairie-plains space on the Euro-American imagination, especially in her early prairie novels *O Pioneers!* (1913), *The Song of the Lark* (1915), and, most pointedly, *My Ántonia* (1918).

My initial discoveries in Calgary drew me into the archives, and not just Munro's. At the time the only way scholars could see Cather's autograph letters was to visit numerous archives all around the United States. Having conceived of a second book project, "Connection: A Woman's Place in the Writing of Emily Carr, Willa Cather, Margaret Laurence, and Alice Munro," one I envisioned as based in the archival materials of each author, I set about visiting archives and gathering materials. It was to be an analysis of each writer's relationship to her own particular "home place"—Wright Morris's phrase—an analysis grounded in feminist and place theory. Although I may yet complete the book (a sizable portion of a draft exists), I ultimately set it aside in order to research and write *Alice Munro: Writing Her Lives*. The effects of my growing familiarity with the Munro archive are evident in my published criticism. It is evident first in "'So Shocking a Verdict in Real Life': Autobiography in Alice Munro's Stories" (1988), but it is probably most evident in "Alice Munro's Willa Cather," which first appeared in *Canadian Literature* in 1992, and in the balance of the essays that followed. As both *Alice Munro: Writing Her Lives* and this book show, once I discovered archival research generally and the Alice Munro fonds at the University of Calgary in particular (I may be the only person who has read the entire Munro archive there), my scholarship was transformed—both in how I have read Munro and how I continue to read her work. And that reading has been continual, for as the years have passed and I have gone from Munro critic and bibliographer to biographer and critic, Munro and her works have loomed ever larger in my personal ken. Although I still do critical and historical work on the North American West, derived from the contexts I examined in *The Great Prairie Fact and Literary Imagination*, Munro and Cather have become the primary subjects of my career.

After the autobiographical crux, there are two others in need of addressing here: first, my decision to republish these essays without revision beyond formatting, mechanical correction, and some new copy-editing—that is, without updating or substantive revision. Second, there is the matter of my repetitions of quoted passages from her published stories and essays, and from some of her statements.

My thoughts regarding Auden on Housman have most to do with this, certainly, but Auden is relevant in another way: in 1945, Random House brought out its edition of *The Collected Poetry of W. H. Auden*. When preparing it, Auden's editor Edward Mendelson has written, "Auden gave many of his earlier poems ironic, distancing titles whose tone was (depending on your point of view) either tellingly or irritatingly at odds with the poems they headed." In subsequent editions Auden "replaced a few of the more flippant titles with neutral ones." (xxvi). Like Munro and

Cather, Auden is an artist of especial interest to me—a wonderful year-long seminar with Chester Duncan at the University of Manitoba during 1977 to 1978 ensured as much. I am certainly no Auden, but his retitling of his poems in the ways Mendelson describes has always struck me as an ill-advised, regrettable act. That is my point of view and, as such, I have no desire to now revise my younger self.

More especially, Munro's own poetics are rooted in her Huron County home place—as I often argued, a place she at first remembered across distance and time from British Columbia (1952–73) and then, once she returned in 1973, has both confronted and lived with (and within) since. Situations, incidents, names, and references echo within her stories. A favourite of mine is Munro's repetition of the name "Mr. Willens" from her "Story for Sunday" (1950), the second story she published in *Folio* while at the University of Western Ontario, in "The Love of a Good Woman" (1996). That university and its location, London, also echo throughout Munro's work, in *Who Do You Think You Are?* (1978), *The Beggar Maid* (1979), "Family Furnishings" (2001), "Wenlock Edge," and elsewhere. Most recently, with "Train" (2012), which begins with the character Jackson, who is returning home from the Second World War, jumping off his train before it reaches his station, Munro returns to the material in unpublished stories that she worked on called, variously, "The War Hero" or "The Boy Murderer"; many fragments in the Calgary archives begin with, for example, "Franklin got off the train at Goldenrod, where he didn't need to" (37.16.28). And of course there is the presence of Munro's mother in her stories from the late 1950s on, including in the "Finale" of *Dear Life* (2012).

My point here is twofold: by publishing the essays in much the same form they appeared originally, I am both leaving myself as I was as a critic when the essays were originally published and encouraging readers toward the critical specifics of that time—the 1980s, 1990s, 2000s, and 2010s. My critical interludes—the review essays devoted to Munro criticism—do this most explicitly, certainly, but my own essays are meant to do much the same thing. There is continuity, growth, and influence in this. Two examples: "Clear Jelly: Alice Munro's Narrative Dialectics" (1983), my first published essay on Munro, defined Munro's retrospective narrative; it has been frequently cited, was recently republished in a volume focused on *Dance of the Happy Shades* edited by a French scholar (Guignery), and is arguably the basis for Isla Duncan's narratological study of Munro, *Alice Munro's Narrative Art* (2011). A second example, which illustrates both the extension of my thinking and the effect that my discovery of the Munro archives had on my work, can be found in the two essays "Connection: Alice Munro and Ontario" (1984) and "Alice Munro's Ontario" (2007), both of which conclude with an analysis of the final scene in "Chaddeleys and Flemings: 1. Connection" (1978). In the earlier essay, I focused on Munro's evocation of the Ontario small town, using "The Peace of Utrecht" (1960) as my central text and offering an argument largely drawn from my University of Waterloo thesis. In "Alice Munro's Ontario"—written, as I have said, before *Alice Munro: Writing Her Lives* but revised after its publication—I examine the original unrevised versions of "Home" (1974) and "Working for a Living" (1981), seeing them as key texts that reveal Munro's palpable, deep connection to her Huron County home place, to her parents, and to her own personal and cultural history. What Munro achieves in the conclusion of "Chaddeleys and Flemings: 1. Connection" is not just the well-made fictional artifice of her early work but a deep and resonate verisimilitude rooted in her return to Huron County. Life *is* but a dream—a dream that is just as it often seems, and often feels—and throughout the late 1970s and into the 1980s Munro was compulsively articulating such feelings about her home place.

And then there is the relationship between Munro and Cather. I had not read Munro's "Dulse" (1980) when I first met her in New York City at one of the publicity events arranged by Alfred A. Knopf for the launch of the US edition of *The Moons of Jupiter* in March 1983 (at that stage of my life I was often aware of her newly published stories, but I allowed them to myself only sparingly). I had arranged to meet her in order to ask some questions connected to my annotated bibliography, which was then in the making, and was seated next to her at a luncheon. Ever polite, but even then not especially drawn to literary critics, she asked about my interests beyond her writing. Not knowing about "Dulse," I told her about my interest in and work on Cather and the prairie west, and we had a lively discussion about Cather. That same day at a friend's place I read "Dulse" and was stunned by its very existence—Munro, of course, had made no mention of it. That evening, at a reading, I told Munro of my discovery.

She said she thought I knew it when we met and talked earlier in the day. No, not at all.

This episode led, a few years later, to a conference paper called "Alice Munro's Willa Cather" (and occasioned my first real interview—on the telephone—with Munro). After several drafts and with increasing use of the archival holdings on "Dulse" at the University of Calgary, it was eventually published in 1992. Without question, part of my motivation for comparing the two writers has been my own interest in and knowledge of each writer, but there is more to it than that. As Munro shows throughout "Dulse," she has been a careful reader of Cather's fiction and of her as a person, too, certainly. But when she visited Grand Manan (around 1978 to 1979) she in effect researched the time Cather spent on the island. That is, she met the prototype for Mr. Stanley—the Cather fanatic in her story—someone whom Cather scholars had met there and been aware of. When I first visited Grand Manan in 1995 to prepare to lead an excursion of a Cather group to the island, I met someone who Munro had also met, and had plucked from those she met there to use in her story. That person had, as Munro writes in "Material," "passed into Art" (*Something* 43), and as it happened was not very happy about it: people read Munro's story and recognized the likeness.

Both Cather and Munro are what I would call organic writers—artists who work with images and memories that both resonate with authenticity and are mimetic in the fullest sense of the term. On reading them, readers stand back, rapt with the way the writing has made them feel, and think that this is how it feels to live, to be alive. Indeed, but in reading them we also feel Munro's drive toward wisdom and the power of affecting "Art"—a word Munro capitalizes in "Material" to emphasize its significance. As I compare the two of them, I am reminded that in our 1987 telephone interview, Munro mentioned that her favourite Cather story is "Old Mrs. Harris" (1932), which Cather wrote as an homage to her dying mother. For her part, Cather has Godfrey St. Peter, her historian protagonist in *The Professor's House* (1925) remark to a class, "'Art and religion (they are the same thing, in the end, of course) have given man the only happiness he has ever had'" (69). Wisdom. Art. Munro belongs in my essay on the influence of Housman on Cather because, just as she sees the same qualities in Cather and enumerates them in "Dulse," so too she senses similar qualities in Housman's *A Shropshire Lad* and invokes them in "Wenlock Edge." (Munro once told me that she could recite whole sections of the poems in *A Shropshire Lad* from memory. More than that, it is a delight to me that Mr. Stanley's favourite Cather novel in "Dulse" is her most perfect one: *A Lost Lady* [1923] [Interview, May 12, 2014; *Moons* 39].) In a review of a small, sharp book on Cather, Joan Acocella's *Willa Cather and the Politics of Criticism* (2000), A. S. Byatt—who has written some of the finest reviews of some of Munro's books—wrote that Munro is the only other writer she knows besides Cather who "has learned to depict whole lives from a distance in the same strangely unworked-up and unaccented way, while also making it entirely new, as her landscape and *moeurs* are new" (53). When Cather reviewed a new edition of *A Shropshire Lad* in 1897, she quoted from "On your midnight pallet lying" (poem 11) and asserted: "That is what it means to write poetry; be able to say the oldest thing in the world as though it had never been said before, to make the old wounds of all bleed fresh, to give a new voice to the *Weltschmerz*, that, perhaps, is the most exalted lyric in the whole collection" (Cather, Review 708). So, too, with Munro. Ruth Scurr's powerful 2011 review of Munro's *New Selected Stories* (published only in Britain) is titled "The Darkness of Alice Munro." Indeed.

A final point about my method here. The reader who reads this book from cover to cover—as opposed to the one who dips in here and there—will doubtless notice that I quote certain passages of Munro's more than once. Munro's 1973 statement in an interview that art involves "approach and recognition" is a favourite of mine, as are lines from "Material," such as "a fine and lucky benevolence" and the one I just used here, "passed into Art." Her 1974 essay in *Weekend Magazine*, "Everything Here Is Touchable and Mysterious," which has never been reprinted, offers such passages along with its title and provenance (Munro's father provided her with factual material about the Maitland River—a significant presence in Munro's imagination, and in this essay—which runs by their farm in Lower Wingham). The ending of "The Ottawa Valley" is key to understanding Munro's depiction of her mother, and, as also just mentioned, the ending of "Chaddeleys and Flemings: 1. Connection." There is also the ending of "Meneseteung" (1988). I also include Byatt's quotation in which she compares Munro's art to Cather's at the outset of my "Alice Munro's

Ontario." One approach to dealing with these repetitions might be to cut the repeats, but I have elected not to do that. It seems appropriate, in a book on a writer who so emphatically and deeply draws from her own place and culture, and who returns to repeat herself, to allow these assertions and passages to repeat—central as they are to Munro's art. "The final four works in this book are not quite stories," Munro writes, introducing her "Finale" in *Dear Life* (255). Here her mother and her father appear yet again, and for a final time: "dear life," indeed. Given this, and given the consistent probing found in her art itself, the repetitions here seem apt, justified by the repetitions and revisitations found throughout Munro's work. As Munro writes: "Connection. That was what was it all about" (*Moons* 6). That one is another favourite.

* * *

As I have gone back and reread these essays, remembering and (at least in some sense) rediscovering their arguments and contexts, I have noticed the recurring ideas, quotations, and references to specific stories that have informed the arguments these essays offer. Reconsidered now, in 2015, when as Munro critics we have a good sense of just what "the rest of the story" is ultimately likely to be, as regards both Munro and the whole corpus of her work, these recurrences seem eerie in their constancy. They serve to map the work of a writer whose intention for her art has never waivered, even if her own estimation of its accomplishment may have. That is, such recurrences are striking in the numerous ways Munro has vivified them throughout her career. Never a writer much inclined to analytical or academic debates about her own work, Munro has nevertheless made comments on that work that consistently display both imaginative precision and truth. Such comments are sharp, pointed, and, what is more, borne out by Munro's own practice. By way of concluding this introduction, I wish to address some of them, and to draw further connections between them and the trajectory of Munro's own life and career.

In my 1987 review of *The Progress of Love*, for example, I began by quoting a comment that Munro made to Jill Gardiner in an interview for Gardiner's 1973 M.A. thesis: "as we grow older: 'life becomes even *more* mysterious and difficult,' so that 'writing is the art of approach and recognition. I believe that we don't solve these things—in fact our explanations take us further away" (*Reading Alice Munro* 73). Gardiner interviewed Munro on June 1, 1973—at a time when Munro had left her marriage for good, would soon return to Ontario, and would soon write and publish three critical "approach and recognition" stories as consequence of that return: "Home" (1974), "The Ottawa Valley" (1974), and "Winter Wind" (1974). These stories, each one confronting memories and situations drawn from her family, offered "recognitions" that were far more raw and far less made and mannered than any Munro had published previously in such family-derived stories, such as "The Peace of Utrecht" (1960), "Boys and Girls" (1964), and "Red Dress—1946" (1965). In those 1973 stories, Munro may be seen, again, approaching and recognizing the mystery of each of her parents—and her grandmother and a great aunt, too—as she would approach them again and again after returning to Huron County in 1975, living there, and continuing to write. Visiting with Munro there myself on September 6, 2013, I asked her about the four pieces that make up the "Finale" section of *Dear Life*: "The Eye," "Night," "Voices," and "Dear Life." Introducing them as "not quite stories," Munro writes that she believes "they are the first and last—and the closest things I have to say about my own life" (255). Her mother and father are each there, and are again approached, wondered over, and recognized. When I asked her if each of these incidents actually happened, she said they had. They were, as she had written, "the closest things about my own life." Munro, writing her lives, still.

Three salient points emerge from such facts that need emphasis here. First, Munro's return to Ontario in 1973, and her return after that to Huron County in 1975, brought about an aesthetic confrontation with the physical surfaces, the cultural mores, and, most especially, her memories of the region that ultimately strengthened both the effect of and their affect on Munro's stories. Once back in Ontario, she continued to write as she had from British Columbia—descriptively, experimenting with form and point of view, writing densely detailed short stories—but as a first project, "Places at Home" (an unpublished piece of writing for a photography book), and then *Who Do You Think You Are?*, demonstrates, she did this with greater immediacy and urgency. Ever an organic writer, Munro revises perpetually—constantly rethinking her ideas for stories, beginning drafts, rejecting beginnings, rejecting characters and scenes, beginning again (the archive reveals boxes of rejected beginnings and, sometimes, whole drafts)—seeking to put on paper the story that exists in her mind. We readers have long thought she succeeds wonderfully—certainly at least since *Dance of the Happy Shades* won her first Governor General's award in 1969—but Munro herself has never been completely sure, nor does she ever seem satisfied. Her uncertainties were most acute during the mid-1970s and into the early 1980s—her famous removal of *Who Do You Think You Are?* from the press in 1978 for restructuring and rewriting being the clearest indication of this.

However, and this is my second point, this was also the time during which Munro was working on a group of stories that proved to be critical to her development as a writer of both unique power and profundity, both immediately and over the course of her career. Among these are the three first-person "Janet" stories that she held back from *Who Do You Think You Are?*, working on them subsequently through magazine publication and into her next book, *The Moons of Jupiter* (1982): "Chaddeleys and Flemings: 1. Connection," "Chaddeleys and Flemings: 2. The Stone in the Field" (1979), and "The Moons of Jupiter." So, too, is "Working for a Living" (1981), which began as fiction, was rejected by the *New Yorker* in that form, then became a memoir—which was rejected by its editors in *that* form as well. These pieces became, in fundamental ways, the basis for what Munro called in 1980 the "family book," which she had in mind then and kept thinking about and working on but did not complete until 2006 as *The View From Castle Rock*. During this time, too, she wrote and published "Dulse" and "Bardon Bus" (1982), two other explorations that showed Munro combining autobiographical materials with non-personal considerations—literary influence and posture, her own position as a writer, and relationships, viewed analytically—and exploring female sexual mores and desires. These latter explorations would prove, from the 1980s on, to be among her most central and enduring, drawing her especially then and as she has aged. Such stories as "Hateship, Friendship, Courtship, Loveship, Marriage" (2001), "The Bear Came Over the Mountain," "Chance" (2004), "Too Much Happiness" (2009), and "Dolly" (2012) confirm as much.

Such constructions of similarity between and among stories as these have to do with Munro's interests, and with the shape of her writing, rather than with the growing critical reputation of that writing. Turning to such matters, my third point is derived from how Munro shaped her career during the late 1970s and into the 1980s. Once she hired Virginia Barber as her agent in New York, Munro effectively began working quite consciously within two literary marketplaces, Canada and the United States, with Barber pursuing connections on her behalf in a third, Great Britain. Munro's decision to pull *Who Do You Think You Are?* from the press was occasioned, in part, by the responses she was getting to the manuscript from her editor at W. W. Norton in New York, who was trying to reshape it into a conventional novel at the same time that it was going into production in Canada. When that editor left Norton, Barber took Munro's book to Alfred A. Knopf and to Ann Close, an editor there. When it was published by Knopf in 1979 as *The Beggar Maid: Stories of Flo and Rose*, the book was slightly different from its Canadian predecessor—Munro had had time for more revision and adopted some of her Norton editor's suggestions, and Close had made some suggestions of her own (see Thacker, *Writing* 336–57). Thus *The Beggar Maid* has a slightly different text and so, technically, is a different book than its Canadian version.

Such details of difference are of less import than the acknowledgement that, with Barber, the *New Yorker* (and its right-of-first-refusal contract from 1977 on), and the reshapings found in *Who Do You Think You Are?/The Beggar Maid*, Munro's career in the late 1970s was becoming deeply enmeshed in two literary cultures, that of Canada and the US, the first overarching the second. Just as Munro herself was rediscovering her home place, shaping it in different and more complex ways, so, too, were the markets for that work changing and expanding. By 1980 she had her literary foundation in place: Barber in New York, her agent; Charles McGrath (and his successors), her editor at the *New Yorker*; Douglas Gibson, her Canadian editor in Toronto, and Close, her US editor, also in New York. By early 1983, when Knopf published the US edition of *The Moons of Jupiter* and the British version appeared from Allen Lane, Munro's critical reputation was well-established, and it was also growing. It was clear that she was already a writer to be reckoned with, and it was equally clear that with the *New Yorker*, Barber's broad efforts, and her two book publishers, Munro's new stories—still increasing in effect—were finding a greater audience. Her reading base was still strongest in Canada, but she was finding ever more readers abroad throughout the 1980s.

Also in 1983, the first critical book on Munro's work was published: *Probable Fictions: Alice Munro's Narrative Acts*, edited by Louis K. MacKendrick and published by ECW Press. It contained an interview with Munro and nine critical essays, and was followed the next year by the first critical monograph and by my annotated bibliography of Munro in the fifth volume of *The Annotated Bibliography of Canada's Major Authors*, also from ECW Press. In 1984 came *The Art of Alice Munro: Saying the Unsayable*, a collection of papers edited by Judith Miller from the first conference on Munro, held in 1982 at the University of Waterloo, and published by its press. As all this suggests, just as Munro's own career was taking off with *The Moons of Jupiter*, an equivalent critical interest in her works was emerging. The appearance of *Probable Fictions* in 1983 began a decade that saw the publication of 10 books on Munro, another two in which she is considered along with other authors, an annotated bibliography, a short monograph as part of a reference work, a brief series biography, and about a hundred critical articles and dissertations. Most of the book publication came from Canada, but not all of it—E. D. Blodgett's *Alice Munro* (1988) was the 800th volume in Twayne's World Authors Series and Ildikó de Papp Carrington's *Controlling the Uncontrollable* (1989) was published by Northern Illinois University Press. Since 1993, this pace of critical book publication has abated, with just five more single-authored books. At the same time, there have been two collections of critical essays, special issues of journals, an extended literary biography, a memoir by one of Munro's daughters, an appreciation, and around another two hundred articles and dissertations. A massive (457 pages) reference book, *Alice Munro: An Annotated Bibliography of Works and Criticism* by Carol Mazur and Cathy Moulder, was published by Scarecrow in 2007.

Given all of this, and given that this is an author who is, as the Nobel Prize Committee asserted in its press release, a "master of the contemporary short story" (October 10, 2013), *Reading Alice Munro, 1973–2013* should be seen as a historical introduction to both Munro and to Munro criticism. The body of critical analysis focused on Munro and her works is now a large and daunting thing, certainly, but the gradual critical understandings revealed here—from 1983 until 2013, along with their coinciding contextual issues—define her emergence and, when seen together, contextualize that emergence within Canadian literature during the last decades of the previous century and first years of the current one.

* * *

I wish to express my gratitude to the editors of the publications in which these essays first appeared for permission to republish them here. The specifics of this publication are to be found in the acknowledgements and also in the works cited. In preparing the essays for *Reading Alice Munro, 1973–2013*, with the exception of the routine copy-editing mentioned above, I have not altered the original text except in a few places to silently correct a factual matter and, in one instance, when two passages were repeated. As well, because these essays appeared using a variety of house citation styles (and for a few using no citations at all), I have elected to follow current MLA citation style. Thus textual citations have been deleted from some endnotes and been incorporated into a Works Cited. Also, when citing materials from the Alice Munro fonds at the University of Calgary, I have given the identification numbers used in one of the two published accession catalogs (*The Alice Munro Papers* 1986, 1987); I refer readers to those two indispensable books. When using material from subsequent accessions—for which there are in-house finding aids only—I have indicated the dates of composition for letters or relevant box and file numbers.

The work involved in a book such as this encourages its author to look back. So I have done here. Revisiting who I was when I was about to become a graduate student, discovering Munro in 1973 to 1976, and then as a more-advanced graduate student discovering Auden and Cather, reminds me of all the support I have enjoyed through the years. First and foremost there is Debbie and the other members of my family. Then, during those graduate student years, there were Stanley E. McMullin at Waterloo and Evelyn J. Hinz and John J. Teunissen at Manitoba. Since 1983 it has been my privilege to teach at St. Lawrence University. Its travel funds, generously and supportively dispensed by a succession of presidents and deans, got me to Calgary and into the Alice Munro fonds, and into many other archives as well. A timely gift to the university by Eric and Jane Molson jump-started *Alice Munro: Writing Her Lives* in 2003. At St. Lawrence I have also enjoyed the enthusiastic and always-generous support of David L. Torrey. I am so very grateful for all of this support. As well, beyond my family, my mentors, and my St. Lawrence connections, there has been a group of like-minded academic friends who have made my own "dear life" a joy: Anne, Evelyn, Florence, John, Laurie, Mark, Matt, Melody, Michael, Richard, Sue, Tracy, and many more. "A fine and lucky benevolence," in fact.

R. T.
Canton, New York
July 15, 2015

Part One

Narrative Techniques, Forms, and Critical Issues: Establishing a Presence

By the early 1980s, Alice Munro was recognized as being among Canada's leading writers. She had won two Governor General's Awards, for *Dance of the Happy Shades* and *Who Do You Think You Are?*; by the end of 1980 she had published six recent stories in the *New Yorker* and several others in competing commercial magazines, both American and Canadian; the first academic conference on her work was held in March 1982 at the University of Waterloo (Munro was there for a reading); and that fall *The Moons of Jupiter*—her strongest collection yet—was published by Macmillan, with its American edition appearing from Knopf early in 1983. Munro's career was not only well established: it was building momentum, and that momentum would deepen and be confirmed in 1986 with *The Progress of Love*, for which she took her third Governor General's Award.

Following in the wake of such ongoing publication and widespread interest, more critics began writing about Munro's stories, and they did so in more technical ways. Critical articles were appearing with increased frequency in literary journals. In 1983 the first critical book on Munro's work, *Probable Fictions*, was published, and it included an interview and nine essays focused on matters of style, technique, diction, syntax, and structure. These critics probed just how Munro was able to affect her readers. Subject and theme, although not altogether ignored, were treated in relation to these matters. This first book was followed over the course of the latter half of the decade by a succession of critical monograph studies that elaborated Munro's art and its effects in extended and detailed ways. Taken together, W. R. Martin's *Alice Munro: Paradox and Parallel* (1987), E. D. Blodgett's *Alice Munro* (1988), Ildikó de Papp Carrington's *Controlling the Uncontrollable* (1989), and Beverly J. Rasporich's *Dance of the Sexes: Art and Gender in the Fiction of Alice Munro* (1990) constitute both deep analysis and protracted critical attention. Each of these studies sought to treat Munro's *oeuvre* as a whole, and in so doing they both furthered the prominence of her fiction and deepened understandings of it. Although they varied in their individual strengths, there is no question that together they established Munro's standing as a major author, a figure whose work deserved and rewarded close analysis.

It was in such contexts—both authorial and critical—that the essays and reviews in this section of *Reading Alice Munro* appeared. Read now together, they assert ways of understanding Munro's stories that had, and continue to have, critical purchase. The first two, "Clear Jelly" and "Connection," published in 1983 and 1984, respectively, examine narrative structure and Munro's handling of persona and time, as well as Munro's relation to and use of her home place, Southwestern Ontario's Huron County. Critical questions on these aspects of Munro's work have continued to vivify her writing throughout her career, up to (and even especially including) her 2012 collection *Dear Life*. Similarly, the third article here, "'So Shocking a Verdict in Real Life'" (originally delivered at the 1987 University of Ottawa symposium on autobiography and Canadian literature and published in 1988), still resonates in Munro criticism, in particular with regard to *Dear Life*'s "Finale" section. Questions of autobiography in Munro's work have always been ubiquitous. Finally, the three reviews included here establish contexts relevant to the 1980s, both aesthetic, in the review of *The Progress of Love*, and critical with the other two—both "Munro's Progress" and "Conferring Munro" appeared in 1987, and "Go Ask Alice" was published in 1991. Read now, each of the latter catch the feeling of Munro's expanding aesthetics at that time and the qualified (and sometimes paltry) reflection of it in the criticism. "Go Ask Alice" in particular does this, its cheekiness and allusive title aside.

"Clear Jelly": Alice Munro's Narrative Dialectics (1983)

Beginning with her first collection, *Dance of the Happy Shades*, Alice Munro has received consistent praise for her style. Yet, strangely enough, most such comments have come from reviewers—of the several articles that treat Munro's work, only three have focused upon her style, and none have analyzed her narrative technique (See New "Pronouns," Hoy "Dull," and Martin "Strange").[1] But a close examination of her early uncollected stories and those contained in *Dance of the Happy Shades* suggests that Munro's style developed from her first stories on; its development, moreover, is best seen through an examination of narrative technique. By the time her first collection appeared, Munro had perfected a distinctive retrospective narrative approach that she has used throughout her subsequent work. It is, in her stories, the means by which past and present commingle, the narrator's humanity is communicated, and each narrator, and several other individual characters besides, is allowed their articulate moments. Simply put, it is the catalytic factor in Munro's substantial art.

Munro's first published stories appeared in the University of Western Ontario's undergraduate literary magazine, *Folio*, while she was a student there. Two of these, "The Dimensions of a Shadow" and "The Widower," reveal no real portents of her later success with the short story. The third-person omniscient narration is heavy handed and Munro's narrative tone didactic, although she does show some facility with descriptions of physical detail. The remaining story, however, entitled "Story for Sunday," reveals a glimpse of the narrative technique that would become her hallmark, while at the same time it shares some of the others' flaws. As the story begins, the youthful protagonist, Evelyn, is hurrying to Sunday school, where she is a teacher's assistant. While Munro's omniscient third-person narrator concerns herself with the story's setting, as in the previous story, Munro concurrently reveals Evelyn's sense of anticipation over seeing Mr. Willens, the Sunday school superintendent, once again. Later, while Evelyn waits for the service to begin in church, the narrator tells us that "[t]oday when she [Evelyn] looked at the pictures it was not quite the same; even in the depth and stillness of the moment she remembered Mr. Willens." (Laidlaw, "Story" n.p.) And, drawing upon Evelyn's memory, the narrator flashes back to the source of the girl's anticipation: the previous Sunday, having returned to an isolated room to retrieve her gloves, Evelyn happened upon Willens. He complimented her on her helpfulness and then took her in his arms and kissed her. As a result, the impressionable Evelyn has transformed him into a special being: "He was not handsome; his face in profile was somewhat flat, almost convex, not handsome at all, but beautiful." In so saying, Munro's narrator has made a key distinction: memory has transformed Willens into a romanticized being. Because of his attention the previous week, Willens has inadvertently altered Evelyn's view of herself. For example, looking at the other girls in church, who were concerned with mere boys, Evelyn considers herself superior because "she moved in a clear, cold flame of love which they [the other girls] could not even see." Of course, Evelyn plans to position herself for another kiss, but, upon returning to the isolated room once again, she finds Willens reenacting their kiss with the church's piano player, Myrtle Fotheringay. Overall, "Story for Sunday" is not profound literary art; it is significant only because it shows Munro, at a very early stage in her career, consciously manipulating past and present, holding the two realms together for the reader to see. Hence, through this commingling of past and present, Evelyn is allowed an articulate moment.

During her first few stories, Munro appears to have experimented with a variety of narrative stances, fluctuating from the first-person point of view to that of the third and back again, something that continued through the *Dance of the Happy Shades* stories and continues still. In the early stories, however, the shifts in narrative perspective are often marked. In "Story for Sunday," Munro uses third-person narration but is primarily concerned with Evelyn's thoughts and feelings. Her next published story, "The Idyllic Summer," also uses third-person narration, but Munro treats its protagonist in a far more objective manner. It deals with the relationship between a wholly cerebral classics professor and his somewhat intellectually disabled daughter who is, therefore, primarily emotive. Munro uses the professor's letters to his colleagues to display the character's pious and pompous manner, while she describes the daughter, Clara, through her third-person narrator's analyses of both the girl's actions and the setting. The focus is on Clara, the inarticulate character, because her father is able to speak for himself. Yet in "The Idyllic Summer" we see Munro dealing with the two character types seen throughout her stories: the articulate character speaking for himself and the inarticulate character rendered through third-person objective description and carefully delineated setting; in her next two stories, Munro concentrates on each separately. Thus, Munro's approach to her subject varied during this period, just as it would in the stories composed after "Thanks for the Ride," alternating between a focus on an individual character's thoughts and feelings as they present them and an emphasis on less articulate characters rendered through their actions and setting.

In her next story, "At the Other Place," Munro adopts for the first time the first-person point of view, a narrative stance that became dominant in her first two books. It is, as well, the first in which a conventional family is depicted and also the first in which an immediate sense of place is vividly described. Because Munro's presentation of setting figures evocatively in her characterization, it is worth noting that from her very first stories on she handled setting well. In "At the Other Place," her narrator creates a definable texture of place for the reader, replete with sights, smells, and colours:

> It was a very hot day, but there had not been enough hot weather yet to burn the country up. The roadside bushes were still green and the money-musk was blooming unfaded in the long grass. Haying-time was over, but in some of the fields the coils were

> still standing. No one was working anywhere; the country was all hot and still in the sun, in the plum-blue shade of the heavy oaks and maples. The cows were lying down in the pastures, the horses dozing on their feet, under the trees. We passed a field of buckwheat in flower; it smelled as sweet as clover. (Laidlaw, "At" 131)

Munro here is finely attuned to the kind of surface detail that allows the reader to mentally recreate the scene she is describing. Through these figurative images, the reader is able to grasp the sensual context of the story, which in turn lends the dramatized scenes a further sense of immediacy.

"At the Other Place" is also the first story in which the narrator's voice reveals two personae: though the narrator is ostensibly a child, her perceptions and the resulting descriptions are not strictly those of a child. Hence, her distinctions are often quite discerning; they are more mature in their judgement than the narrator's age would indicate, and she couches them in language sophisticated beyond her putative years. Munro produces these two aspects of the narrator's sensibility, the child and the remembered child, through an approach that is similar to the way she blends past and present in "Story for Sunday," although here, instead of simply allowing the discrepancy between past and present to be inferred, Munro deliberately cultivates it.

The story describes an afternoon outing to "the other place" owned by the narrator's family, the place where her father grew up. Within the story, Munro recreates the immediacy of a child's understanding through memory and through her narrative approach, and combines this with the weight of understanding of the older narrator (the adult who was the young girl), resulting in descriptions and evaluations that are a merging of past and present. Thus, when considering her father, a farmer dressed incongruously in his Sunday best, the narrator allows that

> my father, in a stiff blue shirt and suit with wide stripes, looked shrunken and stooped, red and grizzled in the face, much less his own man than he was in overalls and mechanic's cap. About this time I began to be puzzled and sad when I saw him in his good clothes—for when we saw him in the fields or holding the

reins of a team or even sawing wood he was sure and powerful, a little more than life-size. (Laidlaw, "At" 131)[2]

Not only does the narrator reveal her sophisticated perception and linguistic sense here, she also reveals that the immediacy of the story is feigned: "About this time." It is an active reminiscence.

While visiting the other place to have a picnic and to care for the family's sheep, the narrator liked to explore the house where her father grew up. Reflecting, she recalls that she "sat on the window-ledge, looking through the open doorway at the big hard-maple that had been there when my father was little, and the slow movement of its branches, the way the sunlight caught on its leaves, gave me a forlorn and beautiful feeling of time and changes, and changelessness" (Laidlaw, "At" 131–32). Once, when her father came to the house to inspect an old wood stove, the narrator states that "[h]e did not look around or grow thoughtful as I thought he should" (Laidlaw, "At" 132). Because of her own pensiveness, revealed here, the narrator is not entirely the 12- to 14-year-old she otherwise seems to be. Rather, as the story's narrator, she is nominally a child, narrating her immediate perceptions and thoughts; but upon closer examination we see that she is actually an adult, or at least an older adolescent, remembering her experiences on a particular day. Just as she uses memory in "Story for Sunday," Munro here holds up past and present together. And by giving the story the appearance of immediacy—she is not trying to hide the fact that an older narrator is remembering—Munro lends her narrator a unique ability. The narrator in "At the Other Place" recreates through memory the immediate reality of the story, while at the same time she is able to infuse the narrative with the subjective importance of the memory, realized only as she matured. Thus, her comments about her father, quoted above, unite both past and present, and so by their interaction expand what Munro is getting at.

Surveying the stories chronologically, it is apparent that Munro came to use this retrospective narration (first seen in "At the Other Place") with increasing frequency; indeed, in later stories she experimented with the technique, shaping and adjusting it to fit her subject, and as her narrators became more articulate, her art became more complex. But this represents only her overall direction; other stories written at this time reveal a different emphasis. In an unpublished interview, Munro comments that in her early stories she was more interested in setting than in character (Gardiner Interview 173).³ Her subsequent story, "The Edge of Town," reflects this. Its protagonist, Harry Brooke, is an incessant talker who, ironically, cannot communicate with those around him, neither the townsfolk nor his own family. Having adopted the third-person point of view, Munro is concerned with setting from the story's very beginning:

> Up here the soil is shallow and stony; the creeks dry up in summer, and a harsh wind from the west blows all year long. There are not many trees, but wild-rose and blackberry bushes in little pockets of the hills, and long sharp sword-grass in the hollows. On an August day if you stand on the road leading out from the town, you can see miles and miles of brown blowing grass, and dust scooped up from the roads, and low, bumpy hills along the rim of the sky, which might be the end of the world. At night the crickets sing in the grass, and every second day, at supper time, a freight train goes through the town. (368)

Into this setting Munro places Harry Brooke, whom she treats objectively, never directly venturing into his thoughts. She delineates Harry's isolation by employing setting as a symbolic index of character and, in a manner analogous to the style of Eudora Welty, transforms details of setting into symbolic counterpoints for character.⁴ As well, having been born and raised in the same sort of social environment in which she places Harry, Munro is able to describe his place in the town knowingly, unequivocally, as she presents the town's reaction to his babblings:

> His expectancy, his seeking, made them wary, uneasily mocking. In a poor town like this, in a poor country, facing the year-long winds and the hard winters, people expect and seek very little; a rooted pessimism is their final wisdom. Among the raw bony faces of the Scotch-Irish, with their unspeaking eyes, the face of Harry was a flickering light, an unsteady blade; his

exaggerated, flowering talk ran riot amongst barren statements and silences. (371)

The opening passage, previously quoted, underscores this detached analysis. Living in such an environment brings about the "rooted pessimism" Munro sees in the townspeople, and their stoicism, indeed, serves to set apart and objectify Harry Brooke, whose questions violate their "barren statements and silences."

"The Edge of Town" is sandwiched in between two stories that use the internalized first-person retrospective technique, "At the Other Place" and "Good-by Myra," suggesting that Munro was working concurrently on two separate ways of rendering character. She chose to present characters like Harry Brooke in this story and Clara in "The Idyllic Summer" objectively, through their actions and through setting; such treatment is, indeed, in keeping with the characters' inability to communicate.

Another story in which she uses this technique is "The Time of Death." But elsewhere, Munro chooses to present first-person narrators who articulate their own experiences, thereby deriving their own understanding. These narrators are found in "At the Other Place" and, as will be seen presently, in "Good-by Myra." In working on each approach separately, Munro was developing greater skill with two major components of fiction: setting and character; and by the time she wrote her mature stories, like "Thanks for the Ride," she was able to fuse observer and participant into one narrative voice. Thus, Munro followed two separate, but by no means divergent, approaches to narration in her early stories.

Because "Good-by Myra" is the first story with a narrator who is actively shaping her memories in a somewhat covert manner, giving the impression of immediacy and a detached understanding, it should be considered in some detail. The story deals with the development of a relationship between Helen, the narrator, and Myra Sayla, the outcast of Helen's grade 6 class. Myra is an outcast because of her family background and her younger brother's dependence on her while they are at school. As Helen tells us: "Jimmy Sayla was not used to going to the bathroom by himself and he would have to come to the grade-six door and ask for Myra and she would take him downstairs" (17). Jimmy's dependence extends to the playground as well: because Jimmy's classmates pick on him, the

Saylas spend play periods standing together along the dividing line between the boys' and girls' playgrounds. Moreover, they do not fit into the Scots-Protestant ethos of the town; their parents are Eastern European immigrants, and the family is Roman Catholic. When a well-meaning teacher attempts to intercede on Myra's behalf, the grade 6 girls, who had previously ignored Myra, turn on her as an object of derision.

Helen takes part in mocking Myra and does so without any apparent qualms. But one day while walking to school, she notices that Myra is ahead of her and is slowing down to wait for her, so she befriends Myra, stating that "[a] role was shaping for me that I could not resist playing." The other girl's "humble, hopeful turnings" (55) affect Helen, and she leaps to the superior role they afford her. Throughout their meeting, Helen responds to Myra as a person; prior to this she had thought of Myra only as an odd presence: "It was queer to think that Myra, too, read the comics, or that she did anything, was anything at all, apart from her role at the school." A bond is forged between the two when Helen persuades Myra to keep the prize she found in Helen's Cracker Jack. After forcing it on Myra, Helen realizes the implications of her act: "We were both surprised. We looked at each other; I flushed but Myra did not. I realized the pledge as our fingers touched; I was panicky, but all right. All right, I thought, I can come early and walk with her other mornings. I can—I can go and talk to her at recess. Why not. Why not?" (56). Despite this realization, Helen has some misgivings about the friendship; she is wary of her peers' reaction. But her fears prove inconsequential because Myra, having become ill with leukemia, stops attending school shortly thereafter.

Miss Darling, the grade 6 teacher, organizes a birthday party for Myra—despite the fact that it is March and Myra's birthday is in July—to be held at the hospital. Typically, Myra's disease grants her new status among her classmates: "The birthday party of Myra Sayla became fashionable" (57). Once the party is over and the girls are leaving, Myra calls Helen back to her bed. She offers Helen a brush and comb set that Helen had earlier noticed, and they make plans to play together when Myra returns from her treatment in London. Helen, however, is apprehensive, having premonitions that Myra will never return:

Then I stood beside the bed wanting to say something else, or to ask something. Outside the hospital window, in the late sunlight, there was a sound like birds calling, but it wasn't, it was somebody playing in the street, maybe chasing with snowballs of the last unmelted snow. Myra heard, too; we were looking at each other. At that clear carrying sound her face changed, and I was scared, I did not know why.

"When you come back—" I said...

Here Helen is faced with the life outside and the fact of Myra's impending death, which she intuits. Helen "understood the demand she [Myra] made. And it was too much." As Helen leaves, she "called back quickly, treacherously, almost gaily, 'Good-by!'" (58). The demand Myra made on Helen was of personal commitment, something that, as Helen herself suggests, is too much for an 11-year-old to bear. Yet by narrating "Good-by Myra," Helen is remembering and purging herself of guilt. In the words of another of Munro's narrators, Myra has been "lifted out of life and held in light, suspended in the marvelous clear jelly that [Munro] has spent all [her] life learning how to make. It is an act of magic, there is no getting around it; it is an act, you might say, of a special, unsparing, unsentimental love. A fine and lucky benevolence." Like the character being spoken of here, Myra "has passed into Art. It doesn't happen to everybody" (*Something* 43).

Such is the intention of Munro's own art. She creates a dialectic within the first-person narrator: Helen, the girl who knew Myra as an 11-year-old, and Helen, the older person actually narrating the story, combine to give the story two levels of reality. Because of Helen's memory and her detailed description, the texture of the story in "Good-by Myra" is a commingling of the remembered event, vividly described so as to lend it immediacy, and Helen's understanding of it, a detached understanding because of the time that has passed since Helen knew Myra. The dynamic interaction between these two aspects of the narrator, the dialectic between them, is at the core of Munro's rhetoric; it is the way by which she creates her own "clear jelly."

Although Munro uses the retrospective technique tentatively in "At the Other Place," she uses it in a thoroughgoing way in "Good-by

Myra"—the first time she does so. Remembering Myra as she was in the schoolyard, Helen recalls the Saylas in mythical terms: "Over their dark eyes the lids were never fully raised; they had a weary look. But it was more than that. They were like children in a medieval painting, they were like small figures carved of wood, for worship or magic, with faces smooth and aged and meekly, cryptically uncommunicative" (17). As perceptive and descriptive as this passage is, it is not the product of the mentality of an 11-year-old girl. The language and diction are too refined, and the narrator's understanding of the scene's ramifications is too acute. In passages such as this, Munro combines her first-person narration with omniscient description. Yet the omniscience does not jar the reader, because it is a suitable intrusion, subtle and illuminating. The central simile contained here expands the reader's understanding of the Saylas quickly and unobtrusively.

This technique embodies the net effect of human memory: the reader is presented with Myra not as she actually was, but as Helen remembers her. Although the two images of Myra may very well be one and the same, they do not have to be, because memory tends to blur the picture, disregarding and enhancing details to create a desired impression. Helen is scared and does not know why because she has instinctively recognized another person's impending death, and the knowledge is beyond her intellectual scope. Yet the sensibility of an older Helen is able to grasp the idea of Myra's eventual death; this recognition is implied throughout the story's last paragraph, as Helen "treacherously" calls "Good-by!" to Myra (58).

Another reason that "Good-by Myra" is central to this consideration of Munro's developing narrative technique is because of major revisions she made before republishing it, as "Day of the Butterfly," in *Dance of the Happy Shades*. Comparing the two versions reveals the direction in which their author was moving. In the stories written and published after "Good-by Myra"—many of which were included in *Dance of the Happy Shades*— Munro moved more and more toward using this retrospective first-person narrator as the teller of the tale. Although this narration was first seen in "At the Other Place," Munro first uses it in a consistent and somewhat covert manner—she neither draws attention to nor provides specific information about the older narrator—in "Good-by Myra." In revising this story in order to sharpen the memory of the older narrator, Munro reveals her main concern. Her remembering narrators inform, judge, understand, and ultimately illuminate—theirs is an essential presence in her fiction, a catalytic one. Munro's desire to sharpen the narrator's understanding of Myra Sayla is, therefore, in keeping with the development of her distinctive narrative voice.

"Day of the Butterfly" bears a greater similarity to those stories in *Dance of the Happy Shades* in which Munro's retrospective narration is most refined—"Boys and Girls," "Red Dress—1946," "Walker Brothers Cowboy," and "Images"—than to her early stories. Thus the earlier version of this story is a harbinger of things to come, whereas the revision suggests an author who has attained a much firmer grasp of her narrative voice in the interim between drafts. The two versions diverge at the point when Helen describes the "clear carrying sound of somebody playing in the street" (*Dance* 110). In the earlier version, Helen echoes Myra's plans for her eventual return, but in "Day of the Butterfly" she does not. In "Good-by Myra," the sound makes Myra's face change, which in turn frightens Helen, but in the revision the sound "made Myra, her triumph and her bounty, and most of all her future in which she had found this place for me, turn shadowy, turn dark" (110). In the first version, Helen's feelings are ambiguous; she is frightened by the change in Myra's face but does "not know why" (58). In the revision there is no ambivalence: Helen knows that Myra will go to London and die. Helen's fright in "Good-by Myra" comes out of her intuition of the eventuality, but in the revision, the adult narrator, with her sharpened memory, states the realization more emphatically.

Further, the delineation of Helen's memory has transformed the presents lying on Myra's bed. In the earlier version, they are without subjective significance, but in "Day of the Butterfly," Helen finds them threatening: "All the presents on the bed, the folded paper and ribbons, those guilt-tinged offerings, had passed into this shadow, they were no longer innocent objects to be touched, exchanged, accepted without danger." Helen's memory here is more exact, and her realization more profound; by characterizing the presents as "guilt-tinged offerings," she links them to the girls' previous cruel treatment of Myra—treatment to which she was a party. Helen's recognition here does not differ in kind from the earlier version, yet its personal exactness leads both the narrator and the reader to a deeper understanding of the relationship. Moreover, Helen's attempt to withdraw quickly from the room, which is stated explicitly in the first version, is stated more subtly in the second. Likewise, Helen tries to give the present back to Myra in the first version, but in the second she mentally denies the "guilt-tinged offering": "I didn't want to take the case now but I could not think how to get out of it, what lie to tell. I'll give it away, I thought, I won't ever play with it. I would let my little brother pull it apart" (110). In this instance, too, the scope of Helen's realization is broadened; because the rejection is thought rather than stated, Helen's older self is shown to be shouldering more responsibility for it. Perhaps Helen recalls her own role when she and her peers were taunting Myra.

Finally, the most important change Munro made is in the last paragraph of "Day of the Butterfly." In "Good-by Myra," Helen's final goodbye is allowed to stand alone, while Helen thinks only of getting outside into the spring air. In "Day of the Butterfly," however, Helen's reaction to a nurse's admonishment to leave is far more explicit:

> So I was released, set free by the barriers which now closed about Myra, her unknown, exalted, ether smelling hospital world, and by the treachery of my own heart. "Well thank you," I said. "Thank you for the thing. Goodbye." Did Myra ever say goodbye? Not likely. She sat in her high bed, her delicate brown neck rising out of a hospital gown too big for her, her brown carved face immune to treachery, her offering perhaps already forgotten, prepared to be set apart for legendary uses, as she was even in the back porch at school. (110)

Myra may be "immune to treachery," but Helen certainly is not. Moreover, since Myra is the subject of the reminiscence that comprises the story, she has been "set apart" for Helen's own "legendary uses." In comparing the two versions, then, it is possible to chart Munro's expansive delineation of memory when applied to a crucial childhood event. Helen's recollections in "Day of the Butterfly" are more precise; the adult recollections of the mature narrator are presented with a higher degree of comprehension in the second version. The narrator in "Day of the Butterfly" recognizes the "treachery" in her own heart, which she does not attempt to avoid, and she understands her "treachery" better than she did in the original version of the story. It is a recognition that, as the narrator, she cannot deny: Helen must deal with her childhood responsibility. Another noteworthy difference is in the differing tones in the two versions of Helen's retreat. In "Good-by Myra," Helen impetuously departs, quickly calling "Good-by!" (58), whereas the second Helen is more cerebral and more serene, as if she is aware of her responsibility toward Myra. Thus, her farewell is not an exclamation; instead, it is a flat statement: "Goodbye" (110). Overall, Munro's revisions produced a more thoughtful evaluation of her narrator's memories.

In an unpublished interview, Munro comments on the differences between the two versions: "I've just changed the rhythm to get the voice of the narrator. I began to do that a lot better.... They [the changes] matter a lot to me. I don't decide to make the changes; it's just [that] when I start rewriting I start hearing the narrator's voice" (Gardiner Interview 176).[5] Her comments reveal her awareness of the separate narrators in the stories and, more importantly, her recognition of her own narrative development. Her comments also implicitly recognize a change in the narrator's situation, dictated by the author's own growth in her perceptive ability during the interim between drafts. Thus, it is fair to say that as Munro changed, her perception of Helen's responsibility changed, and the sharper focus in "Day of the Butterfly" reflects this change. The shift lies with the author and the narrator rather than with the story's essential intent, because Helen's moral responsibility toward Myra remains unaltered.

As indicated earlier, Munro developed as a narrative craftsman along two separate, but by no means divergent, lines. That is, although she tended increasingly toward the type of narration seen in "Good-by Myra,"[6] she still occasionally wrote stories in which characters are presented objectively, without recourse to memory, through a third-person narrator. Such stories as "The Time of Death" and "A Trip to the Coast" are strongly related to "The Edge of Town" in that setting and atmosphere predominate and characters are treated symbolically.[7] They are also Munro's least successful stories in *Dance of the Happy Shades*. Their presence, however, is significant within Munro's work because they forced her to observe in a detached manner. Commenting on "An Ounce of Cure," a story written just after "Good-by Myra" and which is patently a first-person reminiscence, Munro says:

> One thing in it I think is interesting, now that I look back on it: when the girl's circumstances become hopelessly messy, when nothing is going to go right for her, she gets out of it by looking at the way things happen—by changing from a participant to an observer. This is what I used to do myself, it is what a writer does; I think it may be one of the things that make a writer in the first place. When I started to write the dreadful things I did write when I was about fifteen, I made the glorious leap from being a victim of my own ineptness and self-conscious miseries to being a godlike arranger of patterns and destinies, even if they were all in my head; I have never leapt back. ("Author's" 125)

This statement reveals Munro's essentially rhetorical approach to fiction, because like their author, her protagonists are both participants and observers. Through the interaction of these two modes of perception, Munro is able to present coherently the entire significance of a story's events. It is therefore not remarkable that in some stories she prefers to simply observe in the third person—without reference to the participant's thoughts or emotions. This allows her to concentrate on setting and atmosphere as the primary determinants of character, especially in "The Time of Death."

In "Thanks for the Ride," Munro brings her two separate narrative approaches together within one story. Dick, the story's narrator, is one of her finest characters; he is both participant in and observer of the story's action, a "pick-up" liaison, and Munro's sole male first-person narrator.[8] Lois, his partner in their evening activities, is almost wholly inarticulate, meaning her character is defined through Dick's observations of the town's environment, her physical appearance, and her home and family. Because of his function within the story, Dick is a commingling of first-person commitment and third-person detachment. As the story opens, he is sitting in the single café in a small Ontario town, presumably near Lake

Huron, with his cloddish cousin, George. The pair have been thrown together by circumstance and are planning an evening together, though Dick is not overly enthusiastic. His descriptions of the café and town are those of a detached third-person narrator:

> My cousin George and I were sitting in a restaurant called Pop's Cafe, in a little town close to the Lake. It was getting dark in there, and they had not turned the lights on, but you could still read the signs plastered against the mirror between fly-speckled and slightly yellowed cutouts of strawberry sundaes and tomato sandwiches....
>
> It was a town of unpaved, wide, sandy streets and bare yards. Only the hardy things like red and yellow nasturtiums, or a lilac bush with brown curled leaves, grew out of that cracked earth. The houses were set wide apart, with their own pumps and sheds and privies out behind; most of them were built of wood and painted green or grey or yellow. The trees that grew there were big willows or poplars, their fine leaves greyed with the dust. There were no trees along the main street, but spaces of tall grass and dandelions and blowing thistles—open country between the store buildings. The town hall was surprisingly large, with a great bell in a tower, the red brick rather glaring in the midst of the town's walls of faded, pale-painted wood. (*Dance* 44, 46–47)

There is nothing in these descriptions that suggests the first-person narration, except possibly "surprisingly"; they serve to define the setting and, as such, act as a symbolic counterpoint later on for the inarticulate Lois, who is apparently as rough as her environment and is roughly used by boys up from the city, boys like Dick and George. Indeed, this is her town. Later, after Dick and George have met Lois' friend Adelaide and have located Lois walking down a street, they all go to Lois' home so that she can change. Dick follows her into the house to wait for her, and through his observations we observe how adroit Munro is at welding together his roles of observer and participant:

> She opened the front door and said in a clear, stilted voice: "I would like you to meet my family." The little front room had linoleum on the floor and flowered paper curtains at the windows. There was a glossy chesterfield with a Niagara Falls and a To Mother cushion on it, and there was a little black stove with a screen around it for summer, and a big vase of paper apple blossoms. A tall, frail woman came into the room drying her hands on a dishtowel, which she flung into a chair. Her mouth was full of blue-white china teeth, the long cords trembled in her neck. I said how-do-you-do to her, embarrassed by Lois's announcement, so suddenly and purposefully conventional. I wondered if she had any misconceptions about this date, engineered by George for such specific purposes. I did not think so. Her face had no innocence in it that I could see; it was knowledgeable, calm, and hostile. She might have done it, then, to mock me, to make me into this caricature of The Date, the boy who grins and shuffles in the front hall and waits to be presented to the nice girl's family. But that was a little far-fetched. Why should she want to embarrass me when she had agreed to go out with me without even looking into my face? Why should she care enough? (*Dance* 49–50)

Here, in this paragraph, is the essence of Munro's narrative art. Having written stories like "The Edge of Town," in which her third-person narrator describes, analyzes, and pronounces, and having written stories like "At the Other Place" and especially "Good-by Myra," in which her remembering narrators both participated in the action and articulated its significance, Munro brings the two separate approaches together in this finely wrought story. Dick is, as far as the reader can see, observing, describing, participating, and remembering, seemingly all at once. He is both descriptive and thoughtful as a narrator, as the two separate parts of the above paragraph show: at first he describes the room, and once this description is accomplished he falls to musing over Lois' expectations. In this way, in her finest stories—of which this is the first—Munro's adroit narrators communicate by varying their perspective: describing, reacting, confirming, denying, and, above all, remembering—as each is needed.

Thus, her stories are best understood through an analysis of her rhetoric. Munro's narrative technique, usually subtly adjusted for the needs of each story, defines the dialectical basis of her style.

An example of these adjustments is the manner by which Munro communicates Lois' plight of being trapped in the small resort town, for we also see her donning her Saturday night finery for almost every city boy in town during the summer in the (apparently futile) hope that he will be "The Date." Because Lois is presented objectively, from Dick's point of view, Munro draws upon Dick's own curiosity about her character: he is inexperienced in pick-up affairs and so relates to Lois as a person, not as an object. In addition, Dick's description of the town, quoted above, underscores Lois' character, in that she is the human counterpart of those "hardy ... red and yellow nasturtiums." Despite Lois uttering little more than a dozen lines during the entire story, the reader is perfectly aware of her multitude of reasons for an "abusive and forlorn" cry at the story's end (*Dance* 58). Because he is describing what he observed from memory, Dick lends subjective weight to objective facts. Thus, when he first comes into Lois' house, he notices "the smell of stale small rooms, bedclothes, frying, washing, and medicated ointments. And dirt, though it did not look dirty" (*Dance* 50). With his urban middle-class background, Dick is unaccustomed to Lois' mode of life at the edge of poverty, and his memory lends subjective weight to his initial impressions.

As he notes Lois' grandmother, whom he likens to a "collapsed pudding," Dick fills out his impression:

> Some of the smell in the house seemed to come from her. It was a smell of hidden decay, such as there is when some obscure little animal has died under the verandah. The smell, the slovenly, confiding voice—something about this life I had not known, something about these people. I thought: my mother, George's mother, they are innocent. Even George, George is innocent. But these others are born sly and sad and knowing. (*Dance* 51)

This is not to suggest that Dick could not have had such thoughts while glancing at Lois' grandmother peering in from the edge of the living room, but one doubts that they would have been so well articulated. Through her descriptions, Munro is here—as she is throughout her other stories—juggling reminiscence so that it gives the appearance of immediacy. That is, should the readers care to think about it, they would see that the entire story is written in the past tense, and as a result, Dick's emotions are recalled in tranquility. But Munro's descriptions and other details lend such clarity to the presentation of her story that readers think the events are unfolding before them. This ability, based on her narrative technique, allows her to fashion art out of a pick-up affair, a first kiss, or a runaway horse—commonplace events all.

This retrospective technique, which allows the now-older narrator to comment on what happened when they were younger—to become, as she says, a "godlike arranger of patterns and destinies"—is not, by any means, unique to Munro. A more widely known and recognized example of it is in James Joyce's "Araby," one of the stories of childhood in *Dubliners*. In her unpublished interview with Munro, Jill Gardiner presented the author with Cleanth Brooks and Robert Penn Warren's analysis of the technique as it functions within Joyce's story. Munro's response was as follows:

> The adult narrator has the ability to detect and talk about the confusion. I don't feel that the confusion is ever resolved. And there is some kind of a central mystery, as in "Walker Brothers Cowboy," that is there for the adult narrator as it was for the child. I feel that all life becomes even more mysterious and difficult. And the whole act of writing is more an attempt at recognition than of understanding, because I don't understand many things. I feel a kind of satisfaction in just approaching something that is mysterious and important. Then writing is the art of approach and recognition. I believe that we don't solve these things—in fact our explanations take us further away. (Gardiner Interview 178)

Such a statement certainly calls into question the thematic analyses offered by critics who purport to define Munro's vision of the world—because, as her devotion to the short story suggests, Munro sees the world as in flux. Thus, her pronouncements are few and her insights tentative and fleeting. Conversely, the central importance of her rhetoric takes on a greater validity in light of this statement—narrative technique is, after all, the vehicle for Munro's "approach and recognition."

A passage from "Thanks for the Ride" underscores this point. Sitting in a car parked on a lonely country road, passing a bottle of bootleg liquor back and forth, Dick observes Lois and tries to understand her:

> Each time Lois handed the bottle back to me she said "Thank you" in a mannerly and subtly contemptuous way. I put my arm around her, not much wanting to. I was wondering what was the matter. This girl lay against my arm, scornful, acquiescent, angry, inarticulate and out-of-reach. I wanted to talk to her then more than to touch her, and that was out of the question; talk was not so little a thing to her as touching. Meanwhile I was aware that I should be beyond this, beyond the first stage and well into the second (for I had a knowledge, though it was not very comprehensive, of the orderly progression of stages, the ritual of back- and front-seat seduction). Almost I wished I was with Adelaide. (*Dance* 53)

Here Dick is describing, observing, participating, and remembering. This passage could support a study of diction and syntax that would lead inductively, through an understanding of Dick's position as narrator, to a well-grounded presentation of theme. The adjectives define Lois: "contemptuous," "scornful," "acquiescent," "angry," "inarticulate." Lois is all of these, but in using these adjectives, Dick is also both "approaching something that is mysterious and important"—Lois—and revealing his position as a narrator. These adjectives, and others like them throughout the story, suggest that Dick, the narrator, is recalling the entire evening after he has heard Lois' "abusive and forlorn" cry: "'Thanks for the ride!'" (*Dance* 58). It was only after he left Lois that he recognized her to be a "mystic of love." But however important Dick's ruminations are to him, they mean nothing at all to Lois, who knows nothing of them. So far as she is concerned, Dick was just like all the rest of the city boys, perhaps even worse, because he showed her a glimmer of a relationship based on something other than sex and then dashed that hope. His penultimate description of Lois—"this mystic of love" who "sat now on the far side of the carseat, looking cold and rumpled, and utterly closed up in herself" (*Dance* 57)—is apt. She looks "cold and rumpled" because that is the way she is, and that is the way she has every right to be.

Munro's retrospective narrative technique allows the reader to understand both Lois' defiant isolation and Dick's palpable regret—the two emotions held in tandem. This effect is the product of technique. Whatever view of life Munro has and that is reflected in her stories comes, as she says, from "just approaching something that is mysterious and important"—and that, indeed, is achieved through her craft and through her adroit use of a distinctive, retrospective narrative technique. Because the narrative voice is not tied to time, it roams freely through the narrator's current impressions and memories, and illuminates as it evaluates. In "Thanks for the Ride," we see it for the first time in its full flower.

Munro continued to use and refine this technique subsequent to the late 1950s, as can be seen in the balance of the stories contained in *Dance of the Happy Shades*. Five of these—"The Peace of Utrecht," "Boys and Girls," "Red Dress—1946," "Walker Brothers Cowboy," and "Images," in the order of their composition[9]—are her most mature and refined stories in the collection; they are so because Munro employs her retrospective narrative technique subtly and with dexterity. This ability certainly owes to the experience of writing the earlier stories.

Munro refined this technique by the time she published *Dance of the Happy Shades*, and has used it consistently in her subsequent work. Throughout *Lives of Girls and Women*, the book's narrator, Del Jordan, treads a fine line between the two points of view found in stories like "Day of the Butterfly." Her older voice seldom intrudes overtly; instead, it is used subtly to instruct, clarify, and expand the younger narrator's pronouncements. For example, in the last segment of "Baptizing," when Del and Garnet French recognize their differences and tacitly reject one another, the older voice comes in to comment: "We had seen in each other what we could not bear, and we had no idea that people do see that, and go on, and hate and fight and try to kill each other, various ways, then love some more" (*Lives* 240). Such covert intrusions, which contain the older Del's knowledge, are found throughout *Lives of Girls and Women*.

In this way, the technique Munro employs in *Lives of Girls and Women* is a distillation of the one she developed through her early work; it is essentially the same as the technique employed in the earlier stories considered here.

Munro's next published work, *Something I've Been Meaning to Tell You*, is another matter. The reader is startled by its range of narrative points of view, for Munro's narrators are constantly shifting in age, demeanour, and station in life. Some of the stories, such as "The Found Boat" and "The Ottawa Valley," are directly related to Munro's earlier work, focusing upon some remembered childhood experiences. Others suggest a new direction; in "Tell Me Yes or No," the narrator imagines that her lover is dead, which alters the reader's impression of what is real. Munro's range has also widened with this collection, in that she is often concerned with the question of marriages gone sour, as in "Material" and "The Spanish Lady."

But despite the wider range found in the collection, Munro's basic narrative technique is still essentially the same as that developed by the end of *Dance of the Happy Shades*. Within most of the stories is a polarity of perception, either the narrator's or the central character's, and it is partially resolved through some sort of reconciliation or epiphany. Although she uses a wider range of character types for her narrators, the way in which she communicates each of their situations has some precursor in an earlier story. For example, the dramatized reminiscent technique found in "Material," "Memorial," and "The Ottawa Valley" was first used in "The Peace of Utrecht," first published in 1960 and later included in *Dance of the Happy Shades*. By rendering her narrators' memories dramatically, however, Munro treats overtly the dual-voiced retrospective technique she had employed covertly in "Day of the Butterfly" and "Thanks for the Ride." Munro is using essentially the same narrative techniques in *Something I've Been Meaning to Tell You* that she had perfected by the time she published her first collection.

Although Munro uses the third-person narrator much more in *Who Do You Think You Are?* than in her previous work, it, too, continues her use of her characteristic retrospective technique. Here the narrator, Munro, juxtaposes her younger, innocent view of herself and of her life with a more definite and comprehensive understanding, which derives from her subsequent experience. Using the third-person narrator in this way, Munro presents Rose's initial impressions in concert with the character's eventual understanding—and in doing fulfills the role of the first-person narrator of adding subjective weight to earlier impressions, as seen in "Day of the Butterfly" and "Thanks for the Ride." Because of the detachment occasioned by the third-person narrator, Rose's story is less immediate to the reader than Myra's, or Lois' and Dick's, to be sure, but the narrative technique used in *Who Do You Think You Are?* is derived from Munro's experience in writing the earlier stories.

Munro's distinctive narrative technique, which she had perfected by the time her first collection appeared, is the basis of her felicitous style. It has enabled her to create a dialectic between present and past, between experience and understanding. This, in turn, has enabled her to transform commonplace, everyday experiences—like a girlhood acquaintanceship, a pick-up affair, or a first date—into finely wrought art. Munro's narrative dialectics, which balance one point of view against another, allow her to create her own "clear jelly," and to present a comprehensive understanding to her readers. This, in the words of Munro's narrator in "Material," "is an act of magic, there is no getting around it; it is an act, you might say, of a special, unsparing, unsentimental love. A fine and lucky benevolence" (*Something* 43).

Connection: Alice Munro and Ontario (1984)

Critics have long recognized the evocative presence of the small town in Ontario writing: Susanna Moodie's Belleville beckons as an island of civilization within a wilderness prison in *Roughing it in the Bush* (1852), Sara Jeannette Duncan's Elgin plays a central role in *The Imperialist* (1904), and no list of fictional Canadian small towns is complete without Leacock's Mariposa. More recently, Robertson Davies' Deptford trilogy has broadcast the Canadian small town far beyond Canada's borders, probing as it does the legacies of this particular—some would say peculiar—place, inherited by those real and fictional souls who inhabited them and inherit them still (see Reid). Yet the Ontario small town as an archetype is a conundrum: a province that has grown to become urban and sophisticated believes itself rural and simple. Much like the notion Davies calls the Canadian "Myth of Innocence," Ontario prefers to see itself as a place of small towns, its cities notwithstanding; as he writes: "deep in our hearts we Canadians cherish a notion—I do not call it an idea, because an idea may be carefully formulated, whereas a notion is an elusive thing that takes form from every mind that embraces it—we cherish a notion that we are a simple folk, nourished on the simpler truths of Christianity, in whom certain rough and untutored instincts of nobility assert themselves" ("Dark" 43).[1] So, too, Ontario—urban Ontario—persists in seeing itself—through its literature, the stuff of myths—as a place of small towns, formed and informed by the sway of Elgin, Mariposa, Deptford and the like. Such a notion has some basis in fact, in that many Ontarians live in small towns today, though most do not. Thus the small-town ethos in Ontario gains its primary importance as a myth—that is, as a falsehood that is somehow true—of the sort that Davies defines. In contemporary Ontario writing, the small town ethos is a legacy, an inheritance that helps explain the present by assessing and redefining the past. Thus, as an inherited presence, the Ontario small town remains central to contemporary writing in Canada; in the work of Robertson Davies, George Elliott, James Reaney, Alice Munro, Marian Engel, Matt Cohen, and numerous others, the legacy of the small town is palpable.

Of those who focus on the small town as a setting, presence, and legacy, Alice Munro seems to do so in the most pointed manner; in her stories—perhaps because they are stories rather than novels—the presence of Ontario's past is not only recurrent, but ubiquitous. Again and again, Munro takes her reader to Jubilee, to Hanratty, and, more recently, to Dalgleish, Ontario. We see and feel these towns through Munro's descriptions and analyses; her narrators remember rural Ontario during the 1930s and 1940s, balancing it against an often more urban, more sophisticated present of the 1960s through the 1980s. Her characters strive to understand themselves and their surroundings at key moments in their lives, at moments of epiphany, and in order to understand who they are, they first must recognize where they have come from. Almost always this is from rural Ontario, along Lake Huron.[2]

Munro creates Ontario's identifiable surfaces, she says, incidentally; Ontario is important in her stories because it happens to be her place, as she explains in a recent interview: "I don't think the setting matters at all. A lot of people think I'm a regional writer. And I use the region where I grew up a lot. But I don't have any idea of writing to show the kinds of things that happen in a certain place. These things happen and place is part of it. But in a way, it's incidental" (Hancock Interview 88). Despite this attempt to disavow the importance of setting in her work, Munro's fiction defines Ontario as a fictional place; the key comment in this quotation, then, is: "These things happen and place is a part of it." Indeed it is, but to Munro, place is a part of the whole tale she tells; to her, place and character are inextricably connected in a story—it is an interdependence born of the vagaries of birth and life. These associations are, of course, wholly random, but they are nonetheless significant for being so, as one of Munro's narrators explains in "The Moons of Jupiter":

> Once, when my children were little, my father said to me, "You know those years you were growing up—well, that's all a kind of blur to me. I can't sort out one year from another." I was offended. I remembered each separate year with pain and clarity. I could have told how old I was when I went to look at the evening dresses in the window of Benbow's Ladies' Wear. Every week through the winter a new dress, spotlit—the sequins and tulle, the rose and lilac, sapphire, daffodil—and me a cold worshipper on the slushy sidewalk. I could have told how old I was when I forged my mother's signature on a bad report card, when I had measles, when we papered the front room. But the years when [my children] were little, when I lived with their father—yes, blur is the word for it....
>
> Those bumbling years are the years our children will remember all their lives. Corners of the yards I never visited will stay in their heads. (*Moons* 222; 223)

This musing defines Munro's use of place: at the core of her art lies her own experience of Huron County, Ontario, a place remembered, recovered, revised, and, at times, renounced. In Munro's fiction, from her first stories published in the 1950s as an undergraduate through to the recently published "The Ferguson Girls Must Never Marry," Ontario as a fictional place is central to her stories' content and form. Small-town Ontario—its mores, perceptions, and prejudices—infuses Munro's art, allowing Ontario readers to recognize their place, certainly, but ultimately offering us much more. Munro's stories transcend the local and the provincial to reach the universal, which she captures and communicates. She does this by taking her readers, in some sense, to Ontario—if not physically, then through her memory of it.

As such, small-town Ontario is not only of thematic importance to Munro's work, it is technically significant as well, centrally so; indeed, her remembering narrators, in reflexively shifting from present to past and back again, create what one critic has called Munro's "jerky" narrative pace—but those shifts, and thus that pace, are essential to her stories.[3] Munro's work is dependent on a narrative technique that combines the past with the present, intermingling the two so as to reach toward a narrator's understanding of herself. However jerky it is, then, Munro's juxtaposition of an Ontario past with an Ontario present is fundamental to an understanding of her work. Through this juxtaposition she takes her reader to Ontario, sometimes focusing on the past almost exclusively, sometimes focusing on the present in the same way, but most frequently balancing the one with the other, as seen from the narrator's perspective. Consequently, the reader finds a well-defined relationship between the present and the past in Munro's fiction, to which the presence of the Ontario small town is crucial. Even in smug, urban, and sophisticated 1980s Ontario, the legacy of the small town persists, rearing its conscience-stricken head.

Defining her characters by their identities and their connections with rural Ontario, Munro adopts much the same approach as Eudora Welty, whose stories of the American south she has praised. Indeed, Welty's observations on the role of place in fiction define not only her own use of Mississippi, but also Munro's use of Ontario. In "Place in Fiction," Welty writes:

> It is by the nature of itself that fiction is all bound up in the local. The internal reason for that is surely that *feelings* are bound up in place. The human mind is a mass of associations—associations more poetic even than actual. I say, "The Yorkshire Moors," and you will say, "*Wuthering Heights*," and I have only to murmur, "If Father were only alive—" for you to come back with "We could go to Moscow," which certainly is not even so. The truth is, fiction depends for its life on place. Location is the crossroads of circumstance, the proving ground of "What happened? Who's here? Who's coming?"—and that is the heart's field.... Fiction is properly at work on the here and now, or

the past made here and now; for in novels *we* have to be there. Fiction provides the ideal texture through which the feeling and meaning that permeate our own personal, present lives will best show through. (*Eye* 118, 117)

"The past made here and now." This observation, like Welty's and Munro's fictions, emphasizes the relationship between the past and present, and the power of place to conjure up that relationship through memory and to synthesize the two.[4]

Yet that relationship and that power can be misunderstood, as Munro has learned. As her fiction has gained reputation during the last dozen years, Munro has found herself caught up in controversy. Two incidents bear directly on this discussion. In 1976 the Peterborough, Ontario, school board removed *Lives of Girls and Women* (1971)—along with Margaret Laurence's *The Diviners* (1974)—from its approved high school reading list because of its alleged explicit treatment of sex. More recently, the *Wingham Advance-Times*, published weekly in Munro's childhood hometown of Wingham, Ontario, ran an anti-Munro editorial in response to an article on Munro that appeared the week before in *Today* magazine. Entitled "A Genius of Sour Grapes," the editor intones: "Sadly enough Wingham people have never had much chance to enjoy the excellence of [Munro's] writing ability because we have repeatedly been made the butt of soured and cruel introspection on the part of a gifted author." Taking a chamber-of-commerce tone, the editorial disputes the accuracy of Munro's claim that parts of Wingham featured "bootleggers, prostitutes, and hangers on," concluding, "something less than greatness impels her to return again and again to a time and a place in her life where bitterness warped her personality." These incidents suggest, like the ubiquity of the small town in Ontario fiction, the persistence of its myth today ("Genius"). Despite its sophistication and urbanity, Ontario still holds its small-town moralists who, as in Peterborough (certainly not a small town itself), rise up and inveigh against immorality. At the same time, the Wingham paper's stand ironically justifies Munro's consistently held view that such towns are stultifying for the imaginative, however imaginatively escapable. Both incidents show, finally, that the small-town ethos is far from dead: the past continues to weigh upon the present.

After the editorial appeared, Munro discussed the controversy, describing Wingham as a place she can live neither with nor without. She acknowledged her unpopularity there, attributing it to her having told all—"the country gossip tattling her tales to city folk" (Wayne 9). Thus like Leacock, Davies, and other Ontario writers, Munro criticizes the small town at a price; it is stifling, to be sure, for the native with imagination and drive, but it also cannot be escaped. For Munro as a fiction writer, particularly, Wingham is her place—she must live in an uncomfortable connection with it. Munro's narrative technique evolved along two parallel lines: her stories employ either remembering first-person narrators or third-person narrators, usually limited to the protagonist's perspective. The first of these approaches predominated her writing up to and including *Lives of Girls and Women*; the second, though used consistently since Munro's first stories, has appeared far more frequently in her two most recent books: *Who Do You Think You Are?* (1978) and *The Moons of Jupiter* (1982). Munro herself is quite aware of her dual approach, though she does not try to explain it. In a recent interview, for example, she comments: "And you get a feel for what you should do. But a lot of my stuff I write in both first and third person. Or I start off one way, and then I do it the other way" (Struthers Interview 24).

At the same time, Munro has spoken often about her attitude toward objects. For example, she remarks during an interview conducted by Graeme Gibson: "I'm not an intellectual writer. I'm very, very excited by what you might call the surface of life." She is seeking to obtain "the exact tone or texture of how things are," and "can't have anybody in a room without describing all the furniture" (Gibson Interview 241, 256–57). Such concern with evoking surface detail is evident from her earliest stories on. Take, for example, the opening passage of "The Edge of Town," published in 1955:

> Up here the soil is shallow and stony; the creeks dry up in summer, and a harsh wind from the west blows all year long. There are not many trees, but wild-rose and blackberry bushes in little pockets of the hills, and long sharp sword-grass in the hollows. On an August day if you stand on the road leading out from the town, you can see miles and miles of brown blowing grass, and

dust scooped up from the roads, and low, bumpy hills along the rim of the sky, which might be the end of the world. At night the crickets sing in the grass, and every second day, at supper time, a freight train goes through the town. ("Edge" 368)

Munro often refers to her stories as being one of two types: adequate or inadequate (in her most recently published interview, these are "the real material" and "holding-pattern stories"). Without question, "The Edge of Town" is a holding-pattern story, for Munro has rejected it "almost entirely as a contrived and as an artificial story" (Gardiner Interview 173).

Her own condemnation notwithstanding, "The Edge of Town" establishes the texture and surface of place as an important presence in Munro's stories from the beginning—and, as here, that place is virtually always southwestern Ontario, whatever the name of the town. Passages such as the one above are certainly vital to the stories in *Dance of the Happy Shades* (1968): the descriptions of Lois's town in "Thanks for the Ride," the river land walked along by the protagonist and her father in "Images," and the description of Lake Huron in terms of geologic time in "Walker Brothers Cowboy." So, too, are they crucial to *Lives of Girls and Women*: "The Flats Road" and "Heirs of the Living Body" depend on the texture of place.

What has changed is how she has used such passages. In "The Edge of Town," and "Thanks for the Ride," first published in 1957, she uses setting to help the reader understand a character who is essentially inarticulate; environment is a symbolic index to character. In the latter story, Munro is far more successful. "Thanks for the Ride" succeeds while "The Edge of Town" fails largely because of a shift from third- to first-person narration—Dick, the story's narrator, sees Lois in terms of place and so understands her entrapment through setting, caught as she is between two role models, a winkingly knowing mother and a caustically cynical grandmother. Thus "Thanks for the Ride" combines place and character—Dick, as participating narrator, cannot understand Lois without understanding her town—whereas in "The Edge of Town," place is separate from its protagonist, Harry Brooke, as the previously quoted passage, in its evocative description of starkness, suggests.

In the same interview in which she condemns "The Edge of Town" as an artificial story, Munro mentions that when she began writing, setting was much more important to her than character (Gardiner Interview 173).[5] This is borne out by her stories: the different way she uses place in "The Edge of Town" and "Thanks for the Ride" indicates the direction in which she developed. Place was separate from character in many of Munro's early uncollected stories, serving as objective setting only, but became progressively more internalized within her stories as Munro began to tailor her settings to make them subjective and dependent on an individual narrative point of view—one that connects one place to another by uniting sensibility and memory.

Rural Ontario is Munro's own place, her own "past made here and now," in Welty's phrase. Its qualities within her stories are well summarized by the final paragraph of "The Ottawa Valley," published in *Something I've Been Meaning to Tell You* (1974). The story recounts a trip the narrator took to the Ottawa Valley as a pre-teenage girl with her mother and sister. There the narrator sees her mother differently—connected to a world she doesn't know, represented by her Aunt Dodie and other relatives from her mother's girlhood in the Ottawa Valley. More importantly, the narrator realizes that her mother has contracted Parkinson's disease; during the visit she recognizes its presence for the first time and so recognizes, as well, her mother's mortality, and that she will not always be there to provide comfort. This latter recognition, by far the more painful, comes when she questions her mother about Dodie's statement that her mother has had a stroke; nervously, "recklessly, stubbornly," the young girl persists, not really satisfied by her mother's response, saying, "Is your arm going to stop shaking?" The narrator understands in retrospect that she had been demanding that her mother "turn and promise me what I needed. But she did not do it. For the first time she held out altogether against me. She went on as if she had not heard, her familiar bulk ahead of me turning strange, indifferent" (*Something* 244). Here, through memory, the narrator first recognizes the disease that would eventually kill her mother, and she her mother's action as a recognition of her fate. The story's final paragraph encapsulates several of Munro's concerns:

If I had been making a proper story out of this, I would have ended it, I think, with my mother not answering and going ahead of me across the pasture. That would have done. I didn't stop there, I suppose, because I wanted to find out more, remember more. I wanted to bring back all I could. Now I look at what I've done and it is like a series of snapshots, like the brownish snapshots with fancy borders that my parents' old camera used to take. In these snapshots Aunt Dodie and Uncle James and even Aunt Lena, even her children, come out clear enough.... The problem, the only problem, is my mother. And she is the one of course that I am trying to get; it is to reach her that this whole journey has been undertaken. With what purpose? To mark her off, to describe, to illumine, to celebrate, to *get rid* of her; and it did not work, for she looms too close, just as she always did. She is heavy as always, she weighs everything down, and yet she is indistinct, her edges melt and flow. Which means she has stuck to me as close as ever and refused to fall away, and I could go on, and on, applying what skills I have, using what tricks I know, and it would always be the same. (*Something* 246)

Here then is Munro's Ontario, Munro's life, described in her own terms through the perspective of a remembering narrator; place is a web of chance connections—some sensual, some human. In trying to understand one's life, a person must live willy-nilly, concerning herself with the past—past places, past people, past worries. Associations spring forth from memories, often triggered by places or events—as the following discussion will show—and impinge on the present like old, brownish snapshots, leading us back into the past through memory, like the woman who was the young girl in "The Ottawa Valley," trying once more to capture, and so to understand, her mother. These two realms of past and present are inextricably linked in Munro's stories, and the form they take is reflexive: past is ever present; now depends upon then.

This reflexive use of Ontario is seen in most of Munro's stories; one may cite numerous instances of the interlayering techniques she uses. But the discussion here is limited to an examination of "The Peace of Utrecht," one of the first stories to establish Munro's characteristic use of place, and that does so most thoroughly. First published in 1960 and included in a revised form in *Dance of the Happy Shades*, "The Peace of Utrecht" concerns a visit Helen makes with her children to the town of Jubilee to see her sister Maddy for the first time since the death of their mother from a long, lingering illness. Helen begins her narration by emphasizing her estrangement from her sister:

> I have been home for three weeks and it has not been a success. Maddy and I, though we speak cheerfully of our enjoyment of so long and intimate a visit, will be relieved when it is over. Silence disturbs us. We laugh immoderately. I am afraid—very likely we are both afraid—that when the moment comes to say goodbye, unless we are very quick to kiss, and fervently mockingly squeeze each other's shoulders, we will have to look straight into the desert that is between us and acknowledge that we are not merely indifferent; at heart we reject each other, and as for the past we make so much of sharing we do not really share it at all, each of us keeping it jealously to herself, thinking privately that the other has turned alien and forfeited her claim. (*Dance* 190)

Helen begins by opening wounds, asserting her separate pain, and thereby directing and intriguing the reader. She embarks, through memory, on a voyage of self-discovery, moving gradually toward a searing recognition; Helen realizes that she has abandoned both her sister and—far more importantly—her mother to their respective fates. By examining herself, Helen is gauging her own responsibility, and her own interdependence and independence. This dynamic, this drama of memory, is informed by Ontario past; Jubilee brings back memories and thus forms and informs the story—its Protestant ethos demands that Helen acknowledge her responsibility. "I felt," she says at one point, "as if my old life was lying around me, waiting to be picked up again" (*Dance* 201).

Helen's narration reveals Munro's dependence on the evocative effects of memory. Helen begins by acknowledging the rift between her and her sister, and in this way the story's narrative order is not chronological. Instead, its movement depends upon a dialectic relationship between Helen's memory and her perception of her present situation, and is directed by her looming awareness of her dead mother. The mother acts like a wedge between the sisters, a function underscored by Helen's nostalgic recollection of the fullness of their childhood relationship, juxtaposed against the emptiness of their present relationship. But Helen is unable to sustain her nostalgia, because she is aware that the rift between the two of them has been caused by Maddy's life in Jubilee, "the dim world of continuing disaster, of home" (*Dance* 191). Helen managed to escape to a husband and family, to a life far away. So in addition to confronting her mother, Helen must also gauge her responsibility toward her sister's present dissatisfaction, which verges on desperation.

After delineating the effect of their mother's illness and death on her relationship with Maddy, Helen steps back and places their story within the social milieu of the town itself. Thus Jubilee is an informing presence, a source of values—some repudiated, some not. Helen recognizes that her mother's lengthy illness is a part of the town, and encroaching on her own sense of identity: "And now that she is dead I no longer feel that when they say the words 'your mother' they deal a knowing, cunning blow at my pride. I used to feel that; at those words I felt my whole identity, that pretentious adolescent construction, come tumbling down" (*Dance* 194). Helen realizes that when the sisters tried to hide their "Gothic Mother" from the town, it rejected the attempt: "We should have let the town have her; it would have treated her better" (*Dance* 195).

After the sisters' own social history, and the effect of the visit, are explained, Helen begins her self-analysis. From the moment of her arrival three weeks earlier, Helen felt as if she was home—yet she knew she was not:

> There is no easy way to get to Jubilee from anywhere on earth. Then about two o'clock in the afternoon I saw ahead of me, so familiar and unexpected, the gaudy, peeling cupola of the town hall, which is no relation to any of the rest of the town's squarely-built, dingy grey-and-red-brick architecture. (Underneath it hangs a great bell, to be rung in the event of some mythical

> disaster.) I drove up the main street—a new service station, new stucco front on the Queen's Hotel—and turned into the quiet, decaying side streets where old maids live, and have birdbaths and blue delphiniums in their gardens. The big brick houses that I knew, with their wooden verandahs and gaping, dark-screened windows, seemed to me plausible but unreal. (Anyone to whom I have mentioned the dreaming, sunken feeling of these streets wants to take me out to the north side of town where there is a new soft-drink bottling plant, some new ranch-style houses and a Tastee-Freez.) Then I park my car in a little splash of shade in front of the house where I used to live. (*Dance* 196)

Here Munro combines place and character: Helen's recognitions begin with the town itself. Having been long away, Helen assesses the ways in which Jubilee is still the same while, parenthetically, acknowledging the ways in which it has changed. Implicitly, the same might be said of Helen. Remembering, Helen finds the place she left, but now she must identify and digest its changes, literal as well as personal. By defining the rift between Helen and Maddy announced in the story's first paragraph, Munro begins with physical place and the changes it has undergone, which Helen notices, in order to move towards plumbing the psychological changes now separating the two sisters.

Emotional changes—leading inexorably toward their mother's death—are introduced through the family home, still maintained by Maddy. Helen's response to her daughter's incredulity at her first glimpse of Helen's childhood home, gives voice to Munro's awareness of the disparity between imagination and reality. As Helen enters the house she views herself in a mirror:

> Then I paused, one foot on the bottom step, and turned to greet, matter-of-factly, the reflection of a thin, tanned, habitually watchful woman, recognizably a Young Mother, whose hair, pulled into a knot on top of her head, exposed a jawline no longer softly fleshed, a brown neck rising with a look of tension

> from the little sharp knobs of the collarbone—this is the hall mirror that had shown me, last time I looked, a commonplace pretty girl, with a face as smooth as and insensitive as an apple, no matter what panic and disorder lay behind it. (*Dance* 197–198)

Helen realizes that she did not turn to see her reflection; she turned in expectation of hearing her mother call "*Who's There?*" (*Dance* 198). Helen's introspection and her guilt about her mother are, accordingly, thrust toward the reader, and though multifaceted, her guilt stems largely from recognizing that she had gradually become insensitive to her mother's suffering.

The house's rooms—the physical surfaces of place—trigger memories for Helen that help explain her trepidation and that lead her to acknowledge her responsibility toward both her mother and sister. While away from Jubilee, Helen had become detached from the situation at home, something that is evident as she describes her mother's decline:

> In the ordinary world it was not possible to recreate her. The picture of her face which I carried in my mind seemed too terrible, unreal. Similarly the complex strain of living with her, the feelings of hysteria which Maddy and I once dissipated in a great deal of brutal laughter, now began to seem partly imaginary; I felt the beginnings of a secret, guilty estrangement. (*Dance* 200–201)

Despite her absence, Helen is able to be nostalgic about her youth in Jubilee and her relationship with Maddy: "I thought of us walking up and down the main street, arm in arm with two or three other girls, until it got dark, then going in to Al's to dance, under a string of little colored lights. The windows in the dance hall were open; they let in the raw spring air with its smell of earth and the river; the hands of farm boys crumpled and stained our white blouses when we danced" (*Dance* 201). Such experiences, which juxtapose the past with the present, take on an almost mystical significance in Munro's stories. Helen continues, but is unable to sustain a sentimental perspective:

> And now an experience which seemed not at all memorable at the time (in fact Al's was a dismal place and the ritual of walking up and down the street to show ourselves off we thought crude and ridiculous, though we could not resist it) had been transformed into something curiously meaningful for me, and complete; it took in more than the girls dancing and the single street, it spread over the whole town, its rudimentary pattern of streets and its bare trees and muddy yards just free of the snow, over the dirt roads where the lights of cars appeared, jolting towards the town, under an immense pale wash of sky. (*Dance* 201–02)

As with the later passages, quoted earlier from "The Ottawa Valley" and "The Moons of Jupiter," Munro is here defining character through place; identity is dependent on memory, on association, on connection. Helen concludes this musing: "Maddy; her bright skeptical look; my sister" (202). Thus, here her nostalgia is balanced—and deflated—by the perspective and knowledge afforded from looking back from the present —Helen's rueful remembrance of Maddy's "bright skeptical look" is undercut by both her more cynical point of view and her knowledge of Maddy's present desperation.

Because Maddy refuses to discuss their mother's death with her sister, Helen must discover the truth from their maiden aunts Annie and Lou—foils who suggest a shared old age the younger sisters have escaped. The aunts' role, too, is to speak for the town, and to articulate its judgement of Maddy's treatment of their mother. During a visit to the aunts' home, Helen is led upstairs by Annie, ostensibly to give Helen her mother's clothes, which the older woman has neatly mended, washed, and saved. Throughout the exchange, Munro emphasizes the ethical gulf between them, one Helen recognizes and feels guilty about, but can do nothing to bridge. When Annie almost furtively offers the clothes, Helen responds curtly, cementing these differences and defining the gulf between her own inherited values and those she lives by:

> "I would rather buy," I said, and was immediately sorry for the coldness in my voice. Nevertheless, I continued, "When I need something, I do go and buy it." This suggestion that I was not poor any more brought a look of reproach and aloofness into my aunt's face. She said nothing. I went and looked at a picture of Auntie Ann and Auntie Lou and their older brothers and their mother and father which hung over the bureau. They stared back at me with grave accusing Protestant faces, for I had run up against the simple unprepossessing materialism which was the rock of their lives. Things must be used up, saved and mended and made into something else and used again; clothes were to be worn. I felt that I had hurt Aunt Annie's feelings and that furthermore I had probably borne out a prediction of Auntie Lou's, for she was sensitive to certain attitudes in the world that were too sophisticated for Aunt Annie to bother about, and she had very likely said that I would not want my mother's clothes. (*Dance* 206)

Immediately after this exchange, Aunt Annie comments, "'She was gone sooner than anybody would have expected.... Your mother,'" beginning what Helen thinks may be "a necessary part of our visit" (*Dance* 206). The aunt continues to tell Helen, in great detail, the story of her mother's final weeks, which included a January escape from the hospital in bathrobe and slippers. Helen is not surprised; though she prefers a less harsh view, such as her nostalgia about her childhood relationship with her sister, Helen has divined the truth before Annie offers it: Maddy put their mother in the hospital to die.

This scene, focusing as it does on the differing values of successive generations, dramatizes Munro's use of Ontario's past and present in her stories. Each generation is connected to the one that preceded it, just as it is to the one that succeeds it. At the core of Munro's work lies the confrontation between each generation's point of view, each generation's values.

Implicit in such scenes as this, in which no agreement is possible, are the changes that time has wrought, and a recognition of a deep connection, despite these changes. Auntie Annie concludes, telling Helen what they thought of Maddy's treatment of their mother during her final days: "'We thought it was hard,' she said finally. 'Lou and I thought it was hard.'" Helen responds quizzically, capturing the essence of Munro's use of her own Ontario background; she wonders, "Is this the last function of old women, beyond making rag rugs and giving us five dollar bills—making sure the haunts we have contracted for are with us, not one gone without?" (*Dance* 209). This recognition is central to the story, just as it is to Munro's use of place, and just as it is to her art. "The Peace of Utrecht" dramatizes Helen's recognition of her own isolation, and the means by which Munro accomplishes this are through Helen's memories of Jubilee vis-à-vis the Jubilee she finds during her visit. They are, and yet they are not, the same place, Helen learns. Nonetheless, each of these Jubilees is hers, and she must find herself in both versions, because the two are inseparable, held together by her memory and perception. Munro uses both Helen's memories of her past and her realizations about the present to define the changes the character has undergone. In this, setting is accidental, as Munro suggests, but it is also crucial, because it is largely through setting that Helen gauges and articulates her changed perspective.

The story's title, for example, underscores the casualness of association that Munro captures so readily: looking about her former room just after her arrival, Helen opens the drawer of the washstand and discovers some pages "from a looseleaf notebook. I read: 'The Peace of Utrecht, 1713, brought an end to the War of the Spanish Succession.' It struck me that the handwriting was my own. Strange to think of it lying here for ten years—more; it looked as if I might have written it that day" (*Dance* 201). Thus the Peace of Utrecht is also Helen's own personal peace—just as with her decade-old handwriting, Helen recognizes psychological connections that she must acknowledge: her own responsibility for her mother's death, her lost intimacy with Maddy, and, finally, her permanent connection to Jubilee and thus to "the haunts" she has "contracted for." Though she feels "a secret, guilty estrangement" (*Dance* 201) from Jubilee, and would prefer to feel nostalgic, Helen cannot avoid knowing about the more threatening implications of what she has found in Jubilee during this visit. In this way she comes to understand the depth of her own isolation in tandem with Maddy's, which accounts for the phrase at the story's opening: "at heart we reject each other." In her return to Jubilee and in recognizing the changes she herself has undergone, especially through Auntie Annie's tale of her mother's flight and struggle, Helen finds the truth she has sought throughout the story—though it is by no means a gentle truth.

This interpretation is reinforced by the guidance Helen offers Maddy when she returns home after visiting her aunts—after Maddy admits that she put their mother in the hospital to die, Helen tells her, "Take your life, Maddy." (210). For her part, Helen has reconciled her life away from Jubilee and her attachments there. She has come to an understanding that stands in marked contrast to her sister's.

This extended treatment of "The Peace of Utrecht" is justified because the story is central to Munro's canon; she has often called it one of her first "real" stories, and her "first painful autobiographical story" (Metcalf Interview 58; Struthers Interview 23). At the same time, it focuses on the relationships within families, one of her recurring concerns. From her earliest stories, Munro has been using this narrative approach based on memory to tell her stories; in it, the rural Ontario small town is a crucial presence, in that its mores form the basis of both the confusion with which a story begins and the understanding, however tentative, that emerges at its close. In "The Peace of Utrecht," Munro fully dramatizes this process for the first time. Helen's return to and rediscovery of her home place is followed by Del Jordan's in *Lives of Girls and Women*, by various figures' in *Something I've Been Meaning to Tell You*, by Rose's in *Who Do You Think You Are?* and, most recently, by the protagonists' in *The Moons of Jupiter*. Indeed, Helen's rhetorical response to Auntie Annie—wondering if her final function is to ensure the continuation of personal "haunts"—is a restatement of Munro's perpetual attempts to understand each of her characters. For Munro, meaning is created when place and character are intertwined, just like past and present—when associations and connections are brought into focus at a crucial moment. In her early works, like "The Edge of Town," it is possible to see place as separate from character, but from "The Peace of Utrecht" on, this becomes virtually impossible; from this point on, place and character—that is, identity—so control the direction of a Munro story as she focuses on her protagonist's central mystery that they cannot be separated.

Munro's development in this manner—toward a more vital integration of place and character—is something she herself recognizes. In the 1973 interview in which she rejects "The Edge of Town," Munro states: "At first I think I was just overwhelmed by a place, and the story was almost ... a contrived illustration of whatever this place meant to me—O.K.? And yet, you know, [the opening passage from "The Edge of Town"] was not an imagined setting. I actually lived [it] ... it's all real. It's all there. I did not make it for its meaning. I was trying to find a meaning" (Gardiner Interview 173–74).[6] This is what Munro does in her stories: she tries "to find a meaning." At times she complains of the inadequacy of her attempts, such as with the final paragraph of "The Ottawa Valley," but though her triumphs are momentary, her insights fleeting, Munro writes stories that capture the uncertainty of the present. Vital to this is Ontario's past: images of the past, recalled by memory, help her characters understand their current situations, even if those memories are negative ones, such as an Aunt Annie scolding and condemning the younger generation who have inherited a connection.

The recent story "Chaddeleys and Flemings: 1. Connection" illustrates Munro's continued use of the past in the same manner as in "The Peace of Utrecht." The narrator begins by recounting a memorable visit made by four maiden cousins—the Chaddeleys—to the narrator's girlhood home in Huron County. They are irreverent and fun-loving, and fill their hosts with joy and laughter; during their stay, the narrator says: "My parents, all of us, are on holiday" (*Moons* 18). Juxtaposed against this memory is a present-day visit made by the only remaining living member of the four—known by the narrator as Cousin Iris. The narrator—now grown, married, and living in Vancouver with her condescending and supercilious husband—is tense and craves for the evening to go well. Iris approves of the husband but he does not reciprocate; he does not volunteer to take her back to her hotel, and once she leaves, says: "'What a pathetic old tart.'" He continues to mock Iris and, the narrator says, "was still talking as I threw the pyrex plate at his head" (*Moons* 17). Immediately after this revelation, the story concludes in a manner reminiscent of Helen's nostalgic recollections of Maddy and of an earlier Jubilee—Munro places a fond memory, described earlier in the story, in stark contrast to the narrator's hostility toward her husband:

> *Row, row, row your boat*
>
> *Gently down the stream.*
>
> *Merrily, merrily, merrily, merrily,*
>
> *Life is but a dream.*

> I lie in bed beside my little sister, listening to the singing in the yard. Life is transformed, by these voices, by these presences, by their high spirits and grand esteem, for themselves and each other. My parents, all of us, are on holiday. The mixture of voices and words is so complicated and varied it seems that such confusion, such jolly rivalry, will go on forever, and then to my surprise for I am surprised, even though I know the pattern of rounds—the song is thinning out, you can hear the two voices striving.

> *Merrily, merrily, merrily, merrily,*
>
> *Life is but a dream*

> Then the one voice alone, one of them singing on, gamely, to the finish. One voice in which there is an unexpected note of entreaty, of warning, as it hangs the five separate words on the air. Life is. Wait. But a. Now, wait. Dream. (*Moons* 18)

This lyrical, yet somehow frightening, memory contrasts palpably with the glaring ugliness of the act that precedes it, and through it the reader comes to understand the narrator's situation, her present versus her past. This, quite simply, is what Munro does in her stories, and this is how she uses the Ontario small town—earlier in the story the narrator concludes:

"Connection. That was what it was all about" (*Dance* 6). In this final image, which haunts the narrator, Munro recreates and holds in evocative juxtaposition a single delightful memory from that earlier summer visit: a song shared by the visitors as they went to sleep outdoors one night in the cool of the evening, overheard by the narrator. Faced with her husband's sneers, she comes to understand it as her connection to another time and another place that is far preferable to her present situation. As with Helen in "The Peace of Utrecht," it is a connection that cannot be denied, and a vital part of her being. The remembered voice, too, is like the single voice Munro offers in all of her stories: that of a person far away in time or space, confirming a crucial connection to Ontario. This memory defines the narrator's separation from those who do not share this connection; her sneering husband does not, will not, and cannot understand. But the reader, through Munro's art, does understand. For Munro, a connection to Ontario and its past always beckons: "Connection. That was what it was all about."

Critical Interlude:

Conferring Munro (1987)

The Art of Alice Munro: Saying the Unsayable. Ed. Judith Miller. Waterloo: U of Waterloo P, 1984.

A witticism making the literary rounds a few years ago described Canada's preeminent women writers as "the three Margarets": Margaret Laurence, Margaret Atwood, and Alice Munro, thus consigning Munro to odd-woman-out status by virtue of her un-Margareted name. Using critical attention as a measure, one might well see Munro's role within this trinity in much the same fashion—as an odd woman out. Though her stories began appearing around the same time as the other two Margarets' works, and Munro's offerings were as roundly praised as theirs, her work has only recently begun to get the extended critical attention long accorded theirs. *The Art of Alice Munro*, which publishes some of the papers delivered at the March 1982 University of Waterloo conference on Munro's fiction, follows hard on the heels of *Probable Fictions: Alice Munro's Narrative Acts* (1983); together, they are a part of what appears to be an avalanche of critical attention. Five volumes of "Munroviana"—a term coined by one of the critics included here—have been published or were scheduled for publication between 1983 and 1986, and that's not counting Hallvard

Dahlie's monograph on Munro included in *Canadian Writers and Their Works*, nor books in which Munro figures as one of several writers being critiqued.[1] Clearly, Munro has been conferred a new critical status, receiving attention befitting the author of so many stories first published in the *New Yorker* and, ultimately, collected in *Who Do You Think You Are?* and *The Moons of Jupiter*. The latter book has cemented Munro's position as one of Canada's best.

That Munro's art should receive progressively greater scrutiny by critics is hardly surprising, of course, given that readers and reviewers have noted subtleties and complexities in her stories from the very first—refinements belied by their apparent simplicity in subject, narration, structure, and tone. As well, critical attention is at least in part cyclical and faddish, with enthusiasts rushing holus-bolus to the latest rage, whether for purposes of a graduate thesis or the invitation of a handy conference or a call for papers. For good or ill, Munro's time has come. Such concerns are germane in assessing *The Art of Alice Munro: Saying the Unsayable*, because this volume evinces all the strengths and weaknesses its form—the conference collection—usually offers and, at the same time, reflects something of the state of Canadian criticism in relation to Munro's newfound celebrity.

Like most conference collections, the products of occasions, *The Art of Alice Munro* is uneven: two of its essays are excellent by any standard, two are quite good, another makes a reasonable point but is seriously flawed, another offers an oral address—enthusiastic though not especially well-informed—and the remaining two are simple-minded at best and puerile at worst: what they have to say would have been better left unsaid. The collection also includes, inevitably, an interview with Munro, which is balanced, less inevitably, by a fine overview of the Munro papers held by the University of Calgary. Yet this book's flaws exceed the expectations for such occasional volumes. Throughout, there is little evidence of the tough-minded editing necessary to transform conference presentations into a credible volume of essays; what emerges instead is simply a printed record of a conference on Munro.[2]

After Miller's introduction, which offers little more than summaries of the essays (and exaggerates their accomplishments more than a bit), *The Art of Alice Munro* begins with Joseph Gold's "Our Feeling Exactly: The Writing of Alice Munro." Despite its title, the essay does not really take up Munro's writing; it concentrates on *Who Do You Think You Are?*, with asides to *Lives of Girls and Women*. More importantly, Gold's essay is little more than an appreciation, an oral presentation in print. There is little development of argument and Gold quotes far too much; he also indulges in overstatement ("Rose's orgasm blows up Ontario" [8]) without accounting for himself, and leaves his reader adrift. This is a pity, for Gold is a critic of some acuity, and his thesis—the relationship between feeling and language—is central to Munro's work.

Equally troubling, but from another point of view, are Margaret Anne Fitzpatrick's "'Projection' in Alice Munro's *Something I've Been Meaning to Tell You*" and Nora Robson's "Alice Munro and the White American South: The Quest." Neither author has a point worth making. Fitzpatrick sounds as if she has swallowed a psychoanalytical textbook when she is not sounding sophomoric: "In this paper I will first briefly elucidate the psychological nature of projection and then, by example, show how Alice Munro has used projection in the construction of certain of her characters and plots" (16). Her point—that Munro's characters feel self-conscious and so project their anxieties outward in a variety of ways—is obvious in the first place, so Fitzpatrick's five-page "glimpse" adds little and might well have been based on other (and better) examples from Munro's stories. Robson, on the other hand, dips into her M.A. thesis to make a point that has already been made, that Del Jordan "passes through experiences related realistically or symbolically in ways not unlike those of the writers of the American South" (73). J. R. (Tim) Struthers published "Alice Munro and the American South" in 1975; thus Robson's essay—which only points up thematic parallels that Munro freely admits to anyway—seems unnecessary.[3] Both these essays represent the kind of uninformed fannishness that characterized Munro criticism during the late 1970s, and that to some extent characterizes it still.[4]

It is one thing for a critic to expect an essay to be something it is not—and perhaps cannot be—and quite another to ask that it be something it bloody well should have been and is quite capable of being: well-written and to the point. Barbara Godard's "'Heirs of the Living Body': Alice Munro and the Question of a Female Aesthetic" has an excellent point to make, when it gets around to it. Looking at *Lives of Girls and Women*, Godard eventually argues that the book (whatever it is, *Lives* is not the novel so many of these critics simply assume it to be) is a *Bildungsroman* written against James Joyce's male point of view, a revision of both his *A Portrait of the Artist as a Young Man* and *Ulysses*, so that Del ultimately "will dissect and demystify, rewrite tradition to include women's lives while sounding out the limits of language" (70–71). Fine. Excellent point. But seldom have I seen a published essay so in need of an editor: Godard rambles about for almost 10 pages before she gets around to Munro, citing feminist literary theory and trendy criticism (Harold Bloom's "deconstructionist poetics" [50]) galore, making asides to other Canadian writers (Gabrielle Roy, Margaret Atwood), and generally showing us what she's read. Almost 30 pages in printed form, Godard's essay should have been half its length. True, Godard does need the theorists she uses to set up her argument—by no means a simple one—but her 10 pages of rambling should have been a single page and a few windy footnotes. As it is, a fine article on *Lives*—offering the best reading yet on the Joyce connection—is buried beneath a mass of too-detailed allusions.

Before moving on to the better offerings in *The Art of Alice Munro*, I must carp one final time: Harold Horwood's interview with Munro reveals nothing substantively different from other interviews in print, save perhaps its discussion of writing on trains (they both do) and the fact that *Lives of Girls and Women* was written in a laundry room. At the same time, I was struck by how little Horwood seemed to know about Munro prior to the interview.

On to better things. The balance of the essays included are of quite a different order: very good, and two especially are excellent. Jean F. Tener's "The Invisible Iceberg" presents a succinct overview of the history of the Munro papers at the University of Calgary library—how they arrived, something of the problems involved in cataloguing them, what is included, how Munro assisted in setting up the archive—and concludes with an invitation to scholars to come and use them. In addition to the library's more detailed listing—*The Alice Munro Papers: First Accession*—Tener's essay serves as a point of departure for scholars wishing to use the holdings. She certainly arouses our curiosity, especially those of us interested particularly in Munro's style.

If Robson's essay shows how the major purpose of a graduate thesis is not necessarily to contribute to the field as an article, Linda

Lamont-Stewart's "Order From Chaos: Writing as Self-Defense in the Fiction of Alice Munro and Clark Blaise" shows how it can certainly serve such a purpose, as well as become the foundation for additional work. In a precisely written and detailed argument, Lamont-Stewart demonstrates that in both Munro and Blaise's stories, "the writing of fiction is in part a defensive tactic: the writer's ironic awareness of the artificiality of fictional reality affords some protection in a disorderly world" (120). In a similar vein, J. R. (Tim) Struthers argues convincingly in "Alice Munro's Fictive Imagination" that Munro's art is "metafiction" and, though he alludes widely to many of her stories, relevant criticism, and other metafictional writers, he establishes his point mainly through a fine discussion of "Something I've Been Meaning to Tell You." That story "makes the reader swirl in virtually unimaginable psychological depths, in a 'natural confusion' (*Something* 23). It is fiction that questions its own truth and mocks its own telling" (106).

But if these essays are good, then the remaining two are singular, significant contributions both; W. R. Martin and James Carscallen are alive to every nuance in Munro's art, knowing, as Martin puts it, that she "seizes on telling connotations" (31). Martin's essay, "'Hanging Pictures Together': *Something I've Been Meaning to Tell You*," demonstrates a logic of arrangement in the collection based on the very "telling connotations" he sees with sensitivity and precision in the fiction. Following him, we understand the connotations, too, seeing his pairings of stories—"hanging pictures together"—as the product of a compelling internal logic dictated by the stories themselves. Rather than rehearse his argument, I want to offer a passage of Martin's prose that offers a crucial insight:

> I am prepared to guess the reason why [Munro] prefers writing short stories to novels: she feels that writing a novel calls for a deliberate and lengthy setting out in detail of all the connections and relationships between all the characters, episodes and other aspects of a work that is by definition of a certain length, and requires a full analysis of motives as well as a thorough following through of circumstances. If I am right, Alice Munro feels that detailed circumstantiality and exhaustive explanation

soon lead to the obvious and the tedious, which she, with her quick and lively mind, thoroughly abhors. Writing short stories, on the other hand, allows her to create entities which stand apart or move in orbits at some distance from one another, and yet, across the spaces that separate them, powerful, or subtle and at first barely-felt gravitational pulls and ironic repulsions can operate, sometimes over great distances. A reader can become aware of all sorts of tensions, attractions, currents, and cross-currents without being flatly told about them, and can appreciate them the more because his faculties have been roused to act. Someone has said that the most beautiful parts of music are the silences between the notes. Something like this is true of Alice Munro's short stories. (33–34)

While Martin presents a rationale for the arrangement of stories in a collection, Carscallen's "The Shining House: A Group of Stories" presents a group of stories—from across Munro's works—that offer a common perspective. In so doing, Carscallen is impressively sensitive to the whole of Munro's art, for his essay deals with narration, point of view, subject, and character as each is germane, and he ultimately displays an understanding that is refined and cogent. What he sees in many of Munro's stories is an "expansive world" (88), which he likens to the classical biblical Egypt of wealth and power—based on various allusions to Egypt in the stories—and which he calls "Egypt" as a convenient term. Throughout these stories, "the body, what is, finds a reflection in what is not: in thoughts, emotions, pictures, signs—the world, in other words, of 'images'" (91). The power of Munro's stories is derived from the interplay between the body—the narrator/protagonist—and these images.

 A detached reflection—for that is what it is—steals away the life of the thing it reflects, and that life then returns as an alien power: perhaps the current of a river, perhaps the other kind of current that almost electrocutes Dotty (in "Material"); or it may be the emotional shock of Joe Phippen's attack (in "Images"), which leaves the child "electrified," or, as in "Privilege," the "flash flood" of love or hate (93).

Insights like these abound in Carscallen's essay, which I think is one of the best yet on Munro. His argument is compelling, his knowledge of Munro encyclopaedic, and the associations he explains are doubtlessly Munro's own—Carscallen, like Martin, is true to Munro's art.

In sum, *The Art of Alice Munro: Saying the Unsayable* is no more nor no less than it purports to be: the printed record of a conference on Munro. Would that more editorial control had been exerted, although if it had, according to my judgement, there would have been no volume at all. Perhaps there should not have been, letting the half worth reading find homes in journals, as certainly they would have.

I might, in closing, invoke a passage from the narrator of "Material" who, when standing back and assessing her ex-husband Hugo's story about their landlady, Dotty, sums up very nicely—through her ambivalence—my own feeling about *The Art of Alice Munro*: "Don't be offended. Ironical objections are a habit with me. I am half-ashamed of them. I respect what has been done. I respect the intention and the effort and the result. Accept my thanks" (*Something* 43). To qualify this only a bit (just as this narrator does later in the story), I do wish the result had been more impressive. As it is, I am one Munro critic grateful for two of these essays, happy to have another three, and dismayed by the rest. An odd woman out no more, Alice Munro deserves better than this, particularly when a book is called *The Art of Alice Munro*.

Munro's Progress (1987)

Alice Munro, *The Progress of Love*.
McClelland & Stewart, 1986.

Some years ago, while being interviewed for Jill Gardiner's 1973 University of New Brunswick MA thesis, Alice Munro spoke about her use of retrospective narrators and the problems they confront in her stories, saying that as we grow older, "life becomes even *more* mysterious and difficult," and that "writing is the art of approach and recognition. I believe that we don't solve these things—in fact our explanations take us further away" (Gardiner Interview 178). *The Progress of Love*, Munro's sixth collection since she began publishing during the 1950s, displays everywhere its author's unequalled maturity, her unerring control of her materials, and their multitude of interconnections. It leaves its reader enraptured—over the stories as narratives, certainly, but more than that: over their human detail and most of all over the uncompromising *rightness* of the feelings they describe, define, depict, and convey. Yet at the same time, and in keeping with her sense of the mysteries of being, Munro's insights here are both more ambivalent and more technically complex than those she has offered previously.

One does not so much review this collection as savour its delicacies. In "Eskimo," Mary Joe, a doctor's receptionist/mistress, embarks on a plane over the Pacific. Amid the strange things she sees and dreams while aloft, we are offered this recollection of her doctor, and a snippet of their relationship:

> He liked her when the braces were still on. They were on the first time he made love to her. She turned her head aside, conscious that a mouthful of metal might not be pleasing. He shut his eyes, and she wondered if it might be for that reason. Later she learned that he always closed his eyes. He doesn't want to be reminded of himself at such times, and probably not of her, either. His is a fierce but solitary relish. (*Progress* 194)

When the narrator of the title story, now a divorced real estate agent, visits the house she grew up in, her memories drive her to lash out at an offhand remark made by the man she is with, Bob Marks. He immediately apologizes and, conciliatory, asks, "'Was this your room when you were a little girl?'" This question is equally inaccurate, but the narrator acquiesces so as to smooth things over. She then explains to herself, and to us:

> And I thought it would be just as well to let him think that. I said yes, yes, it was my room when I was a little girl. It was just as well to make up right away. Moments of kindness and reconciliation are worth having, even if the parting has to come sooner or later. I wonder if those moments aren't more valued, and deliberately gone after, in the setups some people like myself have now, than they were in those old marriages, where love and grudges could be growing underground, so confused and stubborn, it must have seemed they had forever. (*Progress* 30–31)

Trudy, the protagonist in "Circle of Prayer," recalls her feelings after her husband, Dan, left her for another woman. She holds these feelings together with a memory she has of Dan's mother playing the piano in the ramshackle hotel where the older woman lived, and where Dan and Trudy, years before, had spent their honeymoon. Munro describes Trudy's thoughts:

> Why does Trudy now remember this moment? She sees her young self looking in the window at the old woman playing the piano. The dim room, with its oversize beams and fireplace and lonely leather chairs. The clattering, faltering, persistent piano music. Trudy remembers that so clearly and it seems she stood outside her own body, which ached then from the punishing pleasures of love. She stood outside her own happiness in a tide of sadness. And the opposite thing happened the morning Dan left. Then she stood outside her own unhappiness in a tide of what seemed unreasonably like love. But it was the same thing, really, when you got outside. What are those times that stand out, clear patches in your life—what do they have to do with it? They aren't exactly promises. Breathing spaces. Is that all? (*Progress* 273)

Reading passages such as these in context, we first notice family resemblances with other Munro stories—in subject, technique, tone, and effect—but the maturity of these stories eclipses her earlier efforts and even exceeds those in *The Moons of Jupiter* (1982). "Jesse and Meribeth," for example, which tells of the connections between two girlhood best friends, is related in subject and treatment to "Boys and Girls," "Red Dress—1946," and "The Shining Houses" from *Dance of the Happy Shades* (1968), as well as *Lives of Girls and Women* (1971). At the same time, Munro is extending her range; "The Moon in the Orange Street Skating Rink" has a nostalgic air about it as it matter-of-factly tells the histories of two brothers from the farm boarding in town to attend business school. Calmly and in great detail, Munro recounts their activities and the difficulties that lead to their sudden flight from the town, eventually offering—through perspectives gained a lifetime later—a sense of resolution. The story is beautifully done, and unlike most of Munro's other work. Another story, "A Queer Streak," deals also in familiar materials—weaving the interlayered relations and connections of four generations together—but it does so at much greater length.

But more than such comparisons, *The Progress of Love* offers both greater complexity and, oddly enough, greater uncertainty than we have seen before—not uncertainty of purpose, control, or detail, but rather of meaning and of being: these stories offer a complex wonder at the strangeness of it all. The passage quoted earlier from "Eskimo," for instance, builds matter-of-factly to the telling descriptive line—"His is a fierce but solitary relish." The detail is so precise and right in its focus, encapsulating the doctor's stern, Ontario-WASP demeanour, and yet it is offered only incidentally, a snapped, subtle phrase. In the narrative itself, Mary Jo either misunderstands or misperceives a scene between two fellow passengers on her Tahiti-bound plane, an Inuit man (the "Eskimo" of the title) and a teenaged Métis girl he is travelling with. After she becomes considerably vexed over their disagreement, she offers to help the girl. She then sleeps and has some bizarre dreams that include these passengers, and when Mary Jo awakens she finds that: "Somehow a pillow and a blanket have been provided for her as well. The man and the girl across the aisle are asleep with their mouths open, and Mary Jo is lifted to the surface by their dust of eloquent, innocent snores." Munro concludes "Eskimo" with: "This is the beginning of her holiday" (*Progress* 207). Although generally still offering some sense of ending throughout *The Progress of Love*—through a suitable summary paragraph—Munro now seems, most overtly here in "Eskimo," loath to say what it all means.

Though they may not be composed explicitly to convey the fragility of being and of understanding, the stories here proclaim Munro's uncertainties through their structures and through her masterful interweaving of events disparate in time yet inescapable in connection, and so in the way they resonate with readers. Two differences are striking in this collection: Munro's preference for the third person, evident since *Who Do You Think You Are?* (1978), has persisted, and these stories, more than ever, reflect her own return to Huron County. Indeed, they seem to present southwestern Ontario in something of the same way as *Dance of the Happy Shades*, though balanced now by an older narrative perspective. We no longer see Huron County from the point of view of one growing and going away from her home place—the stories in *The Progress of Love* encompass more time, offering us the longer view, often the cradle-to-middle-age perspective of a returned native. From her earliest stories, Munro's narrative perspective has gradually grown older, and as a result many characters in this collection, like Mary Jo, have personal histories—and therefore perspectives of time and space—roughly equivalent to Munro's own: 40 or 50 years of age, born in rural Ontario, living there still or living there again, divorced, remarried, preoccupied with spouses and mature children, and growing older (though not yet old).

These characters, whose perceptions and perspectives Munro recreates through her emphatic yet detached way, share a common task. In these stories, their "real work," as the narrator in "Miles City, Montana," says, is "a sort of wooing of distant parts" of themselves (Progress 88). Perhaps the most complex story in the collection, "Miles City, Montana" interweaves the narrator's childhood memories of a young acquaintance who drowned, with more recent memories of her own daughter's near drowning on a family holiday. The narrator interconnects memory with incident, and with perspective on both her former self and her now-former marriage, marvelling, in the words of another Munro narrator, at "all this life going on" (*Dance* 31). In these stories we approach the mystery of being, follow the narrative wooing of the self, and, in the end, even if we don't come to an understanding, we come to emphatically recognize life—as it is lived, experienced, and wondered about. Through them, Munro's "real work" proclaims in every way the precise delicacy of her approach, recognition, and progress.

"So Shocking a Verdict in Real Life": Autobiography in Alice Munro's Stories (1988)

In the penultimate scene in Alice Munro's "Chaddeleys and Flemings: 1. Connection," the story that opens her fifth collection, *The Moons of Jupiter* (1982), the narrator throws a pyrex plate with a piece of lemon meringue pie on it at her husband's head; she is responding to his sneering rejection of a cousin of hers, Iris, who has just visited, and whose presence has occasioned for the narrator a flood of memories of a previous visit that Iris and other Chaddeley cousins made to the narrator's girlhood home in Dalgleish, Ontario. Munro describes the scene, and the couple's reactions:

> The plate missed, and hit the refrigerator, but the pie flew out and caught him on the side of the face just as in the old movies or an *I Love Lucy* show. There was the same moment of amazement as there is on the screen, the sudden innocence, for him; his speech stopped, his mouth open. For me, too, amazement, that something people invariably thought funny in those instances should be so shocking a verdict in real life. (*Moons* 18)

The implications of the final phrase are key to understanding both this story and its partner, "Chaddeleys and Flemings: 2. The Stone in the Field," but, more broadly, they also reverberate throughout Munro's entire *oeuvre*. She submitted *Lives of Girls and Women* (1971) to her publisher under the title "Real Life," and "Material" (*Something*) was called "Real People" in an earlier manuscript (37.8.8.); "True Lies" was one of the titles considered for *Who Do You Think You Are?* (1978).[1]

Given these concerns about the relationship between fact and fiction in her titles, we might well begin by asking what Munro means when she uses the phrase "real life." Since the publication of her first collection of stories, *Dance of the Happy Shades* (1968), reviewers and critics have noted parallels between her protagonists' lives and Munro's own life. Indeed, questions of autobiography are commonplace, though they have been asked most frequently concerning *Lives of Girls and Women* and *Who Do You Think You Are?*, collections that concern adolescence in Munro's Huron County, Ontario, most thoroughly. Recently, Margaret Gail Osachoff and Lorna Irvine have examined, respectively, Munro's use of the autobiographical forms of memoir, confession, and meditation, and her treatment of women's power. Although no one has yet attempted a close examination of the relationship between Munro's art and her life, the need for such a study has been given new urgency by the recent publication of her sixth collection, *The Progress of Love* (1986). Here Munro appears to have come full circle, for these stories reflect her return to her "home place,"[2] Huron County, where she has lived for the past 13 years since moving from British Columbia.

Munro, of course, is a writer who prefers to let her writing speak for her, abominating the panels, papers, readings, and receptions that fall to acclaimed authors—here one recalls the caustically sneering descriptions of the celebrated academic writer, Hugo, that open "Material" (*Something*). Like the events in her stories—"deep caves paved with kitchen linoleum" (*Lives* 249)—Munro's own life appears (from the outside) to offer little that is extraordinary: twice married, three children, some travel but mostly living quietly in Ontario or British Columbia; indeed, her celebrity stems wholly from her writing. She does not court notoriety in any way, participating only reluctantly in the publicity that surrounds her as a now-famous writer. But although most readers are ignorant of Munro's own history in its specifics, they know many of its details simply by having read her work: growing up on the edge of Wingham (Jubilee, Hanratty, Dalgleish), her father a sometime fox farmer from Huron County stock, her mother from the Ottawa Valley; the latter dying some time ago after a long battle with Parkinson's disease, the former more recently of heart problems (Tausky, *passim*). "Miles City, Montana" might well be seen as an example of these autobiographical links: the 1961 transcountry trek from British Columbia to Ontario through the States, the two daughters, the former husband who had an office job, the narrator's background and personality—all of which fit the circumstantial details of Munro's own life at the time.

Yet one must emphasize that these details are circumstantial, even though she has confirmed the autobiographical aspects of many of her other stories, most notably "The Office," "The Peace of Utrecht," and "The Ottawa Valley," and she has said that most of her first two books are based on autobiographical elements (Tausky, *passim*). More recently, she has confirmed autobiographical aspects in both "Dulse" and "The Moons of Jupiter."[3] Somewhat ironically, it is the underpinning of autobiography in Munro's stories that lends them considerable validity as fiction. In fact, autobiography lies at the very core of Munro's celebrated ability to offer stories of such precision, haunting beauty, and versimilitude.

Munro's notion of the "wooing of distant parts" of the self directly highlights the issue of autobiography. Thus, whether one sees her fiction as autobiography—in the way William C. Spengemann or Janet Varner Gunn, among others, use the term—or as the kind of confessional fiction that, according to Eugene L. Stelzig, differentiates fiction based on an author's experience from works in which a writer consciously narrates her own life, Munro's stories share the defining of the self—the primary urge in autobiography—as their central aim.

John Metcalf once asked Munro about the autobiographical aspect of her work. Her response, by its very meanderings, suggested that the difficulty in assessing the autobiographical nature of her work is directly related to her primary focus on defining the self. Metcalf asked her, "How far is your work autobiographical," to which she responded:

> Oh. Well. I guess I have a standard answer to this … in incident—no … in emotion—completely. In incident up to a point too but of course, in *Lives of Girls and Women* which is a … I suppose it could be called an autobiographical novel … most of the incidents are changed versions of real incidents. *Some* are completely invented but the emotional reality, the girl's feeling for her mother, for men, for life is all … it's all solidly autobiographical. (Metcalf Interview 58; ellipses in original)

Such uncertainties or equivocations have also consistently characterized Munro's fiction. This wonder speaks directly to the question of autobiography in the stories, and also to Munro's relationship with her narrative personae over time.

Most specifically, autobiography can be seen in the way Munro writes her stories, for she sees her writing as an "art of approach and recognition," a way of looking at and evaluating life's confusions. She goes on to say that "we don't solve" the mysteries surrounding the sorts of incidents she uses in her stories: "in fact, our explanations take us further away." As we grow older, she says, "life becomes even *more* mysterious and difficult" (Gardiner Interview 178). Thus by approaching the mystery inherent in her own life, she has forged an art that offers not understanding but momentary glimpses and fleeting insight—she is ever aware that "people's lives, in Jubilee as elsewhere, were dull, simple, amazing, and unfathomable—deep caves paved with kitchen linoleum" (*Lives* 249). Her stories probe the depths of her characters' lives; throughout them is a complex relationship between the story told and the life lived, a relationship borne of point of view, as the narrator in an unpublished draft of "Bardon Bus" (*Moons*) concludes ruefully:

> But suppose you are going along, making up your story, the story of your life, and at the same time your story is being made up for you, from the outside. This is what happens with everybody, to a certain extent. Only at some points do the two stories coincide. I am making up my story which features X, and Alex Walther is resting his head in Kay's lap. When such

discrepancies are forced on your attention, you have to let go. If you don't want to go crazy you have to let go, and I don't have the stamina, the pure, seething will, for prolonged craziness. I have to let go my story of X though I may recall it, with faded emotions, at a later time. (38.8.5.5.f1)

Munro's narrative focus on self-definition—and its attendant and growing uncertainties—conforms to much theoretical analysis. Indeed, quite eerily, Munro's fiction seems to be almost a correlative of Paul John Eakin's comment that twentieth-century autobiographers "no longer believe that autobiography can offer a faithful and unmediated reconstruction of a historically verifiable past." Their autobiographies express "the play of the autobiographical act itself." In defining this act, Eakin encapsulates Munro's narrative technique:

The materials of the past are shaped by memory and imagination to serve the needs of present consciousness. Autobiography in our time is increasingly understood as both an art of memory and an art of the imagination; indeed, memory and imagination become so intimately complementary in the autobiographical act that it is usually impossible for autobiographers and their readers to distinguish between them in practice. (5–6)

This is, of course, what Munro's narrators do in her stories, in which "the needs of present consciousness" are paramount; indeed, hers is an art that juggles this interplay between past and present—always shifting back and forth, and perpetually understanding the present moment in terms of a newly seen relationship with the past. Put another way by one of Eakin's reviewers, the writer, during the autobiographical act, is able to "repeat and re-stage (often metaphorically) past self-imaginings through which we became who we are" (Sheringham).

Yet, Eakin is focusing on fictional elements in self-conscious autobiographies; Munro's focus is on autobiographical elements in fiction. Here again, though, dividing lines are difficult to distinguish, and autobiographical theory seems particularly apt when applied to Munro's work. Gunn writes of the autobiographical situation, asserting that "autobiography completes no pictures. Instead, it rejects wholeness or harmony, ascribed by formalists to the well-made art object, as a false unity which serves as no more than a defense against the self's deeper knowledge of its finitude" (25). Munro's progress as a writer—viewed from the perspective of her most recent collection—has been a movement away from the very "false unity" Gunn posits toward the absolute certainty of the finiteness of the self, a movement critics have discussed using the term "metafiction" (see Struthers "Fictive"). This movement accounts for the growing authorial equivocation that has emerged in tandem with her growing artistry. Munro's recent stories offer none of the capsule summary conclusions—the "false unity"—found so often in her stories in *Dance of the Happy Shades*. Now instead, Munro's narrators stand back and stare at the mystery of being they have just unfolded, approached, and recognized—either loath or unable to tell what it all means. Beneath this movement—call it metafiction, magic realism, or sure-handed artistry—are Munro's own experiences. The autobiographical impulse is at the core of Munro's art, and although many stories are certainly not explicitly autobiographical ("Thanks for the Ride," in *Dance of the Happy Shades*, for example), we cannot claim with any certainty that any of them escape Munro's autobiographical urge.

Speaking to Metcalf, for example, Munro pointed out that her "first really painful autobiographical story ... the first time I wrote a story that tore me up was 'The Peace of Utrecht' [*Dance*] which I didn't even want to write" (Metcalf Interview 58; see Thacker "Connection"). In it she tackles her mother's death, a subject that she dealt with more directly a second time in "The Ottawa Valley" (*Something*) and that she often aludes to throughout her work, most recently in *The Moons of Jupiter*. In "Utrecht," Munro heavy handedly attempts to create a "false unity" through the supposed "peace" of the story's title and through Maddy's broken bowl at the story's end and her protestations to her sister that she cannot pick up the pieces of her life, now that their mother is finally dead (*Dance* 210). Moving away from such formal symmetry in her next attempt to treat her mother as a character in "The Ottawa Valley," Munro focuses on the narrator's recollection of the first time she noticed her mother's shaking arm, which was the same time that she realized her mother was impotent to stop the disease. Yet here, when Munro steps back and assesses her story, she is quite likely speaking in her own voice:

> If I had been making a proper story out of this, I would have ended it, I think, with my mother not answering and going ahead of me across the pasture. That would have done. I didn't stop there, I suppose, because I wanted to find out more, remember more. I wanted to bring back all I could. Now I look at what I have done and it is like a series of snapshots, like the brownish snapshots with fancy borders that my parents' old camera used to take.... The problem, the only problem, is my mother. And she is the one of course that I am trying to get; it is to reach her that this whole journey has been undertaken. With what purpose? To mark her off, to describe, to illumine, to celebrate, to *get rid* of, her; and it did not work, for she looms too close, just as she always did. She is heavy as always, she weighs everything down, and yet she is indistinct, her edges melt and flow. Which means she has stuck to me as close as ever and refused to fall away, and I could go on, and on, applying what skills I have, using what tricks I know, and it would always be the same. (*Something* 246)

This passage not only demonstrates Munro's autobiographical impulse, it also reveals her doubts over the whole business of fictionalizing—that hers are ineffectual "tricks"—as well as her doubts that she will ever write "the truth."[4]

Three of the stories in *The Moons of Jupiter*, the two "Chaddeleys and Flemings" stories (both "Connection" and "The Stone in the Field") and "The Moons of Jupiter," also take up Munro's relationship with her parents, the first two stories dealing with each side of the narrator's family—she is unnamed but was identified as Janet when the stories were to be included in *Who Do You Think You Are?*—and the title story dealing with her father's final hospitalization. "Connection" ends with the narrator's haunting memory of her cousin Iris' visit to Dalgleish, juxtaposed with the plate she had just thrown at her sneering husband—"so shocking a verdict in real life" (*Moons* 18). "The Stone in the Field," however, is its partner story in that it, too, focuses on a "shocking ... verdict in real life," this time the identity of Mr. Black, the man who lived for a time in a shack across from the narrator's aunts' farm and who died there. And as in "The Ottawa Valley," the narrator closes both "Chaddeleys and Flemings" stories by stepping back and commenting directly on her materials, critical of the younger writer who, one thinks, would have forced a "false unity" on them:

> If I had been younger, I would have figured out a story. I would have insisted on Mr. Black's being in love with one of my aunts, and on one of them—not necessarily the one he was in love with—being in love with him. I would have wished him to confide in them, in one of them, his secret, his reason for living in a shack in Huron County, far from home. Later, I might have believed that he wanted to, but hadn't confided this, or his love either. I would have made a horrible, plausible connection between that silence of his, and the manner of his death. Now I no longer believe that people's secrets are defined and communicable, or their feelings full-blown and easy to recognize. I don't believe so. Now, I can only say, my father's sisters scrubbed the floor with lye, they stooked the oats and milked the cows by hand. They must have taken a quilt to the barn for the hermit to die on, they must have let water dribble from a tin cup into his afflicted mouth. That was their life. My mother's cousins behaved in another way; they dressed up and took pictures of each other; they sallied forth. However they behaved they are all dead. I carry something of them around in me. But the boulder is gone, Mount Hebron is cut down for gravel, and the life buried here is one you have to think twice about regretting. (*Moons* 35)

The narrator's palpable uncertainty about the meaning of it all is characteristic of Munro's recent work. The story from which this passage is taken combines autobiographical and fictional detail—which detail is which, finally, seems to matter less than the combination of memory and imagination that Munro uses to forge her delicious insights. Whether "grafted on from some other reality" ("Material," *Something* 42) or directly experienced, autobiography infuses Munro's stories from first to last.

Munro herself best describes the ultimate effect of this process in "Material," a story that combines her own experience of marriage with a cold-blooded scrutiny of writers' egotism and craft—brought together by memory. Thus after reading her ex-husband's story, which involves their former landlady, the narrator speaks not only for herself but, quite clearly (though self-refexively and ironically), for Munro as well:

> What matters is that this story of Hugo's is a very good story, as far as I can tell, and I think I can tell. How honest this is and how lovely, I had to say as I read. I had to admit. I was moved by Hugo's story; I was, I am, glad of it, and I am not moved by tricks. Or if I am, they have to be good tricks. Lovely tricks, honest tricks. There is Dotty lifted out of life and held in light, suspended in the marvelous clear jelly that Hugo has spent all his life learning how to make. It is an act of magic, there is no getting around it; it is an act, you might say, of a special, unsparing, unsentimental love. A fine and lucky benevolence. Dotty was a lucky person, people who understood and value this act might say (not everybody, of course, does understand and value this act); she was lucky to live in that basement for a few months and eventually to have this done to her, though she doesn't know what has been done and wouldn't care for it, probably, if she did know. She has passed into Art.

So has Alice Munro. "It doesn't happen to everybody" (*Something* 43).

Critical Interlude:

Go Ask Alice: The Progress of Munro Criticism (1991)

Alice Munro. E. D. Blodgett. Twayne's World Author Series 800. Boston: Twayne, 1988.

The Canadian Postmodern: A Study of Contemporary English-Canadian Fiction. Studies in Canadian Literature. Linda Hutcheon. Toronto: Oxford University Press, 1988.

The Canadian Short Story. Michelle Gadpaille. Perspectives on Canadian Culture Series. Toronto: Oxford University Press, 1988.

Controlling the Uncontrollable: The Fiction of Alice Munro. Ildikó de Papp Carrington. DeKalb: Northern Illinois University Press, 1989.

Dance of the Sexes: Art and Gender in the Fiction of Alice Munro. Beverly J. Rasporich. Edmonton: University of Alberta Press, 1990.

Private and Fictional Words: Canadian Women Novelists of the 1970s and 1980s. Coral Ann Howells. London and New York: Methuen, 1987.

Midway through *Private and Fictional Words*, while discussing Mavis Gallant's stories, Coral Ann Howells quotes an evocative and precise passage from Gallant's 1982 essay in the *Canadian Forum*, "What is Style?":

> This is what fiction is about—that something is taking place and that nothing lasts. Against the sustained tick of a watch, fiction takes the measure of a life, a season, a look exchanged, the turning point, desire as brief as a dream, the grief and terror that after childhood we cease to express. The lie, the look, the grief are without permanence, the watch continues to tick where the story stops. (103)

Fiction writers generally and short story writers in particular are drawn, seemingly perversely (they often say), to such moments as this, ever trying to capture their own essence—and the essence of others and imaginary others—on the static page. They strive to make of their art, as Willa Cather wrote in her *The Song of the Lark* (1915), "a sheath, a mould in which to imprison for a moment the shining, elusive element which is life—life hurrying past us and running away, too strong to stop, too sweet to lose." Similarly, W. B. Yeats asked in his "Among School Children": "O body swayed to music, O brightening glance, / How can we know the dancer from the dance?" (Cather, *Song* 254, Yeats, "Among" 217). How, indeed? And if writers are drawn to such moments for the stuff of their art—perversely or otherwise—we critics are drawn to that art—probably doubly perversely—for many of the same reasons. At two removes from "the shining elusive element," life itself, we try to gauge the whole of the art, to understand the ensemble that is the primary text, with reference to the author, with reference to "life" (however that is defined), with reference to the reader (whoever she is), with reference to other texts (thus Cather and Yeats, as will be seen below), with reference to our own readers, with reference, with reference. Dancer and dance, indeed.

The late 1980s seems a particularly propitious time to be a critic and scholar of English-Canadian literature. Others are better able to generalize about the field's breadth and extent, and have done so; what is clear to me, however, is that the criticism and scholarship surrounding Canadian literature in English has, during the last several years, reached new levels of maturity. The evidence is everywhere: as a subject, Canadian literature is accepted in the academy (perhaps begrudgingly); reference books (Gale, ECW), scholarly editions (Carleton University's Centre for Editing Early

Canadian Texts and its attendant publishing program, which is pushing near completion, and the University of Toronto Press's Strickland sisters editions), and critical books and articles of all sorts have appeared; and conferences and symposia have been held and attended. Thus manifestations of serious discussion are everywhere to be seen, and they have taken a multiplicity of forms and points of view. Moreover, and with increasing frequency, some of this has happened outside of Canada, which is probably a healthy sign. In fact, one way of gauging the putative "arrival" of Canadian literature is its recent appearance in the pages of *Critical Inquiry* in the form of an exchange between Robert Lecker and Frank Davey over the Canadian canon.[1]

Such a debate suggests, as well, that Canadian literature in English is in the ironic position of having been forming a canon while the impetus in literary studies has been to deny such privileging of either authors or texts, because canons omit far more than they include and, insidiously, reflect the mores, values, and priorities of the dominant classes. Thus women and minorities have been largely ignored in the canons of imaginative writing in English, as have those who challenged the literary modes of their day. Noting this, Lecker argues that "Canadian literature was canonized in fewer than twenty years" and maintains that "the canon is the conservative product of the conservative institution that brought it to life. The power of the canon and the power of its members are inseparable: the institution *is* the canon; its members *are* the texts" (656, 658). What is more, of course, is that texts are valourized by (the mostly male) critics who select one author's writings over another's, enshrining its values and, typically, singing its praises in the university English classes they teach, at the conferences they attend, and—perhaps most permanently—in the reviews, articles, and books they write.

Yet, though this process continues, any critic writing today knows that "canon"—like "genre"—may well be an outmoded term, whatever its usefulness in defining courses of study; that texts, whatever their form, are mutable; that no single reading is ever enough, nor that "enough" will ever be reached (or, in any case, would more likely be reached not as a critic but as a scholar, with a better understanding of the multiplicity of views and voices); and—and this I say most emphatically—that "he" is a pronoun that refers to an *individual* critic, not *the* critic, just as "she" is as likely—perhaps more likely—to be the author as "he." Much more than this is to be found in the larger critical context, including the seemingly inscrutable jargon that carries many such discussions—all of which is so easy to scorn, while the "significations" they carry concerning texts are difficult, often impossible, to refute.

In Canada, these issues are arising in far more places than the Lecker-Davey exchange—and as the books under review show to varying degrees, postmodernism has gotten down into the trenches, as it were, by serving as the theoretical basis of extended single-author studies. This is seen most clearly in Blodgett's *Alice Munro*, but postmodernism's sway is felt throughout the others as well. Such methods notwithstanding, these books also show that the sociological process of canon-formation that Lecker so decries continues, for each volume takes its place in the edifice that is Canadian literature, and each has been put there by a publisher both aiming at and attempting to define a particular audience. However all of this is understood—any reviewer about to plunge into six critical books loosely configured around Munro and her texts (such are the lines of demarcation that the fuzziness is deliberate here) must remember the dancer and the dance, as well as, for perspective alone, a comment made by one of Munro's characters in "Goodness and Mercy": "Also, professors are dumb. They are dumber than ordinary. I could be nice and say they know about things we don't, but as far as I'm concerned they don't know shit." (*Friend* 158). All of this is necessary context.

1. Alice Munro: A Paradigm Case (or, The Progress of Criticism)

The author, Alice Munro. She has longed seemed in many ways something of a paradigm case of "the canonization of a Canadian Author."[2] Since the publication of *The Moons of Jupiter* (1982)—her first collection composed preponderantly of stories first published in the *New Yorker*—Munro's work has received progressively greater attention, what might be called "the progress of criticism."[3] With the books under review here, her status as a writer of the first rank is utterly confirmed: in the wake of W. R. Martin's *Alice Munro: Paradox and Parallel* (1987), four book-length critical studies of her work have been published, and Linda Hutcheon mentions a fifth, by Magdalene Redekop, apparently in the offing (xv).[4] In addition, Munro's fiction plays a key role in the other three books under review—though Hutcheon notes that it is largely absent from *The Canadian Postmodern*, clearly feeling that Munro ought to have been included, especially because Del Jordan keeps popping up anyway.

Ultimately, these books demonstrate the profound density of Munro's *oeuvre*, and what is more, their differing approaches and insights attest (and not hyperbolically) to what Blodgett calls "the grandeur of [her] writing" (147). Critics are drawn to her power and vision—to what she sees. As the narrator of "An Ounce of Cure" states: "But the development of events on that Saturday night—that fascinated me; I felt that I had had a glimpse of the shameless, marvellous, shattering absurdity with the plots of life, though not of fiction, are improvised. I could not take my eyes off it" (*Dance* 87–88). Such passages are worth keeping in mind as we wade into the warring of preferences that make up critical analysis, for it is in offering illumination of the fiction that the critical act is undertaken, however tentatively or persuasively.

Before taking up the substance of each of these books, some comment on each as a "canon-affirming product" seems in order. Three of these titles are a part of a publisher's series—Gadpaille's *The Canadian Short Story* and Hutcheon's *The Canadian Postmodern* are volumes in two new series offered by Oxford University Press, and Blodgett's *Alice Munro* is the 800th (!) title in Twayne's World Author Series. Being included in a series is, of course, indicative of a certain heft, but I cannot fathom the audience assumed by Oxford's "Perspectives on Canadian Culture," if *The Canadian Short Story* is any indication.[5] Quite apart from whether or not this *mélange* can legitimately be taken as "culture," a series of short (Gadpaille's is 126 pages plus an eight-page introduction) paperbacks on large subjects assumes an audience in need of introductory books that go beyond standard reference discussions on the same subject. Gadpaille's certainly does not; what is more, she offers what amounts to a skewered view of her subject, one that completely ignores relevant scholarship and ultimately would be better off unpublished. I do not really blame the author—her readings of stories and authors are reasonable enough—but the space is too limited; important as their work is, Gallant, Munro, and

Atwood get about half the ink in a book called *The Canadian Short Story*. Even then, Gadpaille's treatment of their work is rushed, and in the remaining chapters dozens of other figures rush by; little more than an annotated bibliography, *The Canadian Short Story* offers nothing of the sort. In 1973, Clare MacCulloch published *The Neglected Genre: The Short Story in Canada*, another short book of about one hundred pages on this same subject. At the time, such spare treatment could be justified as a way of encouraging critical discussion by simply bringing up the subject, but that moment has passed, as any publisher active in the field ought to know.[6]

Happily, the same critique cannot be extended to Oxford's "Studies in Canadian Literature" series under the general editorship of Richard Teleky. Here the press is publishing—in quality paperback form—the writings of noted critics of Canadian literature. These books fill a need. In addition to Hutcheon's *The Canadian Postmodern*, the series includes collected essays by Robert Kroetsch and Adele Wiseman, and Janice Kulyk Keefer's writing on Mavis Gallant. Similarly, Blodgett's book, one of a dozen volumes on Canadian writers in the Twayne World Author Series, also fulfills a need—though the mind boggles at the thought of 800 titles in the series. Indeed, one of the interesting things about Blodgett's *Alice Munro* is the way he is able to stretch the usual Twayne format, although the result may be a book a bit too sophisticated for Twayne's usual undergraduate audience.

Moreover, both Oxford series and Twayne's inclusion of Canadian writers in their series reveals an interest in Canadian fiction abroad, as do both Howells' *Private and Fictional Words* and Carrington's *Controlling the Uncontrollable*. Howells, an Australian living and teaching in Great Britain, addresses a British audience and tailors her arguments in ways wholly appropriate to that audience. The Carrington volume is one of several critical studies on Canadian literary topics published recently by American university presses, a phenomenon that, to my mind, bodes well for Canadian literary studies and Canadian studies more generally.[7]

Finally, though not part of a series, Beverly J. Rasporich's *Dance of the Sexes* could be seen as completing this grouping of books, commenting as it does on the currency of feminist topics—although Munro herself asserts that she does not see herself as a feminist in any political sense, something

Rasporich admits (though she seems to reluctantly) and Carrington too stridently pronounces. Thus in *Dance of the Sexes*, Rasporich—analyzing the "female, feminine, and feminist sensibilities" of Munro's art—offers a critical dance of her own, often trying (despite her disclaimers) to force Munro's fiction "into a feminist's Cinderella slipper." The "honest fit" (viii) Rasporich seeks eludes her because of Munro's own statements and, more importantly, because of the tentative wariness and, ultimately, the complexities of her fiction. Without question, Munro's is as fundamentally a female way of viewing the world as might be found—"I write about myself because I am the only truth I know," she says (xix)—thus the arguments that try to force her work to conform to feminist ideology make as little sense as those of critics who, previously, found garrisons throughout her early work (after all, Munro is Canadian, and Northrop Frye had said that garrisons are Canadian) (See Macdonald, "Madman"). Taken together, these six volumes ultimately confirm, in microcosm, the relevance of the issues debated by Lecker and Davey; they are also the manifestation of the progress of Munro criticism, if only in the sense of its multiple forms, though they offer much more than that. In the balance of this essay I will discuss each of these books in turn and suggest how each may be seen as fitting into Munro criticism, itself part of the larger "edifice" of Canadian literary criticism.

2. Contextualizing Munro: Contemporary Criticism

The subject each of these critics share is the body of texts published by Munro. For its part, Munro's writing has displayed increasing and demonstrable complexity as she has matured as a writer, despite seemingly re-traversing many of the same problems, places, and situations, drawn ever more tightly by her virtuosic command of the genre she writes in almost exclusively, the short story. Critics have moved away from such simplistic conceptions as the garrison mentality and other thematic approaches that characterized earlier discussions of her work, drawn increasingly to style, form, language, and symbolism in her stories, elements that reflect and refract, seemingly endlessly, back and forth upon one another. For a time a consensus appeared to be forming that Munro was essentially "a magic realist" whose work could be legitimately characterized as "metafictional" (Struthers "Fictive"). What the critics at hand ultimately confirm, however, is that such arguments do not go nearly far enough in gauging the complexity and self-reflexivity of Munro's writing. Blodgett summarizes the matter succinctly while commenting on a key story, "The Moons of Jupiter" (1978):

> The art of Munro is an art of accommodating contradictions, and this is what her principal figures, narrators or not, must be brought to learn. Their gradually acquired habit, which comes to fruition in "The Moons of Jupiter," is to learn how to be "at the mercy" without asking for much more. Something of the design within which they are figures must always be beyond their grasp. (126)

The phrase "at the mercy" appears in another seminal story, "Material" (1973)—both of these stories are central to the arguments of each critic who concentrates on Munro's work alone, and "The Moons of Jupiter" is key to Howells' discussion of her work. This is as it should be, for the progress of Munro criticism offers convincing evidence that several stories are pivotal within her *oeuvre*. These are but two.

Given the sensitivity and density of argument offered by scholarly critics like Hutcheon, Blodgett, and Carrington, it is probably unfair to group Gadpaille's *The Canadian Short Story* with their books. Still, publishers need to be told that publishing short introductions to complex and widely discussed subjects simply misses the point. In general, *The Canadian Short Story* is both descriptive and reductive: it rushes through the nineteenth century, offering summaries of well-known and well-discussed figures (McCulloch, Haliburton, Leacock, Roberts, and Seton), then pauses for a chapter to offer a good discussion of Knister and Callaghan before "giving extended attention to Canada's contemporary masters of the short story" (vii), Gallant, Munro, and Atwood. Gadpaille concludes with another quick-and-dirty chapter covering "The Sixties and After." Although some might find Gadpaille's discussions useful, her treatment of Munro offers nothing new. Electing to sidestep *Lives of Girls and Women* (1971) (Munro's putative novel that is not a novel, whatever it is), she discusses the stories through to *The Progress of Love* (1986) reasonably and perceptively, showing familiarity with published criticism on Munro. Oxford provides a detailed index—good for them—but the absence of a suitable bibliography is inexcusable. Whether we like it or not, critics must be scholars, too, and scholars acknowledge their sources. Again, blame rests largely on the publisher here, for scholarly apparatuses are notoriously denigrated; truth, however, derives from critical discourse in these matters, not publishers' preferences. Unfortunately, there has been far too much of this sort of thing in the criticism of Canadian literature, and although the balance of books under review are most heartening in this respect, we still have a ways to go.[8]

Moving on to better things. By looking at 11 writers, *Private and Fictional Words* "attempts to map an exciting new territory of Commonwealth literature and to examine the ways in which these women's Canadianness informs their fiction" (1). In addition to Munro, a chapter each is devoted to selected works by Laurence, Atwood, and Gallant, while two more broadly drawn chapters examine a novel each by Marian Engel, Joy Kogawa, Janette Turner Hospital, Audrey Thomas, and Joan Barfoot. By way of justifying the use of "Canadian" in the book's title (however controversial that decision may be, Howells concedes), a final chapter looks at two novels by Marie-Claire Blais and another by Anne Hébert. With such an approach, Howells is unable to mount extended arguments for any of the books she considers. And yet, though she has only a little more compass than Gadpaille, Howells manages to say something of consequence on her subject.

Beginning with an overview chapter entitled "Canadianness and Women's Fictions," Howells surveys the critical issues impinging on her subject. Throughout, she is sensitive to such matters as thematic criticism (she neither embraces nor rejects "Canadianness" as an approach, wisely, given the introductory nature of her book), nationalism in Canadian writing; generic issues (she looks at Laurence's *A Bird in the House* [1970] along with Munro's *Lives of Girls and Women*), feminist criticism and gender issues, and the distinction between the personal and the public. The fiction she examines offer words that are "private" because they are borne "out of personal and often unconscious emotion and 'fictional' because the experiences have been transformed into the controlled multivoiced discourse of art" (32). This chapter is precise and cogent, thoroughly setting up the discussion that follows.

That discussion is characterized by several features, not the least of which is Howells' evident overbrimming enthusiasm for her subject. Beyond that, her readings often involve analogues to writers not commonly alluded to in other critical texts—such as figures from British literature, especially Virginia Woolf—and a deft precision of analysis. Her discussion of Munro's "novels," *Lives of Girls and Women* and *Who Do You Think You Are?* (1978), in particular, reveals a close attention to textual detail, and a sensitivity to overall design. Howells builds upon the critical consensus available to her in the mid-1980s by using it as a point of departure for her discussion, and in many ways throughout her discussion of Munro's extended narratives she anticipates the more sustained arguments of Blodgett and Carrington.[9] She concludes, in a passage that bears quotation at length:

> Munro's stories are enclosed textual spaces which always throw their windows open onto "inappropriate and unforgettable scenery" [a phrase from "Simon's Luck" in *Who Do You Think You Are?*] which threatens dissolution of her ordered structures. Indeed her fictional order includes such acknowledgements of disorder, but the structures of a Munro story is like a house which contains secret labyrinths within it and does not collapse into a fragmented postmodernist mode. The framework remains realistic while at the same time her shifts of emphasis into fantasy narrative challenge realism as an authoritative account of reality in an awareness shared by readers and narrators of the incompleteness and partial truth of all fictional structures. (88)

It was Hutcheon's overriding concern with what Howells calls here "the fragmented postmodernist mode" that led her to write *The Canadian Postmodern: A Study of Contemporary English-Canadian Fiction*. Clearly, as well, the implied dissolutions and questions of fictional "truth" Munro raises in her stories—especially since *Lives of Girls and Women*—are what make her work particularly attractive to Hutcheon. Still, the negative connotations of "collapse," as Howells has used the word, might evoke Hutcheon's ire, if not an outright disavowal. Hutcheon's book, which grew out of her assignment to write the chapter entitled "The Novel (1972–1984)" in *The Literary History of Canada* (v. 4, 1990) (that chapter is included as an appendix to Hutcheon's book), allowed her to bring several occasional pieces together as a whole, and she sets out to offer, she writes, "an investigation not into the general phenomenon of postmodernism, but into the particular forms in which it appears in contemporary Canadian fiction" (vii). Rather than get into the bases for her definitions or into the definitions themselves, it is perhaps best to let Hutcheon "situate" (a key term in this discourse) the effects of postmodernism herself: "Certainly I no longer read books the way I once did: that eternal universal truth I was taught to find has turned out to be constructed, not found—and anything but eternal and universal. Truth has been replaced by truths, uncapitalized and in the plural" (viii–ix). This passage is representative of Hutcheon's writing: succinct, to the point, and memorable. She uses the jargon of feminism, deconstructionism, post-structuralism, Marxism, and several other isms besides, effortlessly, and with a fluidity borne of extended, extensive, and important work in critical theory (see Hutcheon).

The importance of *The Canadian Postmodern* for this essay is contextual, for, as noted, Hutcheon's references to Munro are fleeting and minor, however numerous. Given her ability as a critic, I do wish she had not deferrred, because Munro's work lends itself to Hutcheon's mode of analysis, and what is more, the context she defines is far more necessary to a sophisticated, thorough treatment of Munro's writing than that offered by Gadpaille, Howells, or (as we shall see) Rasporich—Carrington and Blodgett are another matter, for they recognize the implications of Hutcheon's analysis as intrinsic to Munro's art. Essentially, Hutcheon argues that postmodernism offers "art forms that are fundamentally self-reflexive—in other words, art that is self-consciously art (or artifice), literature that is openly aware that it is written and read as a part of a particular culture, having as much to do with the literary past as the social present" (1). It practice, a postmodern text "both sets up and subverts the powers and conventions of art" (2). Throughout her introduction, which cogently outlines the whole of her argument, Hutcheon advances a compelling case that English-Canadian writing reflects Canada's status as a "borderline case" whereby the facts of its social and cultural marginality—as a colony, as a small-time player in world affairs—have seemingly engendered a postmodern point of view. Thus Canada's writers "may be primed for the paradoxes of the postmodern by their history" (4). What is more, she argues, this imaginative position—which she calls that of the "ex-centric"—aligns Canadians, whether female or male, with feminism: there is a strong analogy between the political position of women and that of the Canadian. Citing Lorna Irvine's *Sub/version*, in which Irvine writes "that the female voice 'politically and culturally personifies Canada,'" Hutcheon argues that "on a national level, male agression is usually associated, by analogy, with the United States, while Britain represents the stiffling force of colonial tradition" (6–7).

These matters are worked out in the literature in a variety of ways. Hutcheon begins by harkening back to what she calls "the Early Postmodernism of Leonard Cohen," through a discussion of his *Beautiful Losers* (1966). She then follows this with chapters on postmodernist technique, historiographic metafiction, the postmodernist challenge to literary genre (mostly Ondaatje), women writers, Atwood, and, finally, the most postmodern of Canadian postmoderns, Kroetsch. Throughout, Hutcheon's writing and arguments are daunting: she is in complete command of her concepts and language, and, what is far more unusual for a theorist, is equally in complete command of her primary texts. She uses her thorough knowledge of each realm to demonstrate that, in contemporary Canadian writing, "art and theory are both actively 'signifying' practices—in other words, that it is we who both make and make sense of our culture" (23). Hutcheon particularly demonstrates how this process occurs in her discussions of Cohen, Ondaatje, Findley, and Atwood, showing how their narrative strategies enforce an the kind of awareness articulated by Kroetsch: "'it would be an error not to perceive the differences between life and art, just as it would be an error not to see that they are the same'" (182).

3. "With honour, if I possibly can": Many Munros

Turning, finally, to the three critics who have written full-length studies of Munro's fiction, I want to acknowledge that in many more ways than I have indicated, Gadpaille, Howells, and, especially, Hutcheon have, if you will, defined the terms of engagement. If Rasporich, Carrington, and Blodgett demonstrate anything, it is that the intricacies of Munro's *oeuvre* not only reward close attention—that should be axiomatic at this point—they also demand our involvement in ways that test our understandings of life itself. (For example—and by way of my own situation—I just reread "Home," largely because of Carrington's discussion of it, a story Munro published in 1974 but which has never been collected. It's certainly eerie, and almost frightening, how this story confirms the whole of Hutcheon's thesis and Kroetsch's assertion. Punctuated by italicized passages that comment on what she has just written, Munro visibly challenges genre, convention, and any knowable version of "truth," ending the story with: "*I don't want any more effects, I tell you, lying. I don't know what I want. I want to do this with honour, if I possibly can*" ["Home" 1974, 153].)

Rasporich's *Dance of the Sexes* has been some time in the making. Her intentions in the book are primarily twofold, she writes: first, to "pay tribute to one of Canada's most accomplished writers, Alice Munro" (vii) and second, to "investigate the feminist possibilities of her art." At the same time, Rasporich writes, she is "primarily concerned with introducing the student of feminist literature, rather than the expert, to the imaginative female worlds of Alice Munro" (viii). These competing intentions make *Dance of the Sexes* a difficult book to get a handle on: it seems to want to be many things—tribute, biography, critical analysis, and something of a polemic—and is addressed to an ill-defined audience, and as a consequence it succeeds in doing none of these things very well.

After a brief introduction that discusses her various points regarding the female, feminine, and feminist perspective in Munro's work, Rasporich offers five chapters. The first, "Alice: The Woman Behind the Art," begins with a brief biography—which includes some new details—before presenting a rather disjointed, even aimless pastiche of interviews that Rasporich conducted with Munro at various times. These are characterized, beyond the usual "why do you write" sorts of questions, by Rasporich attempting to characterize Munro in this way or that, only to have Munro consistently qualify Rasporich's assertion or, at times, slip away altogether. Overall, this is a curious chapter; although I readily concede—and in no way dispute—Rasporich's use of Hutcheon's assertion that women "'must define their subjectivity before they can question it'" (xix), I nevertheless wonder if, beyond a few biographical details, Rasporich's first chapter goes substantially beyond the 15 printed interviews with Munro that Carrington cites (Rasporich cites only a few of these herself). I do not really think so.

The same sort of problem occurs with the second chapter, "Feminist: Her Own Tribe: A Feminist Odyssey," and, although conversely, with the fifth and final chapter, "The Short Story Writer as Female: Forms and Techniques." As suggested above, despite her assertions to the contrary, Rasporich strives mightily to "shoe-horn" (her own term) Munro into "a feminist's cinderella's slipper" (viii). Munro does not really fit, and in any case, Rasporich's attempt is based on a reading of the collected fiction. Rushed as it is (50 pages for Munro's six books) and based on questionable generalizations, Rasporich fails to convince. For example, in discussing the narrator's reaction to her father's former girlfriend, Nora, in "Walker Brothers Cowboy" (*Dance of the Happy Shades*), Rasporich writes: "In contrast to the girl's sick and decorous mother, however, and the grey, naturalistic despondency of the scene, Nora is a flash of color in her 'soft brilliant' dress and a hearty woman capable of uproareous behaviour and active invitation" (40). Although this is true for a short time in the story, Nora ultimately seems lonely and embittered. As well, Rasporich writes that "Munro is even prepared to join that group of nineteenth- and twentieth-century female artists who have used the fictional character of the deranged woman 'as the symbolic representation of the female author's anger against the rigidities of patriarchal tradition'" (85);[10] this despite Munro's assertion in Rasporich's first chapter that "madness doesn't seem to me a gender thing—I have more madwomen simply because I know more women and I know stories through women" (30). Questionable generalizations such as these characterize Rasporich's discussion of Munro's putative feminism. The point here is not that the case Rasporich is trying to make cannot be made; rather that, given her approach to the fiction, her use of it, and the structure of her argument, Rasporich's case has not been made here. Indeed, one might say that it has already been made by

Irvine ("Changing Is the Word I Want," *Sub/version*). In the fifth chapter, on form, Rasporich's problem is the opposite: she treats an extensive topic, forms, and techniques, too briefly. In light of Carrington's masterly discussion of the subject—down, almost, to the slightest nuance of interconnection—*Dance of the Sexes* pales in comparison.

Rasporich's other chapters, "Folk Artist and Ironist: Humor Comes Best to those Who are Down and Out" and "Regionalist: Wawanash County: A Landscape of Mind, a Mythic Place," represent the core of the book's contribution. Arguing first that "food in Munro is charged with feminine value" and, further, that Munro is a "literary folklorist of female culture" (95, 98), Rasporich convincingly cites numerous instances where these assertions are seen to be so. In fact, so compelling is her discussion of humour and irony that I would have liked a much more detailed argument on that subject. Similarly, when in the next chapter Rasporich discusses place and argues that "Munro is able to authenticate a fictional female world by expanding her characters' inner lives into place, and by manipulating place as feminist inquiry" (122), her own "feminist inquiry" springs to life. This part of Rasporich's argument is excellent, although here she is not as fully in command of the scholarly context as she ought to be.[11] Overall, the "introduction to the feminist possibilities of [Munro's] art" (xiii) is, ironically, either too introductory or too ambitious; with regard to three of her chapters, the case has been made elsewhere, or in order to really differentiate Rasporich's perspective, needs to be made more fully here. At the same time, her discussion of folk aspects and place could easily have been expanded into a book itself.

By contrast, Blodgett's *Alice Munro* and Carrington's *Controlling the Uncontrollable* are critical books to celebrate; in each, Munro's work receives the sustained and detailed analysis it demands, proving itself far more than equal to such scrutiny. The two volumes are nicely complementary, moreover, in that Blodgett offers the more sophisticated analysis in terms of theory while Carrington's more thorough control of detail in Munro's writing—extending into the uncollected stories—is exhaustive and compelling. Each volume, finally, is well rooted in a foundation of Munro scholarship.

As earlier noted, one of the intriguing things about Blodgett's volume is the way in which he is able to stretch the normal Twayne format.

Instead of the usual opening biographical chapter, the reader here finds "Signifying a Life," a chapter containing far more than biographical facts. In it Blodgett offers an even-handed discussion of the autobiographical in Munro's fiction—he opts for Munro's own distinction that much of her material is "personal," rather than autobiographical (5)—while offering the factual details of the author's biography almost *passim*. In so doing, Blodgett introduces his critical stance on and approach to Munro's fiction, and the result is compelling. *In medias res*, Blodgett does argue for seeing Munro's life in three stages: Wingham (until her attendance at the University of Western Ontario, 1931–49), Western Ontario and Vancouver/Victoria (1949–72), and her return to rural southwestern Ontario (1972 to the present). This way of approaching Munro and her work—through place and biography—is amplified by Blodgett's highlighting of a comment Munro made in an interview with Peter Gzowski: "'I write about where I am in life'" (6). Though it is seemingly straightforward, Blodgett writes that this "point of departure for Munro's work is deceptively ambiguous, for while the world lies there as a gift, it also lies there as a problem of meaning. Her question as an artist is: How is the world to be understood, and is it possible, finally, to do so?" (6).

Both Blodgett and Carrington, in their own ways, set out to analyze this process as it may be seen in Munro's fiction. Blodgett draws on the writings of Derrida and Barthes, applying their thinking to excellent purpose when he writes: "The narrator, furthermore, is a hermeneutic problem whose presence in the text—separated from her narrated self and vainly trying to re-place herself—exemplifies how hard it is to speak of the presence of the real in Munro, and how every effort to find it is equally vain." Carrying this thinking further—balancing "Munro's life" and fictive versions of "life" (or lives, given Munro's shifting manipulation of points of time in her characters' lives)—Blodgett offers a passage that bears quotation at length:

> It is the process by which the self becomes a text, falling apart as it does so. But as a text, and it is to this perception of the real that Munro seems inevitably to progress, the self becomes no other that what is, returning, so to speak, to itself. Within all

the play of signifiers of which a text and a self are composed, the finished narration acquires a kind of mark of destiny and perfection, some inescapable core. At least this appears as one of the ineluctable signs of Munro's mature work, in which the narrator gradually glides into the narration, and its arrangement into a certain disposition of parts becomes the narrator's as well, illuminating her at once as giver and receiver of the world remade. "I write about where I am in life" [quoting Munro once more]: or should we not say that she writes about where she is in the text that her life, finally, is? (10)

Though passages such as this may well leave those unfamiliar with contemporary literary theory wondering what it could possibly mean, Blodgett's point here—on which a good part of his subsequent argument is based—is crucial. Essentially, the question of reality is central to Munro's way of seeing; lines of demarcation—be they generic, chronological, or, seemingly, factual—are not immutable in the world she delimits in her fiction, and that is just the point of it all. Both Blodgett and Carrington demonstrate this process by looking at "The Progress of Love," another pivotal story. Further, it is probably worth noting that in the same issue of the *Canadian Forum* that included Gallant's "What is Style?," Munro contributed an essay called "What is Real?"

Dancer and the dance, indeed. Limiting his discussion to Munro's collected fiction, Blodgett successively devotes a chapter to each of Munro's books, asking numerous questions about form, technique, and analogues, and using these questions and his answers to them to allow his argument to build force as it proceeds. In *Dance of the Happy Shades*, he writes, "the first problem of Munro's narration is that it assumes the shape of exploration, and the burden for the reader is knowing how to assess the discovery" (16). Similarly, Munro offers in *Lives of Girls and Women* a "search for the right mode of discourse" (60), while in *Something I've Been Meaning to Tell You* (1974) "what we discover is that true authority is not imposed upon the material. It is acquired by surrendering to it. The mark of the narrator is her vulnerability and, consequently, her inability to control loose ends" (68). Ultimately, Blodgett convincingly argues that essential to Munro's art is a process whereby readers see her—through her narrators—"endeavoring to locate the meaning that unifies, yet always wary of it" (68).

Unlike Rasporich's discussion, which seldom seems to be entirely sure of the sum of any particular story or group of stories, Blodgett's analyses convince by their mastery of the whole fabric of Munro's art. To be sure, there are times when one would like him to go into greater detail, or to respond to this or that objection, yet one never wonders over his ability to do so, given the space. Indeed, his chapters are tightly woven and at the same time inclusive of important—and seemingly idiosyncratic—detail. Thus when discussing "Dulse," in *The Moons of Jupiter*, Blodgett is sensitive to how Munro is using the character of Willa Cather in a multiplicity of ways. Lydia, the protagonist of that story, meets a man on Grand Manan Island, New Brunswick (where Cather had a summer cottage), who, quite simply, worships her. Lydia questions his reverential attitude; thus, as Blodgett says, Cather represents a way of knowing that Munro implicitly rejects: "If the knowledge of character is mysterious and perhaps, finally, beyond knowing, we cannot very well put faith in the author, who is required to possess this knowledge" (113).[12] Finally, Blodgett uses this discussion to make a point that, especially in view of his fine subsequent treatment of *The Progress of Love*, may be extended to the whole of his analysis:

> For no one with Munro's sensitivity to the way language fabricates a world can make the reader believe that there is a pure knowledge, unaffected by language. Thus her strategy is one that not only makes one wary of realism, but also heightens one's awareness of how fragile our sense of self and the other is, so utterly dependent as it is upon language and consequent conflict of meanings. (115)

This passage and the discussion around "Dulse," especially, serve as suitable transition to Carrington's *Controlling the Uncontrollable* in that, as Blodgett remarks elsewhere, "one is urged to read Munro as one bent on using fiction as a method for understanding what the limits of fiction are" (121). Central to this process are notions of "control" (highlighted in Carrington's title), which relate to art as artifice, or the fashioning of some "mould," as Cather wrote in *The Song of the Lark*, "in which to imprison for a moment the shining, elusive element which is life itself." "Dulse" illustrates a key difference in Blodgett's and Carrington's studies, for, although Blodgett limits himself to Munro's collected fiction (curiously—and inaccurately—labelled "novels" in his bibliography), Carrington demonstrates again and again that the process of understanding through language continues in Munro's work between published versions of her stories. Thus "Dulse" appeared in the *New Yorker* as a first-person story but in *The Moons of Jupiter* was revised into a third person story.

Carrington begins where a scholar ought: by acknowledging her debts to those who have discussed Munro's "use of paradox in both style and structure" before her. Nevertheless, she maintains that "the most central and creative paradox of Munro's fiction is its repeated but consciously ambivalent attempt to control what is uncontrollable, to split in half to control a suddenly split world. These internal and external splits produce the 'intense … moments of experience' that pattern Munro's stories" (4, 5).[13] Carrington argues persuasively that "these methods of splitting point of view and manipulating narrative time allow Munro's watching narrators to back off—temporally, psychologically, and spatially—from her participating characters. *Back off*, with its consciously cautious connotations of distance and self-protection, is another frequently repeated phrase" (8). Passages such as this characterize *Controlling the Uncontrollable* as a whole, with Carrington balancing generalization with telling and specific detail. Clearly, this is a critic who is also a scholar. She knows Munro's work, and Munro criticism, inside and out.

Unlike Rasporich and Blodgett, who generally structure their analysis chronologically, Carrington devises her own groupings. Thus after an introductory chapter, "The Medium of Control: The Humiliations of Language," she offers successive chapters focused on thematically grouped stories: first, stories that involve "frightening eruptions," such as a character striking out at another, in "The Time of Death" (*Dance of the Happy Shades*) or, more recently, "Fits" (*The Progress of Love*); second, stories that involve the same first-person narrator; third, a large grouping of characters struggling for control; and, finally, parents and daughters. This approach seems eminently sensible and, more importantly, it allows Carrington to move throughout Munro's *oeuvre*; in each instance, moreover, she demonstrates that these concerns have characterized Munro's fiction from first to last. This approach also allows Carrington to argue effectively against notions that have become clichés. For example, when Munro published *Who Do You Think You Are?* (1978), many critics commented that it was reminiscent of *Lives of Girls and Women*, based on much the same material. Examining *Who Do You Think You Are?*, Carrington concludes that Munro does not "repeat herself"; rather, "she demonstrates the validity of her own aesthetic: by returning to the same theme, she clarifies her misconception of what she thought was happening and sees what she had not understood in her earlier attempt" (98).

Again and again, Carrington offers analyses that illuminate Munro's stories in ways that are new. This is especially so in her chapter on parents and daughters, which examines the effects of autobiography, place, shifting authorial perspective, and repeated treatments throughout Munro's writing as the author has attempted to come to terms with her mother on the one hand and with her father (in very different ways, to very different purpose) on the other. As well, her discussion of the influence of Yeats on "Wild Swans" (*Who Do You Think You Are?*), though not an original point, is the most sustained treatment to date (125–28); such a comparison suggests, further, the level of literary stature—in terms of canonical pecking order—that Munro is reaching (See Martin, "Alice" *passim*, and Gold, "Feeling" 10).[14] Her discussion of language, moreover, is simply daunting in its detail. There are problems, to be sure: Carrington is entirely too strident in protecting Munro from feminist readings; I am sympathetic, but I do not think it is that large of an issue, really. She also sees Munro's characters consistently as writers, often when there is little basis in the text for such a designation. These matters are mere quibbles, for the strength of *Controlling the Uncontrollable* lies in its exhaustive scholarship and sensible, well-defined arguments.

The final effect of Carrington's approach—especially when paired with the greater theoretical analysis of Blodgett's *Alice Munro*—is to demonstrate the utter density of Munro's work and, as well, its continuity of both focus and purpose. Clearly, Munro's writing is of a stature to command the attentions of such intense critical scrutiny as is considered here, and it renders the insufficient and uncertain dissemblings of critics like Gadpaille and Rasporich paltry. Indeed, what Blodgett calls Munro's "unassailable moral integrity" (151) is borne out in her fiction by the various shifts, doubts, and re-explanations Munro repeatedly offers, always with an eye to discovering "what is real," and asking how one can really know, ever. This has been so throughout her work, and it has grown in frequency, intensity, and complexity as she has progressed as a writer, as *Friend of My Youth* has just recently demonstrated yet again, if more demonstration were necessary. Munro wrote in "Home": "*I want to do this with honour, if I possibly can.*" That she does in her stories, impeccably, always (though not forever: controlling the uncontrollable). They *are* real. Dancer and the dance, indeed. Go ask Alice.

Part Two

What the Archives Reveal: Reading a Deepening Aesthetic

During the latter half of the 1980s and into the 1990s, Alice Munro's stories appeared in the *New Yorker* with increased frequency and regularity—only occasionally would one be published in another magazine, meaning that the editors at her primary venue had passed on it. With her still-growing reputation, placing stories elsewhere was not difficult. During the 1990s Munro published another three collections—*Friend of My Youth* (1990), *Open Secrets* (1994), and *The Love of a Good Woman* (1998)—and a first volume of her *Selected Stories* (1996). The new collections showed both continuity in her art and also some radical experimentation. In the first collection, for example, the title story connected to and extended other family-based concerns readers had seen before, while another, "Meneseteung" (1988), was unlike anything Munro had done previously. Much the same could be said of the stories found in the other two collections from the 1990s, notably with such stories as "The Albanian Virgin" and "Carried Away," from *Open Secrets*, and the title story of the 1998 collection and others there equally so.

As far as criticism, the first half of the 1990s saw another five single-authored books on Munro (one of which examined Mavis Gallant's work in tandem) and a brief series biography. Three of these asserted a new critical sophistication while attempting to extend, in various ways, what critics during the previous decade had established; the other two, from a series published by ECW Press, made the more significant contribution. The latter half of the decade saw only one critical monograph, by Coral Ann Howells, and published in Britain as part of a series there; it stands out as the best such critical book published during the 1990s. Critical essays appeared in greater numbers with uneven results, some showing both insight and imagination while others, often from abroad, merely "discovered" Munro and asserted the attractive qualities they found in her stories. In 1998 I edited a special issue of *Essays on Canadian Writing*, republished the next year as *The Rest of the Story: Critical Essays on Alice Munro*. It, along with my second review essay from 1998, republished here, is probably the best venue from which to ascertain the issues informing Munro criticism during the 1990s.

In January 1988 I visited the University of Calgary to look for the first time at the Alice Munro fonds there; since then I have returned many times. I spent the fall 2003 semester in Calgary reading the entire archive for my work on *Alice Munro: Writing Her Lives*. Because Munro is an organic writer—that is, she writes with images and ideas of what she is after but without outlines or planning notes—Munro's work is especially amenable to archival investigation. Containing as they do notebook drafts and (often) multiple typescript versions of stories, in both fragmentary and complete forms (there is, for example, a full version of "Bardon Bus," which Munro revised after the version published in *The Moons of Jupiter*), her archives reveal a great deal about her intentions and direction. Perhaps more than any other part of her work, they reveal Munro as a writer ever revising, working repeatedly toward particular phrasings, and most especially working intently on those phrasings that end stories. They also reveal her as a writer who sometimes worked extensively on stories that she later abandoned. As the last essay included in the section here asserts, Munro's archives are filled with a myriad of clues regarding her direction and intentions. That essay, published in 1999, was consciously polemical: I was encouraging other scholars to go read and use the Calgary archives regularly and consistently.

Given these investigations, the essays and review essay in this section are infused with what was then a new awareness of Munro's directions, specific attempts, and textual outcomes, seen in relation to what her archives revealed. This is most evident in "Alice Munro's Willa Cather" (1992) and "Writing 'Home'" (1998)—the latter the introduction to the special issue of *Essays on Canadian Writing* and to *The Rest of the Story* and still bearing the marks of that position here—in the readings they offer of, in the first, "Dulse" (1980) and, in the latter, "Home" (1974), "The Progress of Love" (1985), and "Friend of My Youth" (1990). Details from the archives inform the essay on American literary influence and also the second review essay on criticism—which reviews most of the critical work noted above—and especially the final essay focused on the Munro archive itself.

"Alice Munro and the Anxiety of American Influence" is another essay with a polemic agenda. It proceeds from the twin facts that Munro has always been clear about her American literary influences but that, overall, most Canadian critics have avoided that fact. I delivered it as a paper in 1991 at the University of Ottawa's symposium on Canadian–U. S. Literary Relations, and there were whoops and much consternation when I asked, "Whose anxiety is it, anyway—that of Canadian writers or Canadian critics?" With regard to Munro, it was quite clear that the critics were those who were anxious. During that time I was writing about anti-Americanism as a widely held but largely unspoken prejudice among English-speaking Canadians, especially among those in universities, and this essay reflects these discussions (see Thacker "Gazing"). I was also doing my work on Cather as an influence on Munro and she, along with Eudora Welty, looms large. Later, when I revised *Alice Munro: Writing Her Lives* for the paperback edition, I added a tenth chapter covering 2004 to 2010 and, because of encouragements from Munro herself, explored the influence of William Maxwell. So my question still stands.

The second omnibus review essay to be published in the *Journal of Canadian Studies*, "What's 'Material'?" (1998), also rails a bit about Munro's relationship with the Canadian academy. Unlike its predecessor, "Go Ask Alice," which considered books offering larger discussions of Canadian literature, this review essay looks exclusively at volumes of Munro criticism and at Catherine Sheldrick Ross's short ECW biography. More than a bit polemical, too, it examines the relationship between the life, the fiction, and the criticism, asking uncomfortable questions about the appropriateness of the critical monograph for a writer like Munro and, more uncomfortably still, wondering over the unseemly rush of new PhDs to turn their theses into books so as to secure academic careers. At the same time, it argues that the best books reviewed are those from ECW's series.

Alice Munro's Willa Cather (1992)

The fall and winter of 1927 to 1928 proved a difficult time for Willa Cather. She had been forced to move from her Bank Street apartment in New York City, and just after returning east from a long Christmas visit with family and friends in Red Cloud, Nebraska, she received news of her father's death. Cather's longtime companion, Edith Lewis, later recalled this period of their life together, writing that during the following summer, "Grand Manan seemed the only foothold left on earth." They had been visiting Grand Manan Island, off the coast of New Brunswick in the Bay of Fundy, since 1922, staying at the Whale Cove Inn until 1928, when their newly built cottage was ready (Skaggs 128–30; Brown and Crone 41–46). Lewis continues, saying that "with all her things in storage," owing to the move, Cather "looked forward fervently to her attic at Grand Manan. No palace could have seemed so attractive to her just then as that rough little cottage, with the soft fogs blowing across the flowery fields, and the crystalline quiet of the place" (153).[1]

These summer trips presaged the events of "Before Breakfast," one of Cather's last stories, written in 1944—about three years before her death—and included in the posthumous *The Old Beauty and Others* (1948; Arnold 165). It is set on an island—though off the coast of Nova Scotia—and its protagonist, Henry Grenfell, a well-to-do American businessman, is seeking refuge from his overwhelming sense of ennui. He is fleeing what Alice Munro has described in "Chaddeleys and Flemings:

2. The Stone in the Field" as the "pain of human contact"—her narrator admits to being "hypnotized by it. The fascinating pain; the humiliating necessity" (*Moons* 27). Such sentiments, too, inform Munro's "Dulse" (1980), a story first published in the *New Yorker* and, after revision, collected in *The Moons of Jupiter* (1982). And like Cather's story, Munro's derives from its author's knowledge of Grand Manan Island: Munro has explained that while working on a story involving the character who became Lydia, the protagonist of "Dulse," she visited the island and there met a person steeped in Cather's history on Grand Manan. That person's veneration of the American writer served Munro as a basis for Mr. Stanley in "Dulse"—the two parts of the story, she said, seemed to fit well together (Telephone interview).

Although critics have examined Munro's Cather connection, more consideration of the matter is warranted. Klaus P. Stich has discussed Munro's use of Cather as both presence and authorial icon in "Dulse," pointing out a wide variety of apt thematic and imagistic parallels throughout Cather's works. However, though his article includes much that is relevant to an initial understanding of the Cather–Munro connection, Stich's analysis presents a partial picture only. Even so, his discussion of it is far superior to those offered by the critics who have published extended critical analyses of Munro's fiction: Martin, Blodgett, and Carrington. Although they present detailed readings of "Dulse," none pursues the Cather connection much beyond the superficial—she is merely present, as Blodgett argues, to represent a view of art that is "hermetically sealed," one "that Munro finds wanting" (113).

In "Dulse," Munro offers a story that grew out of her own visit to Grand Manan and that recapitulates the setting, midlife-crisis mood, and cathartic *dénouement* of "Before Breakfast." What is more, Cather appears in effect as a character, one with a compelling presence whose status as a no-nonsense-author-of-consequence needs to be probed and (as far as possible) understood—by Munro, by her protagonist Lydia, and by the readers of "Dulse." Cather's importance to Munro's story, moreover, is further borne out in draft versions of "Dulse," as found in the University of Calgary archives. The connection between them extends beyond this pair of stories, and it is a broader parallel that persists yet: Munro's recently published story, "Carried Away" (1991), features a protagonist who considers Cather to be one of her favourite authors, and takes place in February 1917 when Cather was still rising in fame (34).² This notwithstanding, Cather's presence in "Dulse" remains the central connection in the story, inviting further analysis.

That Munro would be drawn to Cather's work is not surprising. As women who have sought to depict the "home place" (in Wright Morris's phrase)—writing out of their inheritance and lineage to create fictions derived from their protracted and intimate knowledge of their respective rural small towns—the two have much in common. Munro would have been aware of Cather's prominence among American writers from the 1920s on, but more than that she may also have been attracted by the appeal of Cather's work outside of the academy; *My Ántonia* (1918), for example, has not been out of print since its publication. This quality persists, and it would likely not be lost on an aspiring writer of Munro's intelligence and ability. Nor would Cather's penchant for seemingly revisiting the same material, as Merrill Maguire Skaggs has recently argued, for Munro has shown the same tendency.³ Finally, although Munro has been seen as a writer of perception and sensibility, rather than of erudition or allusion, much recent scholarship has confirmed a detailed awareness in her fiction of a wide range of literary forebears, both paternal and maternal (Blodgett; Carrington *Controlling*; York "Rival").

Taken together, these lines of parallel treatment and influence suggest a compatibility and relationship between Cather and Munro that, if not of the same crucial importance as, say, Sarah Orne Jewett on Cather, is far deeper than has been acknowledged thus far.⁴ In fact, Cather's well-known phrase describing Jewett's relationship to her subject, the "gift of sympathy," may be apt to describe Munro's view of her American precursor, Cather (Preface). Thus the appearance of Cather as a major presence in "Dulse," along with a telling invocation of the messages of Cather's *A Lost Lady* (1923) in the story, is not just a singular occurrence within Munro's work: it is a direct acknowledgement of Cather's influence and of their shared values.

* * *

At the beginning of "Before Breakfast," Henry Grenfell glimpses the morning star, the planet Venus, but it brings no solace: he has arisen from a difficult night's sleep brought on by his personal dissatisfactions and aggravated by a chance meeting he had with a geologist the evening before. Going about his morning toilet upon rising, "Grenfell rejected his eyedrops. Why patch up? What was the use ... of anything?" (148, Cather's ellipsis). This final question is what Grenfell—through the mediations and actions of the story, all of which occurs before breakfast—must get beyond. He does, ultimately, finding solace in the passage of time from youth to old age, in reconciling himself to the geological history of "his" island—a perspective that troubled him the night before—and, finally, in the transformative powers of Venus/Aphrodite.

Like Grenfell, Munro's Lydia has come to Grand Manan seeking a refuge, and like him, too, she spends just a single night there during the story. At the story's end, she is left at least hopeful if not, like Grenfell, seemingly transformed. Her feelings at the outset, however, are not as intense as his, though they appear to be more chronic. Even so, Munro is defining the beginnings of a despondency similar to Grenfell's. Lydia is 45, divorced with two grown children living on their own, and working as an editor for a publisher in Toronto; significantly, she is a poet, too—but is not forthcoming about it. She is a person who is particularly unconnected to those around her. Having just broken up with Duncan, with whom she had been living in Kingston, Lydia is travelling, in the words of a rejected draft's phrasing, "hoping to manage some kind of recuperation, or even happiness, before she had to start working again" (38.8.20.1.f1).[5]

Parenthetically, draft versions of the story are being used here both for the greater articulation of authorial intention they reveal and to demonstrate the process of Munro's composition. Passages from rejected drafts—such as this one—are not to be seen as preferable to the final versions, although the papers reveal that Munro is an author who works very hard on crucial passages in a story, consequently rejecting descriptions and phrasings that both add to an understanding of her intentions and might well have been retained.

As well, although this essay is looking at the most direct connections between "Before Breakfast" and "Dulse," there are more subtle parallels as well. Cather uses the planet Venus, replete with its mythological associations and sense of timelessness, for its essentially mysterious quality: it suggests meaning apprehended but not fully understood. Thus Grenfell's dissatisfaction arises in part through the geologist's well-intentioned factualities; these have the effect of dispelling the mysterious attraction he feels to his island, which in turn has been of such solace to him, even when he is away from it—the island is his mainstay, even in just knowing it is there.

Similarly, in the *New Yorker* version of "Dulse," Lydia's ex-lover is Alex, a geologist, one "absorbed ... in the crust and content of the earth and in his own distinct energies" (38). A more interesting parallel is found in Munro's title story for the volume in which "Dulse" was collected: "The Moons of Jupiter." The story, which has the same narrator as the "Chaddeleys and Flemings" stories, Janet, focuses on the apprehended death of Janet's father. Janet, who has just visited a nearby planetarium, jokes with her father—in the hospital awaiting heart surgery—about the names of Jupiter's moons. Throughout, her concern is finding truths that can be believed with absolute certainty. Here, however, even the facts of science fail, and she is drawn inexorably to the mystery of the solar system: its enormity, its mythic proportions (reflected in the names of the moons), and its ultimate inscrutability.

At the outset of "Dulse," Munro describes Lydia's disorientation and her futile attempts to connect to the people and the things around her, then encapsulates her efforts and ultimate detachment with the sentence: "She set little blocks on top of one another and she had a day" (36). Stopping at a guest house for the night, Lydia muses over the movements and motives of the people she meets, seeking to infer and then to understand the source of what made them, apparently, whole.[6] She realizes, Munro writes early in the story, "that people were no longer so interested in getting to know her" (36), and she seeks to understand herself in view of such changes. What Lydia is most bothered by, and wishes most to understand, is "what gave him [Duncan] his power? She knows who did. But she asks what, and when—when did the transfer take place, when was the abdication of all pride and sense?" (50). In a rejected draft version of the same passage, Munro is more precise: "Then what had given him his subsequent power? Easy to say it was the foolishness of Lydia, the abdication of all pride and sense, a most persistent streak of cravenness[.]

But it was no help to her, this explanation, it explained nothing, she was left to sit regarding her own life with sad disbelief." The whole of this passage, part of a typed draft, is struck out and replaced with a holograph insertion, reading: "Then what had given him his subsequent power?" Munro appears to have considered putting the entire section from "Easy" to "disbelief" in parenthesis before rejecting it entirely (38.8.20.1.f10–11).

That evening Lydia meets her fellow guests, including Mr. Stanley, to whom she is introduced, and with whom she eats dinner and discusses Willa Cather. At the same meal she acknowledges at another table three men who work for the telephone company. Throughout the story, Lydia's thoughts focus primarily on her own concerns, especially on Duncan and their relationship (at one point we read about her discussion of it with a psychiatrist), and on their recent breakup. She thinks as well about the members of the telephone crew, with whom she plays cards later in the evening, imagining each as lovers (one of them, Eugene, tries to beckon her to his bed). She evaluates each relative to Duncan, whom she recalls in considerable detail as to habits, preferences, and peculiarities. She knows she is now, for him, merely the latest in a long line of former girlfriends—"morose, messy, unsatisfactory Lydia. The unsatisfactory poet" (52).

Even though such thoughts make up most of the story, Lydia meets Mr. Stanley first, and through him she meets the personage of Cather. They talk of Cather generally at dinner, and the next day at breakfast they have a second—and far more pertinent—exchange about her, one that defines her presence in "Dulse." As such, Stanley and Cather frame the story. By using Cather in this way, Munro provides Lydia with another person's (relevant) life to wonder over at this crucial moment in the protagonist's own life. Munro offers Cather—the author of *A Lost Lady*, whose Marian Forrester is, like Lydia, a woman whose entire identity is dependent on men—as a frame for Lydia's "recuperation." And Lydia, for her part, might well be seen as Munro's "lost lady."

* * *

Just as Munro is offering us her version of Cather, so too is Mr. Stanley offering Lydia his version of Cather, itself a persona to be probed. Mr. Stanley, opening their first conversation with "'Are you familiar with the writer Willa Cather?'" (38), uses his enthusiasm for Cather as mealtime chit-chat. He tells Lydia of Cather's summers on Grand Manan Island, mentioning her view of the sea and how she composed most of *A Lost Lady* (his "favorite") on the island, and telling Lydia of his plans to talk that evening with an 88-year-old woman "'who knew Willa.'" "'I read and reread her,'" Stanley says, "'and my admiration grows. It simply grows'" (39). Evaluating Stanley's conversational manner, Lydia thinks of "a time when a few people, just a few people, had never concerned themselves with being democratic, or ingratiating, in their speech; they spoke in formal, well-thought-out, slightly self-congratulating sentences, though they lived in a country where their formality, their pedantry, could bring them nothing but mockery. No, that was not the whole truth. It brought mockery, and an uncomfortable admiration.... And his adoration of the chosen writer was of a piece with this," Lydia decides, "it was just as out-of-date as his speech" (39–40).

Lydia suggests creating some sort of memorial on the island, but Stanley rejects the idea, saying that on the island many "thought her [Cather] unfriendly and did not like her." Lydia, however, realizes that for him this is a "private pilgrimage," so he wants nothing to do with a memorial, which would see, Lydia thinks, their guest house "renamed *Shadows on the Rock*[.] He would let the house fall down and the grass grow over it, sooner than see that" (41).[7]

The draft versions of "Dulse" suggest that Munro worked hard at getting Stanley's character—and so the Cather connection—right. Initially, Stanley was named Middleton, "from Boston, a brisk and courtly and menacing old fellow," and Lydia accompanies him to Cather's cottage; Grand Manan is mentioned, as is *My Ántonia*. Munro sets the date of Cather's death over 20 years early, 1925 rather than 1947, and refers to Edith Lewis as "Edith Head" (38.8.19). Munro subsequently replaces *My Ántonia* with *A Lost Lady*—parts of which were written on the island—and refers to Lewis by her real name (38.8.21). In earlier drafts as well, Lydia was a university teacher of American literature, then worked in a bookstore but "had majored in American literature at university" (38.8.20; these are alternate versions, the first typed, crossed out, with the latter as a holograph correction). What these changes suggest—beyond getting a series of plausible connections to hang together—is that Munro was trying various ways to make the Cather connections resonate and, equally, to make Lydia a person of suitable background for understanding them.

Stanley, based on a person Munro actually met, is developed so as to create a particular version of Cather that Munro seeks to first establish and then probe. Within the story's structure, he is foregrounded: after introducing Lydia and her situation at the outset (presenting only a bit of her fundamental malaise, wondering if she can find a way to support herself and so live on the island), Munro moves at once to Mr. Stanley and the discussion of Cather, which takes up the story's first portion. Lydia anticipates the telephone crew mocking Stanley, which they eventually do—during dinner as the men overhear his conversation with Lydia, and later when he returns for the night after his visit with the woman who knew Cather (48). At the same time, Stanley's formal manner recalls aspects of Grenfell's character; the latter, for example, signs cheques for his family's expenses without looking at what they are for, because to do so would be unseemly (*Old Beauty* 154–55), and Stanley's devotion to Cather is akin to Grenfell's devotion to his island retreat.

Finally and most tellingly, Stanley's version of Cather, his "durable shelter" (59), shows him to be hopelessly "out of date," and almost insignificant. Given Cather's critical reputation throughout her later years (from the 1930s on, she was often seen as a kind of aged literary dinosaur, charmingly still concerned with the romance of the past while American fiction had moved on to social relevance), Munro's characterization of Stanley has particular resonance, both for Lydia and for Munro herself (see O'Brien "Becoming"). In view of Lydia's awareness that "people were no longer so interested in getting to know her" (36), she fears becoming passé and, like Stanley, a nonentity. Equally, Cather's parallel fate within literary renown—being a benign throwback to a simpler time—may be a fear felt by both Lydia, the poet, and her creator, Munro.

Yet Munro counters this view of Mr. Stanley with another, more positive, one. When the two meet, Lydia is vague as to Mr. Stanley's age. Later, during a brief chat with Lydia, the woman who runs the guest house says, almost triumphantly (because Lydia has been unable to guess Mr. Stanley's age accurately), that he "'is eighty-one. Isn't that amazing? I really admire people like that. I really do. I admire people that keep going'" (43). It is an assessment that applies equally well to Cather's Grenfell. Cather and Munro are writing about such people: both Grenfell and Lydia reach moments on their respective islands in which they must decide how to "keep going"; throughout their work, both writers have focused on such moments, Cather most clearly in *The Professor's House* (1925) and Munro throughout her fiction, though most precisely in her last two books.

* * *

Munro's characterization of Cather lies at the heart of "Dulse." What the draft versions suggest is that Munro endeavoured to make Cather's characterization more inscrutable by probing the author's known public persona in tandem with Cather's largely unknown, private persona. Thus Lydia, whose poetic vocation seems equivocal, because she seldom mentions her work to others and has decided "that probably she would not write any more poems" (37), has reason to wonder about the persona presented by a famous woman writer, in view of her own uncertainties, generally, but more specifically because of the vocation she shares with Cather. More precisely, Cather is directly relevant to Lydia's situation because of the unwavering persona she presented to the world throughout her life. For Cather, the preeminence of art, and of her own vocation as an artist was always *the* uncompromised value. Mr. Stanley, for his part, understands this. Speaking of Cather's reputation on Grand Manan during dinner, he says: "'The people here, you know, while they were very impressed with Willa, and some of them recognized her genius—I mean the genius of her personality, for they would not be able to recognize the genius of her work—others of them thought her unfriendly and did not like her. They took offense because she was unsociable, as she had to be, to do her writing'" (40–41).[8]

In the *New Yorker* version of this passage, Munro uses the word "person" rather than "personality" (31), and the tension between the two words—between the externality of the first and the interiority of the second—suggests Munro's direction. For Lydia's sake as well as her own, she is probing the distance between person and personality, between what a person is seen to be and what she shows herself to be—that adumbration of actions, speech, appearance, and presence that make a person who she is. For Munro as for Cather, this is no easy matter, nor are answers in any way unequivocal. This issue, finally, is crucial to Munro's Cather: in "Dulse," Munro offers up Cather as a difficult case in being human, in being an artist, and in being a woman writer—difficult for Lydia, for the reader, and for Munro herself.

During their initial discussion, Lydia passes over Mr. Stanley's assertion that Cather had to be "unsociable ... to do her writing," but they return to the idea the next morning during breakfast, after Lydia has meditated on her own situation and problems. A paragraph about Lydia's lover and their relationship—included in the *New Yorker* but omitted from the book—is directive; its omission, no doubt, was due to changes in the lover's character between versions (his name, his profession, and his encounter with bears), but it speaks directly to why Munro felt it necessary to include Cather:

> All this points to a grand self-absorption. A natural question follows: What did I think would be left over? But self-absorption honest as that [Alex's] can be pure relief, once you've seen a few disguises. He was a great man for not lying, and blithe about it; none of your wordy justifications. He had real hopes for us. He thought we could be true companions: me, a poet, a grownup, hardworking woman absorbed in that, as he was in the crust and content of the earth and in his own distinct energies. He hadn't known poets. (38)

Although the final sentence here is equivocal, it points back at Lydia herself (as well as at her poet colleagues, Cather and Munro)[9] and, accordingly, toward Munro's point: her version of Cather in "Dulse" is essentially a meditation on the artist's need for both self-absorption and disguises.

Thus in the *New Yorker* version, Munro may be seen to be pursuing this issue by sidestepping Lydia as a first-person narrator and addressing her reader directly:

But there is more to it than that; take a look at Lydia. Her self-absorption equals Alex's, but it is more artfully concealed. She is in competition with him, and with all other women, even when it is ludicrous for her to be so. She cannot stand to hear them praised or know they are well remembered. Like many women of her generation, she has an idea of love which is ruinous but not serious in some way, not respectful.

Lydia catalogues the sacrifices she made for her relationship, then concludes, saying of them: "They were indecent. She made him a present of such power, then complained relentlessly to herself, and much later to him, that he had got it. She was out to defeat him" (38). This paragraph is retained in the revised book version of the story, but Munro moves it, in effect, away from herself as the author; it is placed far more clearly in relation to Lydia's psychiatric analysis. The key to these meanderings—both perceptual and textual—is found, in the *New Yorker* version, in the question that abruptly follows the words "defeat him": "Is that the truth?" (38). In *The Moons of Jupiter*, the question becomes: "That is what she said to the doctor. But is it the truth?" (55).

The difference between these two versions—along, one thinks, with the need to shift from first to third person—is crucial. In the *New Yorker*, owing to the narrative fissure between narrator and author demanded by the story, the question encompasses more than Lydia's situation: it expands, given Munro's detached commentary on it, to include herself as the author. In the book version, Munro has revised and backed away from these implications, and the passage becomes more circumscribed and focused on Lydia herself. In both cases, however, the issue is what self-absorption actually looks like, and all the characters in the story—including Cather—are decidedly self-absorbed.

* * *

The overall effect of the shift from the first-person perspective of the *New Yorker* version to the third person in *The Moons of Jupiter* is one of distancing: Lydia seems more disconnected and detached in the revised version. At the same time, these two articulations of Lydia's self-analysis confirm

Judith Kegan Gardiner's argument concerning narrative techniques employed by women writers in relation to their personal identity and, more specifically, offer a parallel to Cather's *A Lost Lady*. Cather uses a third-person point of view in her novel (although an early use of "us" [10] reveals the authorial presence behind the narrative), but she creates Niel Herbert's vision of Marian Forrester so vividly that readers often recall the narrative as his first-person account.[10] The fact that Munro comments directly on Lydia in the *New Yorker* version and her subsequent shift to third person suggest a similar situation, a problem she solved through the creative distance afforded by the more detached narrative approach.

The shift in point of view between the published versions of "Dulse" was not a last-minute change, however; there are drafts using each point of view: the holograph drafts (38.11.7 and 38.8.19) are, respectively, in third and first, and the typescript drafts (38.8.20, 21, 22) are third, first, and third. Munro frequently tries both points of view to see which is the more appropriate, although the shifting back and forth throughout this story's composition and publication indicates more than the usual difficulty in settling on a narrative perspective. As well, the change from Alex to Duncan, from a geologist bothered by polar bears to a historian nudged by black bears, may be part of this self-absorption: the ordinariness of Duncan's life being preferable to the more exotic nature of Alex's. Or it may have to do with the demands of the *New Yorker* and its audience—there is something of an American cliché about Canada in Alex's polar bears—although Alex's background is present in the draft materials (38.8.20).

When Lydia joins Mr. Stanley for breakfast, "the telephone crew had eaten and gone off to work before daylight." She inquires after "his visit with the woman who had known Willa Cather," whereupon Stanley launches into a full report, and the ensuing discussion goes directly to the heart of "the case of Willa Cather." The woman had run a restaurant when Cather was staying on the island, and she and Lewis would often have their meals sent up. Sometimes, however, Cather would not like the meal and would send it back, asking "'for another dinner to be sent.' He smiled, and said in a confidential way, 'Willa could be imperious. Oh, yes. She was not perfect. All people of great abilities are apt to be a bit impatient in daily matters'" (56–57). Here the narrator comments on Lydia's mood at this moment: "Sometimes waking up was all right, and sometimes it was very bad. This morning she had wakened with the cold conviction of a mistake—something avoidable and irreparable." This is by way of accounting for Lydia's response to Stanley's last comment: "'Rubbish, Lydia wanted to say, she sounds a proper bitch" (57).

Mr. Stanley continues, reporting that sometimes, "'If they felt they wanted some company,'" Cather and Lewis would eat in the restaurant. On one such occasion, Cather discussed a proposal of marriage the woman was considering: "'Of course,'" Stanley says, Cather "'did not advise her directly to do one thing or the other, she talked to her in general terms very sensibly and kindly and the woman still remembers it vividly. I was happy to hear that but I was not surprised.'" Lydia's reaction to this, and the ensuing discussion, bears quoting at length:

> "What would she know about it, anyway?" Lydia said.
> Mr. Stanley lifted his eyes from his plate and looked at her in grieved amazement.
> "Willa Cather lived with a woman," Lydia said.
> When Mr. Stanley answered he sounded flustered, and mildly upbraiding.
> "They were devoted," he said.
> "She never lived with a man."
> "She knew things as an artist knows them. Not necessarily by experience."
> "But what if they don't know them?" Lydia persisted. "What if they don't?"
> He went back to eating his egg as if he had not heard that. Finally he said, "The woman considered Willa's conversation very helpful to her."
> Lydia made a sound of doubtful assent. She knew she had been rude, even cruel. She knew she would have to apologize. (57–58)

Retreating to the sideboard and feeling bad for the hurt she has just inflicted, Lydia talks briefly to the owner of the guest house, who talks about longing to get away, then, remembering something, gives Lydia a bag full of dulse—an edible seaweed that she professes to have a taste for—left for her by Vincent, the man on the telephone crew she found the most attractive as a potential lover. She takes it back to the table as "a conciliatory joke," asking "I wonder if Willa Cather ever ate dulse?'" Stanley ponders the question seriously, looking at the leaves, and "Lydia knew he was seeing what Willa Cather might have seen."

The three paragraphs that conclude the story encapsulate the essential question posed by "Dulse," and so speak most directly to Munro's Willa Cather; they need to be quoted together because of their mutuality, amounting to a symbiosis:

> But was she lucky or was she not, and was it all right with that woman? How did she live? That was what Lydia wanted to say. Would Mr. Stanley have known what she was talking about? If she had asked how did Willa Cather live, would he not have replied that she did not have to find a way to live, as other people did, that she was Willa Cather?
>
> What a lovely, durable shelter he had made for himself. He could carry it everywhere and nobody could interfere with it. The day may come when Lydia will count herself lucky to do the same. In the meantime, she'll be up and down. "Up and down," they used to say in her childhood, talking of the health of people who weren't going to recover. "Ah. She's up and down."
>
> Yet look how this present slyly warmed her, from a distance. (58–59)

Some readers have made much of the exchange over Cather's relationship with Lewis, assuming the lesbian cast that has been a central concern of some Cather critics. Thus Munro is seen as either taking a swipe at lesbians on behalf of heterosexual women or, more charitably, adopting the point of view of some of the marginalized.[11] Without engaging either view, the partiality of such arguments needs to be recognized, as does the partiality of any analysis. The story, and Munro's creation of a particularly resonate version of Cather, is far more complicated than that. Munro's work is open to alternative ways of seeing any single event in a character's life; this is true throughout "Dulse," but especially so in its concluding paragraphs, where Munro can be seen—through successive drafts—honing her version of Cather by making that writer's presence more, not less, ambiguous.

Overall, the book version is more articulate and, equally, more open-ended. In the *New Yorker,* Lydia thinks that Mr. Stanley "wouldn't have known what I was talking about" in the face of her question, "How did she live?" (39); in the book, that assertion has been expanded to include: "Would Mr. Stanley have known…?" Likewise, the flat statement in the *New Yorker*: "She was Willa Cather" (italicized in an earlier draft: 38.8.21.f 19) becomes "If she had asked … would he not have replied … that she was Willa Cather." Finally, "The day might come when I'd find myself doing the same," becomes: "when Lydia will count herself lucky" to be doing the same. Indeed, given the open-endedness of Munro's conclusion, it is not far-fetched to see the rejected paragraph from the *New Yorker* version, which describes Cather and Lewis as "true companions," as describing Lydia and Alex as well.

Eudora Welty—one of Munro's acknowledged influences (Metcalf Interview)—has asserted that "the story is a vision; while it's being written, all choices must be its choices, and as these choices multiply upon one another, their field is growing too" ("How" 245). Cather's presence in "Dulse" is central to the story and essential to the choices Munro has made in writing it: through the echoes of "Before Breakfast," through her presence on Grand Manan Island as a shade and a local character, and most fundamentally by "the mystery of her life"—to paraphrase Munro's own words in "The Stone in the Field" (*Moons* 33). Taken together, the choices Munro made created a version of Cather that resonates throughout "Dulse," amplifying the mysteries and uncertainties that characterize Lydia's confusions. The case study that Cather represents for both the self-absorption of the artist and the disguises of the artist, most particularly the woman artist, continues to whet the imagination for Munro, for Mr. Stanley, for Lydia, and for the reader, even after the story has been laid aside.

According to Munro, she was working on a story involving Lydia when she visited Grand Manan with a friend and there met a Cather "fanatic"; the two parts of the story just seemed to fit well together (Telephone interview). The inaccuracies of the references to Cather in the initial draft bear out this gestation of the story, as, indeed, does the flavour of Mr. Stanley's character generally. More significant than a holiday incident providing a new element for a story in process, however, is how Munro used her experience of meeting a Cather "fanatic." It became the basis for a complex invocation of and meditation upon Cather that is, at once, something of an homage, an acknowledgement of their shared vision and purpose, and a caustic analysis of "fanatical" self-absorption—Cather's, Mr. Stanley's, Lydia's, and, finally, her own. This invocation, moreover, serves as a precise object lesson for Lydia, though the matters it raises are not resolved, only intimated and essayed.

* * *

The complexity of the issues Munro confronts in "Dulse" become evident by moving backward through the story's final three paragraphs. Lydia is "slyly warmed" because—Marian Forrester-like—she sees that she still has her ability to attract a man, as confirmed with Vincent's present of dulse. Yet the obverse of her pleasure here is the implication that her identity is still defined by men—giving them the same "power" over her that she allowed of Duncan, a situation that so obsesses her, and that Cather and Munro both confronted as artists in a male-dominated world. The notion of being "up and down" to describe "the health of people who weren't going to recover," recalls, with its connection to Mr. Stanley's "durable shelter," Grenfell's predicament in "Before Breakfast"; throughout each writer's work, moreover, is the acknowledgement that none of us, ultimately, is "going to recover." Thus the central questions posed by "Dulse," by way of both point and counterpoint, are those that directly engage the "mystery" that was—and is—Cather: "But was she lucky or was she not, and was it all right with that woman? How did she live?"

Writing of both biography and autobiography, James Olney quotes an observation by Clarissa M. Lorenz: "'What ordinary mortals can't swallow about artists is the ravaging of others. But the daemon will continue to destroy with impunity. Art, after all, is born of a colossal ego re-creating the world in its image. "A creative person has little power over his own life," said Jung. "Those pay dearly who have the creative fire." So do those who are closest to them'" (436).[12] Elsewhere in the same essay, Olney asserts that "it is autobiography, or the presence of the biographer's life, the presence of the authorial 'I,' that draws biography across the vague, wavering, and indistinct line that separates history from literature…" (429).

Munro has often shown herself to be uncomfortable with the "authority" the role of writer seems to demand of her, and is here writing what amounts to a meditation on the artist's self-absorption. Perhaps, too, "Dulse" should be seen as a meditation on the self-absorption of us all. Similarly, the implications of Cather's work beyond *A Lost Lady* and "Before Breakfast"—all of which, including these two works, is now seen as nowhere near as simple as it was once regarded—are also an unstated but clearly implied presence in the story. In "Dulse," too, Munro is writing autobiography, biography, and fiction: the commingling is indeed, following Olney, literature, but it is also an acknowledgement on Munro's part of her fundamental kinship with Cather. Its sense of an ending that is not really conclusive echoes both *A Lost Lady* and "Before Breakfast," and is an acknowledgement of their shared values. Yet in keeping with each woman's distrust of absolutes, Lydia's unanswered questions about Cather acknowledge, finally, the very mystery of being that drives any artist: "But was she lucky or was she not, and was it all right with that woman? How did she live?" Mr. Stanley does not know, Lydia does not know, Munro does not know. Nor, really, do we. But by asking these unanswerable questions, Munro both acknowledges and celebrates Cather's ability to take the mystery of her life with her. Rather than being an emissary from a simpler time, an anachronism, Munro's Cather is a kindred spirit, an influence, a foremother.

Alice Munro and the Anxiety of American Influence (1994)

In one of the interviews she gave when *The Progress of Love* (1986) had just been published, Alice Munro was asked—in the usual way of such occasions—about "the effects of other writers on" her. She replied, with typical directness:

> "Oh, writing makes my life possible, it always has. I started serious reading and writing at about the same time, during adolescence when my life was difficult, as everybody's is, and it still makes life possible. I read something like that Chekhov story, I can't see how people get through the day without reading something like that."

Taken by itself, such a comment is unremarkable: it is hardly surprising that such a fine writer as Munro would also be a frequent, sharp, and detailed reader. The implied symbiosis seems only natural. And such comments are common in literary interviews generally, and in hers in particular. Yet Munro's assertion here of reading-as-being is notable in another way: it raises the question of influence. She comes back to it herself later in the same interview when she cites William Trevor's work, saying that it has been "a great encouragement" to her: "I brought this up because sometimes you need—I need—reassurance. And I go to a lot of writers, I think, for reassurance, in different ways" (Freake Interview 8, 10).

Munro's comments here and others like them elsewhere confirm that she is quite open to and very much interested in the work of other writers. In the course of this particular interview, in fact, she mentions many others—classical as well as contemporary—whose work she is evidently very familiar with. What is no less evident is that Munro is not shy about naming names. And yet, Chekhov and Trevor notwithstanding, these names are—and have been throughout her celebrity—mainly American. In an early and oft-cited interview with John Metcalf, Munro says that "in terms of vision, the writers who have influenced me are probably the writers of the American South ... Eudora Welty, Flannery O'Connor, Carson McCullers ... Reynolds Price. Another writer who's influenced me a lot is Wright Morris." She then adds a tag line that, for my purposes at least, is crucial: "I'm sorry these are all Americans but that's the way it is" (Metcalf Interview 56, ellipses in original).[1]

Questions of influence have been receiving progressively more attention in Munro criticism these days. Some critics have pursued the Joycean connection first noted by J. R. (Tim) Struthers ("Reality"); others, most notably Ildikó de Papp Carrington, have discovered and discussed a Yeats connection; Lorraine York has examined both Tennyson and Browning ("Rival"); and W. R. Martin, like Carrington and E. D. Blodgett, has noted a wide variety of connections with British and European traditions. Others have detailed Munro's connections to the Gothic. As Janet, the narrator of "Chaddeleys and Flemings," asserts in a much different context, "Connection. That was what it was all about" (*Moons* 6). So it is with Munro herself.[2] Although critics have not exactly ignored Munro's American connections, they have looked for them not very often or very closely. True enough, one of the first critical articles on Munro was Struthers' "Alice Munro and the American South" (1975), but apart from this piece—which really just elaborates on the comment Munro made in the Metcalf interview—only Klaus P. Stich has sought to probe what is perhaps the deepest of Munro's American connections—that with Willa Cather, which, though unmentioned in any interview, is rather evident in her story "Dulse."[3] Beyond these articles and the superficial comments offered in the critical books, no one to my knowledge has attempted to connect Munro's work with that of McCullers, O'Connor, Price, Morris, or several other American writers whom she has acknowledged as influences.[4] My first question, then, is, why is this? The omission seems odd, given Munro's acknowledgements, both about her own reading and about specific influences; it seems especially so in view of the considerable work done on her British and continental connections.[5]

* * *

Without question, the whole business of literary influence is a slippery slope, and taking up questions of influence in Munro's writing poses some particularly knotty problems. Although she has shown herself to be attentive to the work of others, Munro has produced fictions that on the surface appear to be marvelously self-contained. There are some fairly obvious literary allusions in *Dance of the Happy Shades* (1968) (notably in the title story), and she even more successfully (as critics have demonstrated) uses allusions to certain Victorian poets and to James Joyce's *A Portrait of the Artist as a Young Man* in *Lives of Girls and Women* (1971). Since then, however, and with the very notable exception of "Dulse," Munro's display of the influence of others has been, like her fiction itself, quite subtle indeed.

The work of several critics on theories of influence is useful here. Harold Bloom, to whom I obviously owe a portion of my title, has written the best-known discussion of the subject. In *The Anxiety of Influence*, he asserts that "the profundities of poetic influence cannot be reduced to source-study, to the history of ideas, to the patterning of images. Poetic influence, or as I shall more frequently term it, poetic misprision, is necessarily the study of the life-cycle of the poet as poet" (7). His account of literary influence envisions a "psychodrama" (O'Brien *Willa Cather* 260) impelled by the artist's "fear that he is not his own creator and that the works of his predecessors, existing before and beyond him, assume essential priority over his own writings" (Gilbert and Gubar, *Madwoman* 46). Postulating an alternative reading of their own, and rejecting the phallocentrist assumptions of authorship assumed by Bloom and his likes, Sandra Gilbert and Susan Gubar have argued that the woman writer's problem has been less an "anxiety of influence" than an "anxiety of authorship." In both *The Madwoman in the Attic* (1979) and the first two volumes of their projected three-volume study, *No Man's Land* (1988–), Gilbert and Gubar probe "the terrible odds against which a creative female subculture was established" from the eighteenth century to the present; they deal specifically in their first book with" the difficult paths by which nineteenth-century women overcame their "anxiety of authorship" (51, 59).

All of this is germane to Munro's fiction, for, influence aside, she has certainly displayed her own anxiety of authorship, and continues to do so, as her "for reassurance, in different ways" comment suggests. Her early story "The Office" (in *Dance of the Happy Shades*) demonstrates this, as does the title of her *Who Do You Think You Are?* (1978). What is more, the context adopted by Gilbert and Gubar—as opposed to Bloom's Freudian, "life-cycle of the poet as poet" approach—makes much more sense as regards Munro: her art, which she has described as "the art of approach and recognition," is rooted in the present, seen always in the context of its relationship to the people, places, and perceptions of the past, and conjoined with utter delight over language and its myriad inabilities to fully articulate the moment described. Munro expands on this notion of "approach and recognition" in another early interview, explaining as best she can: she believes "that we don't solve" the mysteries surrounding the incidents she uses in her stories; "in fact, our explanations take us further away." As we grow older, according to Munro, "life becomes even more mysterious and difficult" (Gardiner Interview 178). Thus, by approaching the mystery she finds inherent in her own life, she has forged an art that offers not understanding but momentary glimpses and fleeting insight.

Thus, to study Munro's relationship to her forebears—both literal and literary—is to acknowledge, in the words of Terry Eagleton, that "all literary texts are woven out of other literary texts, not in the conventional sense that they bear the traces of 'influence' but in the more radical sense that every word, phrase or segment is a reworking of other writings which precede or surround the individual work" (138). As becomes evident to anyone who follows the process of composition traced in the University of Calgary's Munro papers—in which she can be seen groping for a story's vision, making changes right down to the final instant (and sometimes even almost after the final page proofs have been sent in, as with the first version of *Who Do You Think You Are?* [Hoy "Rose and Janet"])—Munro is a writer whose work confirms Eagleton's point, and in its most radical sense.[6]

Eagleton offers a second, related observation that is perhaps even more apt for a reading of Munro, given the repeated questioning by critics of the relationship between her life and her fiction. Because "there is no such thing as literary 'originality,' no such thing as the 'first' literary work," writes Eagleton, "the biography of the author is, after all, merely another text, which need not be ascribed any special privilege: this text too can be deconstructed" (138). I would argue that this is the way in which Munro uses her own life in her fiction: as a text to be shaped in accordance with a story's particular vision. Indeed, although her techniques in this regard have become much more subtle, the uncollected story "Home" (1974) is something of a watershed in this regard, as are "The Ottawa Valley" (*Something I've Been Meaning to Tell You*) and "Chaddeleys and Flemings" (*The Moons of Jupiter*). In "Home," punctuated as it is by italicized passages that comment on what she has just written, Munro engages in metafiction to challenge genre, convention, and any knowable version of truth, ending, "*I don't want any more effects, I tell you, lying. I don't know what I want. I want to do this with honour, if I possibly can*" (153).[7] Following this same line, Munro has expressed some desire to write straight biography, pointing to Elizabeth Hardwick's *Sleepless Nights*, with its combined autobiographical and fictive elements: "I'd love to do something like that. It's one of the books I can't read, because I start imitating it. It has very seductive prose you want to imitate, though nobody else could do it, I think" (Freake Interview 9).[8] Detail, strength of voice, the narrator's (and often the author's) doubts about understanding the significance of things, "jerky" shifts of focus (Irvine, "Changing" 99)—all of these elements that make up a Munro story bear the marks of other texts, whether literal, literary, or autobiographical. The extent of this has been, thus far, only remotely understood.

That Munro's critics have largely ignored her own acknowledged American influences, preferring instead to focus on her British antecedents, is surely a curious thing. This reader is tempted to wonder aloud if this gap is not in some way a reflection of anti-American attitudes on the part of many Canadian critics, some of whom seem to prefer to concern themselves with her European influences—more distant, more familiar, and more "literary"—rather than the not-so-attractive American "sources." As Munro felt compelled to say to Metcalf, "I'm sorry these are all Americans but that's the way it is." My second question, then, is, whose anxiety is it, anyway—that of Canadian writers or Canadian critics?

W. R. Martin sees reflections of Eudora Welty's *The Golden Apples* (1947) throughout Munro's first two books. Though his argument is insufficient due to his brevity—three paragraphs in all—Martin is on the right track, especially when he concludes by noting that both writers are "historians of the working of the human imagination, and both are celebrants of strangeness and mystery, and 'all the opposites on earth'" (*Paradox* 204).[9] They certainly are. But I would go much further than this and look at the commonalities of vision and technique, which Martin discusses, as part of a larger similarity, one born of place. Cather enters into this, too, not as some sort of daunting version of "the imperiously important author" whom Munro is rejecting (as Blodgett seems to suggest), but as an acknowledged precursor in the fictional depiction of place and as a "prickly" personality who could indeed be imperious.[10] In short, both of these figures may be seen as Munro's foremothers. Although one may point up the many differences between, as well as the similarities among, Cather's and Welty's works on the one hand and Cather's and Munro's on the other, each writer reflects in her fiction what might be called a sympathy of place. As noted earlier, Munro herself preferred the term "vision" when describing Welty's influence. Whether this preference is conscious or not, it recalls one of the critical statements Welty published in the mid-1950s, "How I Write," in which she makes two assertions that are relevant here. The first assertion is:

> The story is a vision; while it's being written, all choices must be its choices, and as these choices multiply upon one another, their field is growing too. The choices remain inevitable, in fact, through moving in a growing maze of possibilities that the writer, far from being dismayed at his presence on unknown ground (which might frighten him as a critic) has learned to be grateful for, and excited by. The fiction writer has learned (and

here is my generalization) that it is the very existence, the very multitude and clamor and threat and lure of possibility—all possibilities his work calls up for itself as it goes—that guide his story most delicately. (245)

Earlier, I recalled having followed Munro's process of composition as documented in some of her papers in Calgary. My sense is that Welty's description here might well have been offered by Munro herself (and, indeed, her published discussions suggest the same process).[11]

The second assertion from Welty's "How I Write" that I'd like to highlight is: "Relationship is a pervading and changing mystery; it is not words that make it so in life, but words have to make it so in a story. Brutal or lovely, the mystery waits for people wherever they go, whatever extreme they run to" (250). This is moving closer to what I mean by "sympathy of place," for what each of these writers does in her fiction is offer texts that—each in its various ways—are ensembles of relationships. These are seen over time, empathetically re-created, replete with the textures of their physical space. Welty writes, in "The House of Willa Cather" (1973):

> She saw the landscape had mystery as well as reality. She was undaunted by both. And when she writes of the vast spaces of the world lying out in the extending night [Welty's reference is to *A Lost Lady*], mystery comes to her page, and has a presence....
>
> Willa Cather saw her broad land in a sweep, but she saw selectively too—the detail that made all the difference. She never lost sight of the particular in the panorama. Her eye was on the human being. In her continuous, acutely conscious and responsible act of bringing human value into focus, it was her accomplishment to bring her gaze from that wide horizon, across the stretches of both space and time, to the intimacy and immediacy of the lives of a handful of human beings.
>
> People she saw slowly, with care, in their differences: her chosen characters. They stood up out of their soil and against their sky, making, each of them and one by one, a figure to reckon with. (*Eye* 43–44)

"The gift of sympathy" is a common phrase in Cather criticism; it is Cather's own, taken from her preface to Sarah Orne Jewett's *The Country of the Pointed Firs* (1896), which she edited. The context here bears remarking on, for it applies as readily to Welty or Munro or Cather as it does to Jewett:

> It is a common fallacy that a writer, if he is talented enough, can achieve this poignant quality by improving upon his subject-matter, by using his "imagination" upon it and twisting it to suit his purpose.... If he achieves anything noble, anything enduring, it must be by giving himself absolutely to his material. And this gift of sympathy is his great gift; is the fine thing in him that alone can make his work fine. He fades away into the land and people of his heart, he dies of love only to be born again. The artist spends a lifetime in loving the things that haunt him, in having his mind "teased" by them, in trying to get these conceptions down on paper exactly as they are to him and not in conventional poses supposed to reveal their character; trying this method and that.... And at the end of a lifetime he emerges with much that is more or less happy experimenting, and comparatively little that is the very flower of himself and his genius. (7–8)[12]

In effect, Cather is expanding on Welty here (though, of course, the chronology is reversed) by broadening the point from "place" to, if you will, "the home place." This phrase, which is usually identified with the 1948 Wright Morris novel that bears the phrase as its title, is closer to what Cather appreciates in Jewett's work and to what, in the final analysis, unites these writers. Without question, too, those who know Cather know that she could be prickly, that she was something of a snob, and that she was the aloof and imperious authorial presence Munro alludes to in "Dulse." But she also produced—for such was her devotion to her art—the sympathetic fictions that Jewett foresaw for her and that Welty would celebrate.

What Cather was doing anticipated both Welty and Munro. Thus Sharon O'Brien writes of Cather in a manner that might be applied equally to the other two, and much more than superficially: "When Cather became a writer of fiction she likewise practiced an art of connection: she retold and reworked some of these community stories, passing them on to her readers, weaving together oral and written narratives, farm women and artists, past and future in her fiction" (*Emerging* 29). There's that word again: connection. Indeed, it is each woman's particular connection with her place that, in effect, sets her fictional world apart from the writing of others. In each case, a characteristic style and, what is more, an emphasis on voice and the peculiar details of locale serve to define character as the writers probe the "pervading mystery" that is "relationship." As Munro writes: "Connection. That is what it was all about" (*Moons* 6). This is why Munro's use of Cather is so very important in "Dulse" and why, for me at least, Stich's discussion of shared names, themes, and other details of the story is fine, but not enough. Given the contexts I have alluded to here—especially, I would maintain, in light of Gilbert and Gubar's argument in *No Man's Land*—the correspondences go much deeper than Stich suggests.

Although I cannot offer a fully developed argument, I would like to point up some other matters that derive, in effect, from Munro's Cather.[13] Then, to conclude, I want to suggest other avenues for studies of Munro's influences. First of all, there is the matter of autobiography. As I have noted elsewhere, Munro's use of Cather derives in part from her own visit to Grand Manan Island, off the coast of New Brunswick, where Cather owned a cottage (at Whale Cove) and spent portions of her summers between the early twenties and the war years (Thacker, "So Shocking" *Reading Alice Munro* 274 n3; Woodress 415–16). There she met a person whom she described as "a Cather fanatic," a person (I have confirmed) well known to Cather critics. Munro was working on the story involving Lydia at the time, and subsequently brought the two matters together (Telephone interview). Second, there is the evidence of the University of Calgary's Munro papers, which suggest that Munro worked to get the Cather dimension of the story right, shifting the allusion from *My Ántonia* (1918)—as it was in an earlier draft—to the much more suitable choice, given Lydia's character, of *A Lost Lady* (1923).[14]

Neither of these matters affects Stich's treatment fundamentally, really, but another seems of much more urgency: Munro's greatest debt to Cather in "Dulse" may well stem from somewhere other than the various novels Stich notes, although his argument concerning *My Mortal Enemy* (1926), based on various parallels and the shared use of the name "Lydia," seems quite convincing. Rather, Munro's best source for her story may be "Before Breakfast," one of Cather's last stories. Written in 1944, about three years before Cather's death (Arnold 165), it was included in the posthumous *The Old Beauty and Others* (1948). It anticipates the situation, mood, character, and dénouement of "Dulse." More to the point, Cather's story is set on an island (though off the coast of Nova Scotia) and its protagonist, Henry Grenfell, has come out to the island suffering from the same sort of ennui that plagues Lydia, though his stems from sources different than hers. What the two stories share, most fundamentally, is their protagonists' need to seek an island refuge from what Munro elsewhere characterizes, through her character Janet, as the "pain of human contact." Janet continues: "I was hypnotized by it. The fascinating pain; the humiliating necessity" (*Moons* 27). So, too, was Cather.

Thus, though "Dulse" is derived from different sources, the stamp of Cather's story upon it is unmistakable. So, too, is the stamp of Cather's personality, which Munro portrays accurately enough to make us wonder about her sources—if indeed she consulted any—and how she used them.[15] Stich also notes echoes between other stories in *The Moons of Jupiter* and some of Cather's works, but there are more than he suggests.[16]

These matters are raised not to dispute a critic who has already done good work on a subject of some interest to me, but to point up the need for further, and deeper, analyses of these matters. Munro's relationship to a whole raft of American precursors demands such attention, most particularly that to Welty and Cather, but to her forefathers, too. Her relationship to Morris, whom she singled out in that early Metcalf interview, needs a much closer examination, especially in light of their shared interest in photography.[17] Indeed—though this is speculation on my part—Munro may have been consciously imitating Morris during her attempt in the seventies to write a text for a book of Ontario photographs (the unpublished "Places at Home"): Morris produced several phototexts, including *The Home Place* (1948) and *God's Country and My People* (1968). Walker

Evans and James Agee probably figure here, too. Or, moving back to fiction, Katherine Anne Porter, or John Cheever, or Sherwood Anderson, or Tillie Olsen, or Walker Percy... The list is long indeed, however it is made and whoever makes it. With Munro it is not surprising that this is so: she is an artist utterly beyond any chauvinism, aware to her very core that "relationship is a pervading and changing mystery," whatever form that relationship takes.

Alice Munro, Writing "Home":
"Seeing This Trickle in Time" (1998)

> A place that ever was lived in is like a fire that never goes out. It flares up, it smolders for a time, it is fanned or smothered by circumstance, but its being is intact, forever fluttering within it, the result of some original ignition. Sometimes it gives out glory, sometimes its little light must be sought out to be seen, small and tender as a candle flame, but as certain.
> —Eudora Welty, "Some Notes on River Country" (1944; *Eye* 286)

> This ordinary place is sufficient, everything here touchable and mysterious.
> —Alice Munro, "Everything Here Is Touchable and Mysterious" (1974)

"Look at the road map of Huron County," begins Magdelene Redekop in her essay in this volume, and this advice seems ever more pertinent to readers who approach, take up, savour, and—as much as possible—understand the art of Alice Munro. With her ninth volume, *The Love of a Good Woman* (1998), just awarded the Giller Prize (having been passed over, ridiculously, in the Governor General's Literary Award competition), with its title story inspiring the cover of the *New Yorker*'s 1996 holiday fiction issue (itself reprised for the 1997 issue containing Munro's "The Children Stay") and featured in the O. Henry Awards "Best of 1997," and with the bulk of her *Selected Stories* (1996) confirmed, Munro's accomplishment is now both unquestioned and unquestionable. And in ways not altogether clear to reader and critic alike, "The Love of a Good Woman" became, almost at the instant of its publication in the *New Yorker* in 1996, a central Munro text. Such are its style and its extent, so clear are its echoes of previous Munro stories, so comprehensive and mysterious are its interleavings that critics—most emphatically Dennis Duffy—saw in it a key, virtuoso instance of its author circling back, re-taking up, and probing once more the "open secrets" of being, and of having grown up, lived in, left, remembered, returned to, and above all made texts out of Huron County, Ontario.

Indicative passages, chosen almost at random, resonate within and between Munro's works. In "Walker Brothers Cowboy," for instance, the narrator recalls her younger self and especially her amazement over her father's attitude toward time: "The tiny share we have of time appalls me, though my father seems to regard it with tranquillity" (*Dance* 3). Equally indicative and even more resonant is: "Of course it's my mother I'm thinking of," which Munro writes as she concludes "Friend of My Youth," just before she offers as the literal conclusion (relevant to some of the story's characters) a historical summary of the sect called the Cameronians—or Reformed Presbyterians—one of whose "ministers, in a mood of firm rejoicing at his own hanging, excommunicated all the other preachers in the world" (*Friend* 26). Beyond this panache, the explicit meaning of this paragraph in relation to the story just told stands contextual but mysterious.

In another story in *Friend of My Youth*, "Meneseteung," Munro imagines the discovery of a nineteenth-century Huron County poet, Almeda Joynt Roth, whose book of poems, *Offerings*, said to have been published in 1873, contains a poem entitled "Champlain at the Mouth of the Meneseteung" (52). Writing of the relationship between the character Roth and the first-person narrator (also, of course, a character), who discovers Roth through the local paper, the *Vidette*, Pam Houston asks a question and offers an answer that together are a fit departure for meditating on Munro's intricate time- and place-based art: "'Does the landscape, then, exist separately from the way these women see it?' And neither woman can answer. The two women have momentarily become one voice, bound together by the metonymic qualities of language, and by the inability of a metaphor to speak its name" (89).

Also bound up with these two women's voices is Munro's own voice through her pen, moving across pages, making and remaking texts. Munro, the creator, made a change between the first publication of "Meneseteung" in the *New Yorker* and its inclusion in *Friend of My Youth*—as she often has done (in *The Love of a Good Woman*, notably, she even points out the extent of the changes between the *New Yorker* publication of the stories and their appearance in the book). In "Meneseteung," the narrator describes her search for Roth's gravestone and her discovery of it; the *New Yorker* version ends thus:

> I made sure I had got to the edge of the stone. That was all the name there was—Meda. So it was true that she was called by that name in the family. Not just in the poem. Or perhaps she chose her name from the poem, to be written on her stone.
>
> I thought that there wasn't anybody alive in the world but me who would know this, who would make the connection. And I would be the last person to do so. But perhaps this isn't so. People are curious. A few people are. They will be driven to find things out, even trivial things. They will put things together, knowing all along that they may be mistaken. You see them going around with notebooks, scraping the dirt off gravestones, reading microfilm, just in the hope of seeing this trickle in time, making a connection, rescuing one thing from the rubbish. (38)

Munro left her *New Yorker* readers with a hopeful sign—making sense of what in "Carried Away" she has referred to as a "devouring muddle" (*Open* 50). Yet when "Meneseteung" appeared in *Friend of My Youth*, Munro had dropped the phrase "knowing ... mistaken," and an additional paragraph had been added (or reattached, once the editors at the *New Yorker* had been satisfied) to offer a different ending: "And they may get it wrong, after all. I may have got it wrong. I don't know if she ever took laudanum. Many ladies did. I don't know if she ever made grape jelly" (73). With this addition, the previous hopeful sign has been dashed and, more troubling to some (though certainly not to Munro herself, given her various comments, especially surrounding *Open Secrets*), the narrator's authority, despite the foregoing 20 pages, is utterly compromised if not altogether dashed. Welcome, again, to Munro, in whose fiction everything is both "touchable and mysterious," and each character, especially those who narrate or serve as vehicles for Munro's wonderings, is keenly aware of the myriad difficulties in the way of "seeing this trickle in time" or "making a connection." It is a world rooted in the times and the touchable surfaces and characters of Huron County, a place inhabited since the early 1850s by Munro's ancestors (as she writes in "A Wilderness Station" in *Open Secrets*), a place she has explored fully and deeply.

Take, for example, a key instance in Munro's art: the story "Home," published in 1974. It offers a basis for further meditation on the ways by which Munro makes her connections. It is one of her few published stories not collected in a book (those first appearing in the *New Yorker*, Carol Beran points out here, are "Wood" [1980] and "Hired Girl" [1994]). In "Home," Munro writes of the circumstances of her father's declining health—a subject that she returned to in "The Moons of Jupiter" (1978). Like "The Ottawa Valley," also published in 1974, "Home" is patently autobiographical and metafictional; it reflects the circumstances of Munro's return to Ontario after living in British Columbia for over 20 years. That it has not been republished in a book, I would guess, has as much to do with its metafictional uncertainties—the narrator shows herself to be tentative and uncertain—as with anything else (though Munro has commented in interviews in a tone of resigned rejection over these attempts at metafictional techniques; see, for example, Freake). Yet "Home" is an apt text for both this essay and this volume: set in the centre of Munro's *oeuvre*, "Home" reveals her techniques, her focus, and her concerns. As such, it introduces, connects with, and illustrates her own hopeful "seeing" of "this trickle in time."

In "Home," accompanying her ill father to the hospital, the narrator/Munro—I conflate the two knowingly, be assured—writes:

> So I sit beside him ... and we follow that old usual route. Victoria Street. Minnie Street. John Street. Catherine Street. The town, unlike the house, stays very much the same, nobody is renovating or changing it. Nevertheless it has faded, for me. I have written about it and used it up. The same banks and barber shops and town hall tower, but all their secret, plentiful messages drained away. Not for my father, perhaps. He has lived here, nowhere else; he has not escaped things by this use. (143)

This passage proclaims a conclusion—"used it up"—that has since been proven false by Munro's further writings: Munro returned to southwestern Ontario after her marriage ended, but she had not at all "used it up," whatever she may have thought then. Rather, she began to use it differently—another story title—the difference born of her time away, and her changed perspective born of distance and experience, the deepened complexities of her art, and her myriad imaginative connections within and between her stories.

Thus Munro wrote, also in 1974, of the Maitland River (which the Indigenous people called the Menesetung), contradicting some of what she had written in "Home":

> We believed there were deep holes in the river. We went looking for them, scared and hopeful, and never found them, but did not stop believing for that. Even now I believe that there were deep holes, ominous beckoning places, but that they have probably silted up. But maybe not all. Because I am still partly convinced that this river—not even the whole river but this little stretch of it—will provide whatever myths you want, whatever adventures. I name the plants, I name the fish, and every name seems to me triumphant, every leaf and quick fish remarkably valuable. This ordinary place is sufficient, everything here touchable and mysterious. ("Everything")

This short essay, published when Munro was described as "a writer living in London, Ontario," shortly after the appearance of *Something I've Been Meaning to Tell You*, was prescient: her art since then has largely been one of visiting and revisiting the same places and the same people, shifting emphases, altering structures, moving in time, "rescuing one thing from the rubbish." The narrator in "Home" heads out from a London-like city on a succession of buses to visit her father and stepmother, Irlma, who live outside a Wingham-like town. The "Meneseteung"—the spelling altered from Munro's first use of it—becomes the title of a story in which the character Almeda Joynt Roth uses the Indigenous name for the Maitland River in her poem. That same river, renamed the Peregrine, manages with its holes to obscure Mr. Willens's fate in "The Love of a Good Woman." This river proves to be, in Munro's imagination, an "ominous beckoning place" indeed, its flow is a metaphor for the passage of time, to the ongoing processes of her art.

Meandering thus through the lowlands of Huron County, near the lake, following the river's flow from Wingham to Goderich—"this little stretch of it"—is what Munro's fiction has done from the first stories of the early 1950s up to *The Love of a Good Woman*. In its own flow, her art defines and details the way in which Munro explores the mystery of being, setting out a complex web of connections, reconnections, summations, and seeming conclusions that hold for a time but ultimately are insufficient. Like Robert Frost's notion that every poem clarifies something, Munro's stories offer readers moments of insight, perhaps even epiphanies: "Breathing spaces, is that all?" one of her narrators wonders (*Progress* 273). These moments both clarify and mystify—and Munro has returned to them, as *The Love of a Good Woman* shows, in progressively more complex ways.

Critics have tried to keep up to Munro yet largely have not—although 11 single-author critical books on Munro have been published, the ability of critics to encompass her and her work within an overarching rationale has been paltry (see Thacker, "Conferring Munro," "Go Ask Alice," and "What's 'Material'?"). Indeed, due to the shape and the scope of Munro's art—story following upon story, reconnecting, redefining—the critical monograph is not really up to Munro at all. Rather, individual articles on individual stories or connected groups of them now seem, to me at least, to offer the better critical course. Thus, the rationale for this volume is that it better follows its subject's inclinations, its subject's art. Following up on Louis K. MacKendrick's *Probable Fictions: Alice Munro's Narrative Acts* (1983), this volume offers essays that explore little-examined aspects of Munro's art—JoAnn McCaig and Carol Beran, for instance, make significant use of the Alice Munro Papers at the University of Calgary to define and understand Munro's long relationships with, respectively, Virginia Barber, her agent, and the *New Yorker*, the showcase magazine in which many of Munro's stories have first been published through Barber's agency. As I have said elsewhere and am about to demonstrate again through my discussion of "The Progress of Love," based on the Calgary archive, the Alice Munro Papers represent an exceptional resource still largely ignored by her critics. Several authors here take up the stories contained in *Open Secrets*, a volume that has not yet received much attention, save from Ildikó de Papp Carrington, who here has continued her analyses into the stories in *The Love of a Good Woman* with her source study of "The Children Stay." Broadening the textual relationships within *Open Secrets*, Nathalie Foy, W. R. Martin and Warren U. Ober, and Robert Lecker examine stories that resonate both within and beyond that volume; the latter two essays also extend historian John Weaver's important characterization of Munro as a historian of her time and place. Likewise, Marianne Micros and Magdalene Redekop define influences on Munro that have not yet been examined, and Deborah Heller deals broadly with *Friend of My Youth*.

Following "Home" to "The Progress of Love"

Returning to "Home," I want to continue this introduction with an extended quotation that will be useful for the remainder of this essay, and with my consideration of the ways by which Munro's stories lend themselves to what Helen M. Buss has called "mapping." That is, "Home" offers a textual grounding that, when understood in relation to what is available in the Calgary archive, forecasts a subsequent relationship to "The Progress of Love" and to "Friend of My Youth." At the same time, "Home" looks both backward and forward in its detailing of Munro's characteristic concern, even obsession, fictional renderings of her relationship with each of her parents. "My Mother's Dream" in *The Love of a Good Woman* offers yet another version—fantastic and delightful as it is—of the mother–daughter relationship. So, when seen at the centre of Munro's work, "Home" both resonates with and illustrates the ongoing connections in her art, wherever one looks.

Toward the beginning of "Home," the narrator/Munro meditates on changes made to the house in which she grew up:

> The front rooms have been re-papered. The paper has red and silver vertical stripes. Wall-to-wall carpeting—moss green—has been put down....
>
> Even the outside of the house, the red brick whose crumbling mortar let in the east wind, is disappearing under clean white metal siding. My father is putting this on himself. So it seems now that the whole house is being covered up, lost, changed into something ordinary and comfortable, and I do not lament this loss as I would have done at one time. I do say that the red brick was really lovely, and that people in the city pay a good price for old bricks, but I do this mostly because I think my father expects it. He can explain again about the east wind and the cost in fuel and the difficulties of repair. It cannot be claimed that the house now being lost was a fine or handsome house in any way. A poor man's house, always, with the stairs going up between the walls. A house where people have lived close to the bone for a hundred years; and if my father and Irlma, combining their modest prosperities, wish it to be comfortable, and—this word is used by them without quotation marks, quite simply and positively—*modern*, I am really not going to wail about the loss of a few charming bricks, a crumbling wall. But I am shy of letting my father see that [the] house does not mean to me what it once did, and that it really does not matter much to me how he changes it. 'I know you love this place,' he says to me, apologetically yet with satisfaction. I don't tell him that I am not sure now if I

love any place, any house, and that it seems to me it was myself I loved here, some self I have finished with, and none too soon. I used to go into the front rooms and rummage around looking for old photographs, and sheet music. I would sit at the piano where mice were nesting—banished now by Irlma—and try to play the opening bit of the Moonlight Sonata. I would go through the bookcase looking for my old Latin Poetry, and find the best sellers of some year in the nineteen-forties when my mother belonged to the Book-of-the-Month-Club (a fine year for novels about the wives of Henry the Eighth, and for three-name women writers, and for understanding books about Soviet Russia). Also limp-covered classics bought by mother before she was married, her maiden name written in lovely, level, school-teacher's writing on the watered end-paper. *Everyman I will go with thee, in thy most need be by thy side*, it says above my mother's name. Reminders of my mother in this house are not easy to find, though she dominated it for so long, filled it with her astonishing, embarrassing hopes, and her dark and helpless, justified complaint. She was dying for many years of Parkinson's disease, which was an illness so little known to us, and so bizarre in its effects, that it did seem just the sort of thing she might have made up, out of perversity, and her true need for attention, and stranger dimensions to her life. This attention was what I was bound not to give, not to be blackmailed into giving. I give it now, being safe. (135–36)

Readers of Munro will see at once the connection between this passage and "The Progress of Love," the title story of her sixth story collection—there the story's narrator, Phemie, revisits the house that she grew up in and notices, among many other things, that in one place the wallpaper—which she had put up with her mother—"hadn't been stripped off when this new paper went on." She can "see an edge of it, the cornflowers on a white ground" (*Progress* 27). Equally, readers will see similar figures to the narrator's mother in "Home" in "The Peace of Utrecht," "The Ottawa Valley," and "Friend of My Youth," to name only the best-known instances. For all of them, Munro's mother, Anne Chamney Laidlaw, who died in 1959 of Parkinson's disease, served as a model for much of the detail about a character and her circumstances.

What readers do not generally know, though, is the path by which Munro arrived at her finished stories—thus, the balance of this essay will, first, examine the composition of "The Progress of Love" and, second, extend the consideration beyond this single story to the larger issue of Munro's continuing writing and rewriting of her parents, especially her mother. I am arguing that in writing "Home," Munro has literally and emphatically been writing home—that her life has been her text, that Huron County has been her imaginative nexus, and ultimately that her career has demonstrated that this "ordinary place" has been "sufficient" for her needs. "The Love of a Good Woman," whether in the *New Yorker*, *Prize Stories 1997*, or *The Love of a Good Woman*, has shown as much, yet again, and most complexly.

One might argue that the title story in each of Munro's collections is the pivotal story, which would set apart "The Progress of Love," as well as "The Moons of Jupiter" and "Friend of My Youth" in their respective collections. (One might wonder, though, if this pivotal status is always correct: "The Moons of Jupiter" was to be the penultimate story in *Who Do You Think You Are?* as it was originally configured [38.4.6.f6], and the arrangement of the stories in *The Progress of Love* was established late in the process, and at one point "The Progress of Love" had been the seventh story [Third accession, 11.3].) Each story, however, is pivotal for arguably better reasons: each continues Munro's apparently lifelong meditations on who is fit for parenthood, on her relationships with her parents (especially her mother—here "Chaddeleys and Flemings," both parts, needs to be added as a companion to "The Moons of Jupiter"), and on the cultural legacy of a Protestant, rural, southwestern Ontario upbringing during the 1930s and 1940s.

The first appearance in the Alice Munro Papers of one of the central incidents in "The Progress of Love," Phemie's grandmother's suicide threat, is in "Suicide Corners," one of the vignettes for an Ontario photo album by Peter D'Angelo, for which Munro was to have written the text; although she worked on it for some time during the mid-1970s, the book was never published (37.13.10.14). According to Catherine Sheldrick Ross,

Munro got the idea of the hanging from her second husband, Gerald Fremlin, whose father had been a policeman in Clinton and had been called to stop just such a suicide (87). It appears again in a fragment, apparently part of *Who Do You Think You Are?* In it, Flop Morgan threatens to hang himself because his wife has called him a liar, but Rose's father talks him out of it. The scene contains a detail that also appears in "The Progress of Love": the rope is not tied, but subsequently the character still succeeds—"Flop dangling from the beam in his barn was just doing what his name has always predicted" (37.16.12).

The hanging appears in a draft story in a notebook included in the second accession, a story that Munro entitled "Suicide Ladies." It is told from the point of view of a girl named Winona (drafts exist of both first- and third-person versions), and the suicide attempt is made by a Mrs. Cole at the end of a pregnancy. Three relatives (Iris, Marianne, and Flor) are visiting Winona's mother, Winifred, and her family, and the news of Mrs. Cole's attempt at suicide is delivered by her son, Franklin, who says, "'She says she's going to hang herself in the barn' ... and then he did laugh, in embarrassment and dread and apology. He began to hiccup." The text continues:

> Franklin's mother was in the barn, just as he had said. She was standing on a kitchen chair in the middle of the space her husband usually parked the car in, and she had a noose around her neck. Phylis and Margory and the dog were hanging around the barn door.
> "Oh, Mrs. Cole!" said Winona's mother in a tired voice[.] "Come down out of that."
> Mrs. Cole's figure made a stunning impression on Winona. At that time women did not go out when in an advanced state of pregnancy, and she had never seen anyone so disfigured. Mrs. Cole was a tall, thin woman normally and as sometimes happens with narrow hipped women she seemed to be carrying the baby not as something fitted into her body but as something precariously hinged on; it didn't seem possible her skin could have stretched so far. She wore the shapeless kind of housedress

that poor women wore, several sizes too big; it kept sliding off one shoulder; her hair also was cut in the style of a poor woman[:] short, straight, held back with a bobby pin.

"I said I was going to do it." She said in a high voice. This was the first time I had heard her say anything except when she called the children or dog Wig, from her back door. (38.11.2)

Such passages—coupled with the advantages of hindsight—define connections between stories. This one suggests that Munro had included the hanging incident in the story that became "Chaddeleys and Flemings: 1. Connection" (1978), given that Iris, Marianne, and Flora are likely the visiting cousins in that story (here they see the threatened hanging as the "entertainment" of a summer's morning). There are, as well, connections between this passage and "Miles City, Montana" (1985), another meditation on parenting and parenthood. Thus, this anecdote, consistent in its particulars, was to have been included in (at least) the photo text, *Who Do You Think You Are?*, and "Chaddeleys and Flemings: 1. Connection" (itself once just "Chaddeleys and Flemings"—it was first submitted for publication as one very long story but later divided into "Connection" and "The Stone in the Field") before becoming an essential part of "The Progress of Love." There, of course, it is a visible explanation of Phemie's mother's hatred for her father, a hatred so deep that she burns the money he left her in his will—her legacy—in the family stove.

This, the second major incident in "The Progress of Love," may also be seen being developed toward its ultimate place through more than one version. There is, for example, an autograph draft story called "Money to Burn" for which there are two versions of the beginning. The first begins with the unnamed narrator going to town one evening with her aunt Tizzy, who is referred to simply as Tizzy. The time period is probably the early 1940s: "The radio ran on batteries. There was no electricity in the house—a fact I remembered only when the lamps were lit. The news we listened to at home made you feel the world was full of doom, but under control. The news here indicated that the world beyond the farm was a jumble of disasters and sprees and jokes of nature that even a man as cocky and worldly wise as the newscaster has trouble crediting" (Third accession 6.7).

Tizzy has been married twice, and there is a mystery to her first marriage: she went on her honeymoon but came back unmarried, though pregnant, and then lived with her parents before marrying Wyck, the narrator's uncle. In the second draft, the details are much the same, though Tizzy has become Aunty and Wyck has become Wick.

Munro uses the name Wick in "A Queer Streak" (1985–86), and the aunt is reminiscent of Beryl in "The Progress of Love" (whose visit in that story echoes the visits of Del Jordan's American uncle in *Lives of Girls and Women* [1971] and of the cousins in "Chaddeleys and Flemings: 1. Connection"). In the same notebook is evidence that Munro tried to use the burning-money episode in the story that became "Fits" (Third accession 6.7). Here, too, she was working on the story about Franklin; it is much bigger than "The Progress of Love" and derives from the notebook work that uses characters from "Chaddeleys and Flemings: 1. Connection." It contextualizes Marietta—the grandmother in "The Progress of Love"—offering much more family detail. Indeed, as the story developed, Franklin's role became Marietta's in the finished version.

I could continue to compare details; my comparisons here address some of the material found in autograph drafts. In another one, for example, Bob Marks initiates sex with Phemie while the two are visiting her girlhood home—his desires are evident in the completed story. Such handwritten material is then changed further—and sometimes changed back again—in the authorial typescripts that follow and in the typist's typescripts that follow those. The story could be taken further yet, into the differences between its first publication in the *New Yorker*, where the point of view is third person, and its subsequent publication in book form, where the point of view is first person (both points of view are found in draft materials).

Elsewhere I have argued for the appropriateness of Eudora Welty's essay "How I Write" to Munro's compositional methods; two passages from that essay are worth quoting here: first, "The story is a vision; while it's being written, all choices must be its choices, and as these choices multiply upon one another, their field is growing too," and second, "Relationship is a pervading and changing mystery; it is not words that make it so in life, but words have to make it so in a story. Brutal or lovely, the mystery waits for people wherever they go, whatever extreme they run to" (245, 250). Both comments—from one of Munro's admitted influences—speak directly to her composition of "The Progress of Love," as revealed in the little-examined Alice Munro papers at the University of Calgary Library. "The story is a vision": in the archive, which admittedly is random in that it is made up of what has been saved (doubtless much was lost, and probably some burned; see 37.14.28), one can see several stories in gestation at the same time, each overlapping the other, some destined to emerge transformed, many destined not to emerge at all.

Throughout, Munro may be seen shaping, adjusting, honing, and sharpening her articulation until she finds it satisfactory. This trying out of incidents, such as a suicide threat or the seemingly senseless burning of three thousand dollars, is at the source of her method. Her immediate source of material is almost always Huron County. Such personal anecdotes are necessary for Munro, as she wrote eloquently in a story called "Material"—in it, the story's narrator considers a story written by her ex-husband, Hugo, that he derived from their time together: "how strange it was for me to realize that what was all scraps and oddments, useless baggage, for me, was ripe and useable, a paying investment, for him" (*Something* 43). Welty wrote that "relationship is a pervading and changing mystery," and Munro uses words "to make it so in a story. Brutal or lovely, the mystery waits for people." For Munro, the mystery of being shapes her stories, doing so until the shapes cohere, until they seem fit and proper.

In "Suicide Corners," one of the vignettes from the photo text, Munro wonders: "More men seem to come to it [suicide] than women. Is that the truth? And if it is the truth, why?" (37.13.10.14.f2). What the Munro archive reveals is that, after trying it out numerous times in various stories drafted over a decade, the threatened hanging at the core of "The Progress of Love" still yields a mystery. It is the incident through which the story's most essential question is asked; it is the incident that prompts the burning of money, which perplexes Phemie still. As she says, wondering about her parents in a phrase that echoes "Suicide Corners," "It seems so much the truth it is the truth; it's what I believe about them. I haven't stopped believing it. But I have stopped telling that story" (*Progress* 30). Munro may have stopped telling the story that is "The Progress of Love," but the Calgary archive reveals that the story will always confirm that "relationship is a pervading and changing mystery," and her words certainly make it so.

"The Bitter Lump of Love": Mothers, Fathers, and Autobiographical Sequence

The image of Phemie wondering about her parents might be seen as something of a tableau in Munro's writing; as is widely acknowledged, one of her key focal points is the relationships between generations, especially between daughters and mothers. Although well known among critics, the means by which Munro managed this—as seen, like the previous discussion, in the Calgary archive—indicate ways in which her stories might be better understood. I have put forward an autobiographical approach to Munro generally; nowhere, probably, does that approach better apply than in her various depictions of her father and, especially, her mother: figures based on them are commonplace throughout her work (see Thacker, "So Shocking"). Two groups of stories are relevant to this configuration, one involving the mother, the other the father. In the first group, most depict Munro's mother as someone who is dying or has died of Parkinson's disease. She is usually characterized by the narrator as an overtly haunting, now long-dead presence. Intimations of this figure are found in other stories in *Dance of the Happy Shades*, but the first extended treatment of her is in "The Peace of Utrecht" (1960), included in that first collection. She appears—emotionally if not precisely—in *Lives of Girls and Women* as Ida, in *Something I've Been Meaning to Tell You* in the stories "Winter Wind" and "The Ottawa Valley," and, during the same year of publication, in "Home." She returns in "Friend of My Youth." These stories offer a "family resemblance" born of their autobiographical provenance, and when looked at sequentially they create a deeper understanding of Munro's process.

By returning again and again to subjects of autobiographical obsession, Munro is, as she has said, editing her life as she goes along (Carrington, *Controlling* 196). But she is also creating a broader fictional world, one born of her sequences and that, given time and continued publication, may eventually be seen as almost Faulknerian in its complexity. James Carscallen has tried to argue as much in *The Other Country: Patterns in the Writing of Alice Munro* (1993), and given Duffy's analysis, the argument can also apply to "The Love of a Good Woman." Indeed, Munro's sequencing may well help to account for the minimal—though not unheard—dissent over her return to material that readers have seen before in her stories—most obviously in *Who Do You Think You Are?*, which many reviewers considered in many ways a redone *Lives of Girls and Women*.

Although some critics consider mothers to have a more important place in Munro's work than fathers and offer good reasons for thinking so—gender identity, female desire, among others (Irvine, *Sub/version* 91–110)—such judgements are of less moment than their presences throughout the stories. Moreover, the amount of time Munro had with each parent offers some insight into the very different relationships she had with each parent: her mother died in 1959, when Munro was 27, and her father lived until 1976, when she was 45. Looking at her earlier fiction, if we divide the stories in *Dance of the Happy Shades* on the basis of mothers and fathers, it comes out to a draw, with two stories concerned primarily with mothers ("The Peace of Utrecht" and "Red Dress—1946"), two with fathers ("Walker Brothers Cowboy" and "Images"), and one pitting the roles against each other ("Boys and Girls"). In *Lives of Girls and Women*, however, Del's father is something of a nonpresence, living out at the farm bachelor-style with the hired man, while Del, her mother, and their boarder live in Jubilee; yet throughout that book the theme of gender roles dominates, and, although not represented by fathers, male characters—Mr. Chamberlain and Del's boyfriends, Gerry Story and Garnet French—are still certainly important.

* * *

These themes continue in diverse ways in *Something I've Been Meaning to Tell You*, such as with the story "Material," a meditation on men's power, and the title story, about secrets. In "The Ottawa Valley," though, Munro's mother reappears; although the story focuses on a moment in their relationship other than that found in its predecessor, "The Peace of Utrecht," the relationship is unmistakable. In the earlier story, the narrator returns to Jubilee from the West Coast to visit her sister, Helen, and her two small children. Their mother, who suffered a long decline, died earlier, and the purported "peace" of the story's title is as much between the two sisters as it is between the narrator, the facts that she learns about her mother's death, and the responsibility that she shares with her sister (see Thacker "Connection"). Carrington discusses the autobiographical details of this story thoroughly, noting that Munro, in her reminiscence "Working for a Living," describes her "adolescent attitude toward her mother's disease: 'Most of the time I was angry at her, for her abdication and self-absorption. We argued'" (186).

In "The Ottawa Valley," Munro focuses not on the details of death but on the memory of that critical moment when the narrator, as a young girl visiting the valley, tested what she knows about the valley against her mother's mythic descriptions of it as her home place, and recognized for the first time that her mother's infirmity would get the best of her:

> "So, are you not going to get sick at all?" I said, pushing further. I was very much relieved that she had decided against strokes, and that I would not have to be the mother, and wash and wipe and feed her lying in bed, as Aunt Dodie had had to do with her mother. For I did feel that it was she who decided, she gave her consent. As long as she lived, and through all the changes that happened to her, and after I had received the medical explanations of what was happening, I still felt secretly that she had given her consent. For her own purposes, I felt she did it: display, of a sort; revenge of a sort as well. More, that nobody could ever understand. (*Something* 195)

Such a passage is precisely Munro: the immediacy of the here and now is connected with the then and gone, with what is remembered. The "reckless" and "stubborn" inquisitiveness of the young girl is not to be allayed, so she pushes on, asking, "Is your arm going to stop shaking?" and demanding that her mother "promise" her what she needs. "But she did not do it. For the first time she held out altogether against me. She went on as if she had not heard, her familiar bulk ahead of me turning strange, indifferent" (195).

However, the passage from the story that has received the most attention from critics—and which I have quoted myself elsewhere—is the final, metafictional paragraph, a separate summing up in which Munro questions the very process of creating fiction; indeed, she comments on what has gone before in her own voice or perhaps in the narrator's, beginning with, "If I had been making a proper story out of this," and going on to realize that the central impetus of this story has been to purge herself of her mother, to "*get rid* of her." Munro concludes that this attempt has not worked, because her mother is still there in memory; "she weighs everything down," for "she looms too close, just as she always did" (246). Memory is obsessive, indeed.

Judging from "Friend of My Youth" and "My Mother's Dream," Munro's mother is still looming. The former, a story within a story, tells of the family relationships of Flora Grieves, with whom the narrator's mother boarded while teaching school before her marriage, and whose story is fascinating to the narrator herself; it is framed by the narrator's description of her dreams of her dead mother, a woman who bears the attributes of the mothers in "The Peace of Utrecht," "The Ottawa Valley," and "Home." The frame begins thus:

> I used to dream about my mother, and though the details in the dream varied, the surprise in it was always the same. The dream stopped, I suppose because it was too transparent in its hopefulness, too easy in its forgiveness.
>
> In the dream I would be the age I really was, living the life I was really living, and I would discover that my mother was still alive. (The fact is, she died when I was in my early twenties and she in her early fifties.) ... She would be looking quite well—not exactly youthful, not entirely untouched by the paralyzing disease that held her in its grip for a decade or more before her death, but so much better than I remembered that I would be astonished. Oh, I just have this little tremor in my

> arm, she would say, and a little stiffness up this side of my face. It is a nuisance but I get around.
>
> ... I would say that I was sorry I hadn't been to see her in such a long time—meaning not that I felt guilty but that I was sorry I had kept a bugbear in my mind, instead of this reality—and the strangest, kindest thing of all to me was her matter-of-fact reply.
>
> Oh, well, she said, better late than never. I was sure I'd see you someday. (*Friend* 3–4)

Munro then turns to the story of Flora and her sister, Ellie, who has been impregnated by Robert, Flora's betrothed. Robert marries Ellie, continuing to live with both sisters, though they physically divide the house into separate apartments. Ellie dies of too many failed pregnancies, followed by cancer, and, romance be damned, instead of marrying Flora (finally), Robert marries Audrey Atkinson, an officious nurse who looked after Ellie. Atkinson is reminiscent of Mary McQuade in "Images" and anticipates Enid in "The Love of a Good Woman" (this is another textual "progress" derived from the mother figure that ought to be traced further). Eventually, Flora leaves the farm to them and takes a clerk's job in town. The connection to the narrator's mother is left hanging in the air, as it were, until deftly taken up again: Flora is the "friend of my youth" of the title, a form of address that the narrator once saw on one of the numerous letters that her mother, in her infirmity, began but seldom completed—written in the same schoolteacher's handwriting mentioned in "Home." Munro's concerns are with the mysteries of sex in her mother's generation ("sex was a dark undertaking for women. She knew that you could die of it" [*Friend* 22]), her attachments to long-unseen friends such as Flora, and ultimately the narrator's connection with her mother.

Through a frequently used device that characterizes her later stories, Munro concludes her story, completes her frame, echoes her earlier stories, and offers an equivocal insight in her final paragraphs:

> Of course it's my mother I'm thinking of, my mother as she was in those dreams, saying, It's nothing, just this little tremor;

saying with such astonishing lighthearted forgiveness, Oh, I knew you'd come someday. My mother surprising me, and doing it almost indifferently. Her mask, her fate, and most of her affliction taken away. How relieved I was, and happy. But now I recall that I was disconcerted as well. I would have to say that I felt slightly cheated. Yes. Offended, tricked, cheated, by this welcome turnaround, this reprieve. My mother moving rather carelessly out of her old prison, showing options and powers I never dreamed she had, changes more than herself. She changes the bitter lump of love I have carried all this time into a phantom—something useless and uncalled for, like a phantom pregnancy. (26)

Adding to the equivocation here, or to the mystery, is the story's final paragraph. There Munro offers the seemingly factual, but also ambiguous, definition of the Cameronians—the sect to which the Grieveses belonged—ending, as I noted at the outset, with the panache of one of the Cameronian "ministers," who, "in a mood of firm rejoicing at his own hanging, excommunicated all the other preachers in the world" (26). Although it is tempting to brush this paragraph aside and deal merely with the concluding, resonant image of the story proper (the narrator's "bitter lump of love" transformed "into a phantom"), Munro does not allow it. The penultimate ending echoes numerous other stories—"The Peace of Utrecht" and "Home" generally, and "The Ottawa Valley" explicitly, even down to some of the same language ("Of course" with reference to summarizing her mother)—and it extends to the main substance of the "Janet Stories" ("Chaddeleys and Flemings" and "The Moons of Jupiter") through their multiple mysteries of the bonds in families. It also suggests a reasonably clear summing up—an epiphany—of the sort found in Munro's early stories in *Dance of the Happy Shades* and in some of the recent stories in *The Love of a Good Woman* (such as "Rich as Stink"). Yet "Friend of My Youth" ends not with the words "something useless and uncalled for, like a phantom pregnancy," but with the triumphant Cameronian minister excommunicating all the others. And there that paragraph sits, mysterious, suggesting its meaning, offering not closure but continuance, "just in the hope of seeing this trickle in time, making a connection, rescuing one thing from the rubbish." Munro, writing "Home," tracing "The Progress of Love," finding "The Friend of [Her] Youth," wondering over the touchability and mystery of being, of being from and in Huron County. Munro, writing on…

Critical Interlude:

What's "Material": The Progress of Munro Criticism, Part 2 (1998)

Introducing Alice Munro's Lives of Girls and Women. Neil K. Besner. Toronto: ECW Press, 1990.

The Other Country: Patterns in the Writing of Alice Munro. James Carscallen. Toronto: ECW Press, 1993.

The Tumble of Reason: Alice Munro's Discourse of Absence. Ajay Heble. Toronto: University of Toronto Press, 1994.

Some Other Reality: Alice Munro's Something I've Been Meaning to Tell You. Louis K. MacKendrick. Toronto: ECW Press, 1993.

Mothers and Other Clowns: The Stories of Alice Munro. Magdalene Redekop, London and New York: Routledge, 1992.

Alice Munro: A Double Life. Catherine Sheldrick Ross. Toronto: ECW Press, 1992.

Figuring Grief: Gallant, Munro, and the Poetics of Elegy. Karen E. Smythe. Kingston and Montreal: McGill-Queen's UP, 1992.

In one of the holograph drafts of Alice Munro's "Dulse" (1980), the narrator meets a "Mr. Middleton from Boston," who in the finished story becomes Mr. Stanley, the man fixated on Willa Cather's writing, her person, and the refuge that was hers on Grand Manan Island. Hearing that Middleton has spent his life working on newspapers, the narrator says:

"I was surprised, I had taken him for a university man, a professor of literature, I had thought that no other job in the world would allow him his pedantic preening[,] his serene absorption" (38.8.19.f1, 3). In what looks like a subsequent typescript in which the narrative has been shifted to third person, the now-named Lydia notes "the fact" of this man's "admiration, his adoration, of the chosen writer. It was not faked. It was true, fervent, engrossing. She thought he could not be a teacher, such worship being too far out of style, too unlikely even in his day" (38.8.20.f3). Also among the papers held at the University of Calgary is an autobiographical note in which Munro recounts the first time she heard from John Metcalf regarding her work; his letter buoyed her because Munro was "reeling" from "a painful session with a man [at the University of Victoria] who told me that my work reminded him of the kind of thing he himself had been writing when he was fifteen and had abandoned with the first glimmerings of maturity." This view, she writes, "was damaging only because I had a most exaggerated respect, then, for academic opinion" (6.6).

Beginning here, speaking for myself, this is the second time I have taken up a group of critical books focused on Munro's writing. In the first review, I ended by citing a phrase from E. D. Blodgett's *Alice Munro* (1988), which asserts that Munro's "'unassailable moral integrity' is borne out in the fiction by the various shifts, doubts, and re-explanations she repeatedly offers, but always with an eye to discovering 'what is real,' and how can one really know, ever?" Concluding, I offered one of Munro's own doubts from her uncollected story, "Home" (1974): "*I want to do this with honour, if I possibly can,*" and left readers with the perhaps wry, though still apt, invocation: "Go ask Alice" (*Reading Alice Munro* 109).

Embarking on this second assay at Munro criticism, I am thinking about these threads: the compelling mass of Munro's *oeuvre*, emphatically including the still largely unstudied intricacies of the Munro archive in Calgary; "'the pedantic preening' of academics" (38.8.19.3); the commonplace and not-at-all-abandoned "adoration" many of us bring to "the chosen writer," Munro; and Munro's own skepticism toward academics generally and literary critics in particular. She wrote, after all, the two scathing paragraphs that begin "Material" (1973), as well as—and here I am again reminding those of us who do this for a living—this notable trio of sentences from "Goodness and Mercy" (1989): "'Also, professors are dumb. They are dumber than ordinary. I could be nice and say they know about things we don't, but as far as I'm concerned they don't know shit'" (*Friend* 158). *I want to do this with honour, if I possibly can.*

Of Critical and "Munrovian" Contexts

One of the reviewers of two of these titles begins by asserting that they "belong to the 'second generation' of Munro criticism, one that is no longer in awe of the mimetic qualities detected by first-phase Munro critics but brings sophisticated theoretical frameworks to bear on her work" (Canitz 247). Although I will address such matters as "mimesis," "awe," and "sophistication" presently, the notion of "second generation" seems a good point of departure for the examination of the current critical contexts surrounding Munro's writing. Clearly, the books reviewed in my first attempt—Blodgett, Carrington, Rasporich—had followed others published during the 1980s; together, they constituted the first extended attempts to evaluate Munro's writing (see Dahlie, MacKendrick *Probable*, Martin, Miller, Pfaus). So the books taken up here do represent, as Canitz asserts, a second phase. What is more, they appear within a context in which Munro has been lionized—the reception accorded *Open Secrets* (1994) having surpassed those of her two previous books, however improbable that might have seemed. More broadly, critical articles abound and appear to be published with increasing frequency. Munro has clearly done far more than arrive: she has established herself as a writer of the first rank—like, she knows very well, Cather—and so, as "the chosen writer" herself, is more than fit to be a subject for adoration. As well, like Cather and others, she has been set upon by critics in a way that is daunting in its extent and in its intensity. Like Cather, too, she is skeptical of such attention.[1]

Like the various quotations from the archives with which I began, this, too, is a necessary context here. There is more: apart from my previous review essay and various articles and bibliography that I have contributed to Munro criticism myself, I bring to this task the perspective of a critic who has been working on Munro's fiction consistently since 1973, when I read my first Munro story, "Material" in *The Tamarack Review*; my M.A. thesis on her early stories and *Dance of the Happy Shades* (1968) was among the earliest critical assessments. Although Canitz and others are free to identify and deprecate the "naïve awe" such critics as I putatively felt at Munro's mimesis in the first phase, I find myself equally dubious—and this while fully appreciative of its so-called critical sophistication—of much of what I have reviewed here. Together with many recent critical articles, some of these books—Heble's, and Smythe's, certainly, and perhaps even Carscallen's—are of doubtful worth; they establish their authors' presence and fulfill academic career needs—probably their most urgent function—but do very little for Munro studies. Indeed, much of Canitz's vaunted "second generation" criticism merely reiterates the first using other terms.

Before taking up each book and detailing such evaluation, a word of my own on Munro's fiction after reading these books and surveying journal articles from the late 1980s through 1996 (the most recent article I found appeared in *Contemporary Literature* [Clark]). Reading over such a disparate grouping, one is struck by several things having to do with the relationship of Munro's work to its critics. Foremost among these are the ways by which Munro's writing creates what amounts to almost an empathetic connection among readers, most especially among critics. We are drawn to her writing by its verisimilitude—not of mimesis, so-called and much maligned by Heble as "realism," but rather its feeling of being itself, or as I have said elsewhere in a review of *The Progress of Love* (1986), of just being human. Thus what seems to drive critics who have taken up Munro's work—and this is especially so of those who have embarked on book-length studies—is a desire to articulate some personal relationship to the work, to replicate in the criticism our feelings upon reading Munro's work. I certainly feel this myself.[2]

What is more, a passage from "Circle of Prayer" (1986) that I quoted in the review of *The Progress of Love* is relevant here: "What are those times that stand out, clear patches in your life—what do they have to do with it? They aren't exactly promises. Breathing spaces. Is that all?" (*Progress* 273). The beginnings of this passage are found in a draft holograph fragment of "Dulse" (38.11.7), and this relationship encapsulates a quality in Munro that seems ever to beckon reader and critic alike. The "progress" of insight, from momentary vision to larger understanding—fleeting, tentative, illusory, yet powerful. Standing back from this recent body of Munro criticism, I am struck by this same quality, the desire of the critic to, as Redekop writes, identify "the story that I hear Munro telling me" (*Mothers* x). Each critic does this, of course, according to her or his lights—however bright or dim—seizing Munro's work most often at these "clear patches"; that is, at those moments of story where her artistry is most evident, and most pointed. There is consensus among critics that her work is never transparent, always elusive, with compounding points of view and meanings, and patterns emerging out of other patterns. Katherine J. Mayberry has stated the matter succinctly:

> Munro's understanding of the function of narrative is mordantly paradoxical. Throughout her career, she has insisted on the existence of prelinguistic experience, of a truth that originates outside of, independent of language. This truth is wholly experiential and wholly personal, never going beyond the bounds of individual perception. Particular and circumscribed, it would seem a simple truth, though as Munro's vision matures, its constitution grows increasingly intricate, its excision from the surrounding web of falsehoods, uncertainties, silence, and alternative perceptions increasingly difficult. But simple or complex, this truth admits little access. The approaches attempted by most of Munro's characters are memory and narrative—virtually equivalent faculties in that they both order past experience, re-collect lived moments within a chronological frame.

She concludes that in Munro, "narrative is finally not the province of truth; to tell is at best to revise, but never to perfectly review" (540).[3]

What Mayberry calls "lived moments" here are Munro's "clear patches," her "breathing spaces"—insights based on moments or incidents that appear briefly in a draft or earlier story, only to emerge as central in a later one.[4] This process—one that Carscallen balloons out of proportion in *The Other Country*—has resulted in a group of Munro stories that might themselves be seen as especially indicative of her work's complexity. That is, owing to what seems their centrality to Munro's work—one of the functions of this being the extent to which they attract critical attention—these stories are most often seen as paradigmatic. "Walker Brothers Cowboy" (1968), "Images" (1968), "Thanks for the Ride" (1957), "The Peace of Utrecht" (1960) and "Dance of the Happy Shades" (1961) are arguably among this group in *Dance of the Happy Shades*. In *Lives of Girls and Women* (1971) it would include "The Flats Road," "Changes and Ceremonies," "Baptizing," and "Epilogue: The Photographer." In *Something I've Been Meaning to Tell You* (1974), three stand out: the title story, "Material," and most especially "The Ottawa Valley" (1974). Most recently, "Meneseteung" (1988) and "Carried Away" (1991) appear to qualify. This is not the place to elaborate a theory of such selection; it is sufficient, however, to see such stories as embodying Munro's most urgent concerns and displaying her most artful effects—the moments that resonate with each of us, as readers more than as critics. Such instances demand our attention, as readers and as critics. Carscallen articulates this point: "In a way opaque to ordinary logic, though implicit in it, we know that the one and the many, like truth and reality, do not ultimately shut each other out. We are our fully individual selves; we are also members of one another—participants in a humanity that is no bare abstraction" (*Other* 88). What this has meant to Munro criticism, especially regarding Carscallen's *The Other Country*, is that beyond moments of epiphany—the "clear patches"—Munro's art is about "Connection. That was what it was all about" (*Moons* 6). Interpersonal connections, perceptual connections, echoes of other stories, other incidents, other characters, other scenes: Munro's art is shaped by a sensibility defined by the weight of her own separateness, her own connection, of who she is.

"This is not enough, Hugo. You think it is, but it isn't."

In *Some Other Reality*, Louis K. MacKendrick challenges the view that "Material" is primarily Munro's own meditation on writing and writers. He maintains, rather, that the unnamed narrator is a nasty person who has not forgiven her former husband, Hugo, and the story she writes is something of a calling him to reckoning (39–45)—thus the assertion used here as a section heading. However viewed, we need to remember that

Hugo is a particular kind of writer: an academic writer—not, as Munro ultimately implies, a "real" one. Hugo is one of those "vain quarrelsome men," she says, "bloated, opinionated, untidy men ... cosseted by the academic life, the literary life, by women" (*Something* 24). Clearly from this, Munro has thought about the university as a place in which people live, pursue careers, succeed and fail—as, I expect, have we all. Indeed, part of this calling to reckoning in "Material" is the narrator's wonderment that someone as irresponsible, capricious, and incapable as Hugo has found a place in which he is able to not only survive, but thrive: "Do you wash, Hugo?" she asks. "Do you call your girl students fond exasperated dirty names, are there phone calls from insulted parents, does the Dean or somebody have to explain that no harm is meant, that writers are not as other men are?" (*Something* 28–29).

Recognizing, as she does here, the hierarchy animating the academy, Munro provides a fit point of departure for this review project. I wonder: What need do these books fill? What audience do they address? Do we need them? By my count, we now have 11 sole-author critical books on Munro's work—another, by Coral Ann Howells, is in press—a couple of collections of critical essays, one short biography, a monograph, and about 100 critical essays and shorter pieces. Munro, of course, has herself published eight books, a dozen uncollected stories, and some fugitive pieces. A *Selected Stories* appeared in the fall of 1996, and the fall of 1998 will see the publication of another collection, *The Love of a Good Woman*. Given such a field, I have elected to approach these books skeptically, wondering in the first instance over their very existence.

Introducing his argument in *The Tumble of Reason*, Ajay Heble notes "a few revisionist studies which" he thinks "warrant consideration in the present context." Later, though, he complains about this, saying:

> On the one hand, I ought, perhaps, to feel inconvenienced by the fact that I am no longer the only one to respond to Munro's fiction in the context of this renewed critical framework. On the other hand, of course, I am pleased to see that Munro's stories are finally beginning to receive the kind of critical attention they deserve. (15, 17)

My first response to these comments is, oh? But then I see that Heble is attempting to assert his own version of Munro. In any case, here is his argument:

> As a result we find Munro abandoning a kind of rational discourse—which assumes that reality is stable, intelligible, and masterable—and replacing it with an equivocal discourse which signifies on the level of the paradigm....
>
> [Munro's] paradigmatic discourse enables us, as it often enables Munro's characters, to imagine possible correlations between sets of phenomena and consider how "reality" might be different if something absent or potential were substituted for the way things are. In making use of this kind of discourse, Munro will substitute direct referentiality with what contemporary critical theory might call "textuality." Her fiction, in part, attempts to force us to reconsider the metaphysical category of reality in textual terms. The world of facts, details, and objects, which, at first, serves to ground the reader in a safe and recognizable reality, is suddenly called into question as Munro makes us aware that we are reading only an attempt to represent these things in fiction, that language is being used to re-present reality. (6–7)

Thus there is, in these terms, disruption in Munro's writing—critically totted up for the present moment—and Heble demonstrates his case in seven chapters, one for each of the books in print up to *Friend of My Youth* (1990).

Though intelligent, precise and thorough with respect to those of Munro's texts it examines, *The Tumble of Reason* need not have been a book; it should not have been a book. It was already a dissertation—one I have not read, though I have looked at its abstract—and what this book offers beyond that publication is not, likely, very much. Heble's introductory chapter posits his "corrective" theory well enough, and his readings of Munro's books demonstrate his ability, but they certainly do not challenge our understanding of Munro's writing in any way sufficient to justify another book. Heble's readings are selective, they are not based in the full scholarly record—archival, sequential, or critical—and they do not advance our understanding of Munro's art very much, if at all. This is a book that should have remained a dissertation and been published as one or two good articles. One need only read the last paragraph of each chapter: there is its point.

The same assessment is inevitable regarding Smythe's *Figuring Grief,* though in her case she managed four published articles before the book. Smythe posits a theory of the "fiction-elegy" and argues that

> in the late modern fiction of Gallant and Munro, the trust in language and art is questioned, and the exploration of grief and loss is conducted not only on the formal level of representation but also on the conceptual and tropological levels in terms of figuring memory, history, and the past. (21)

(Given the context of this review, I will forebear any comment on Smythe's reading of Gallant, though I suspect that my comments below would apply there as well.)

Smythe offers two chapters on Munro. The first, "Munro and Modern Elegy," suffices to demonstrate the limitations of her approach. Without question, Smythe is on to something: death—whether impending, recalled, actual, or imagined—figures often and to great effect in Munro's "material"; indeed, how it figures in a Munro story is often as interesting as its specifics. Smythe insists on identifying an elegiac figuring in the works of both writers, as per her thesis; for her it is paramount. Thus in a subsection of "Munro and Modern Elegy" entitled "Shapes of Death: the Meaning of Loss in Munro's Early Stories" (112–22), Smythe examines the following stories in this order: "Walker Brother Cowboy" (1968), "Images" (1968), "Memorial" (1974), "The Time of Death" (1956), "Day of the Butterfly" (1956), "Winter Wind" (1974), "Material" (1973), and "Tell Me Yes or No" (1974). It may be that my own work on these stories has valorized chronology, but I would not call stories written over nearly 20 years "early," nor would I treat the earliest stories within the frame of later stories. Smythe also manages to assign *Something I've Been Meaning to Tell You* (1974) the wrong year of publication. And when she turns, in the next subsection, to Munro's intervening volume, *Lives of Girls and Women*, Smythe makes no mention of Besner's book.

More than matters of scholarship and structure, what strikes me most in *Figuring Grief* is the drive to apply a thesis. Smythe's reading of Munro is essentially a thematic overview. She sets out to illustrate her points—and treats Munro's stories seemingly randomly, without any clear order—doing so only with an eye toward her own thesis. The argument is well informed by and rooted in relevant authorial statements and critical texts—though, as noted, there are lapses—but ultimately the whole is reductive. Smythe's own thesis is of far more importance than Munro's fiction, which, to my mind, is frequently shoehorned into a series of thesis-driven points. Overall, *Figuring Grief* reads like the academic exercise it was; like *The Tumble of Reason*, this should have remained a dissertation and a series of articles.

That this is the best I am able to offer regarding Heble and Smythe is unfortunate, and it reflects poorly on the present state of the profession of English criticism. Readily conceding that others will disagree with my assessment of these two books—seeing them as effective, necessary critical texts—I nevertheless wonder how each of these authors came to be advised to publish them in their present form. True, they are published by reputable academic presses, but each author would have benefited from a few more years of post-PhD rumination, whether presses, granting agencies, mentors, and authors think so or not. The smug self-congratulation of Heble's comments on Munro criticism, quoted above, and the dissertationese of Smythe's writing, chock full of "I argues" and "I perceives" (vii), fail to hide the fact that neither has much depth of understanding—theirs is quite appropriate for a doctoral degree that, still, should be the beginning of a career as a professional scholar and teacher, not the ending. Yet books like these, which many of us think are needed to ensure that our students do begin an academic career, are sad affairs. It may be that any bright PhD student needs to have a book forthcoming to ensure any hope of a place in university, but it should not be.[5] Without question, each of these volumes testifies more to the currency of Munro's (and Gallant's, in Smythe's case) critical reputation than to the abilities of these critics.

"I respect the intention and the effort and the result"

Willa Cather, when writing about Sarah Orne Jewett (arguably the single most important artistic influence on her own work), makes an observation that is apt for a consideration of Carscallen's *The Other Country* and Redekop's *Mothers and Other Clowns* in this section, and for the balance of these volumes in the next.

> If [a writer] achieves anything noble, anything enduring, it must be by giving himself absolutely to his material. And this gift of sympathy is his great gift; is the fine thing in him that alone can make his work fine.
>
> The artist spends a lifetime in pursuing the things that haunt him, in having his mind "teased" by them, in trying to get these conceptions down on paper exactly as they are to him and not in conventional poses supposed to reveal their character; trying this method and that, as a painter tries different lightings and different attitudes with his subject to catch the one that presents it more suggestively than any other. And at the end of a lifetime he emerges with much that is more or less happy experimenting, and comparatively little that is the very flower of himself and his genius. ("Miss Jewett" 79–80)

Something of Cather's idea is working in each of the volumes yet to be considered, because each is the product of quite a number of years spent reading, ruminating, and weighing Munro's substantive art, itself the product of just the sort of imaginative process Cather describes.

As he concludes his massive, delightful, and peculiar book, *The Other Country*, Carscallen takes up a little-known piece Munro published in 1974, "Everything Here Is Touchable and Mysterious," which deals with her sense of Huron County, particularly her "home place," "'Loretown'—a 'straggling, unincorporated, sometimes legendary non-part' of Wingham, Ontario." "'I am still partly convinced that this river,'" he quotes Munro, describing her hometown's river, the Maitland, "'not even the whole river, but this little stretch of it—will provide whatever myths you want, whatever adventures.'" Carscallen continues with a passage that bears quoting at length:

> The same thing, as I have tried to indicate, is true of Munro's writing itself as it follows its not very extensive course. And while its adventures may often come to tragic ends—the river itself supposedly has "deep holes, ominous beckoning places," eerie enough to satisfy Uncle Benny—there is something here that transforms even the depths.
>
> We saw how an unincorporated region like the Ottawa Valley can equally be the Church of St. John, where the Creator is celebrated for the bright and beautiful things he has made. Munro speaks with the same wonder of the living creatures along the river, or the names which they also are: "I name the plants, I name the fish, and every name seems to me triumphant, every leaf and quick fish remarkably valuable." And so, she concludes, "this ordinary place is sufficient, everything here touchable and mysterious." The touchability of things is their reality, the mystery of them is their truth—or, if we prefer, their truth is what can be grasped and their reality remains mysterious, as in a way reality always does; but in either case it is by the grace of naming, and its counterpart story-telling, that these contraries are gathered into one. Through names and stories, then, Munro offers us true reality: the ordinary made marvellous in its distinctness and the abundance of its life. (534–35)

Before commenting on Carscallen's last words, here, I want to go back—over 535 pages back—to his first: "The following book is offered, not just to Munro specialists, but to anyone who has found her work enjoyable and moving" (vii). Carscallen has been working on Munro, so far as I can tell, since the late 1970s; he published an early profile of Munro in 1980 and then two other essays a few years later. Judging by *The Other Country*, Munro's fiction has certainly "teased" his mind for some time, and to a very considerable extent.

I called this book "peculiar" for several different reasons. Though written in what he calls "plain English"—doubtless his rejection of the hipcrit jargon offered by others, such as Heble and Smythe, about the University of Toronto's English Department—the density of language and, especially, of argument belies any hope that this book will be read in its entirety by anyone but Munro specialists. Indeed, such are the shifts, asides, allusions, promises, and recollections in *The Other Country* that even a person with a detailed command of Munro's writings will have trouble following Carscallen's meanderings. (Indicative of this are the twin facts that I had trouble following his numerous arguments when reading the book toward the end of a semester-long seminar on Munro during which I reread her entire *oeuvre*.) Clearly peculiar, this approach may be a major problem. This is all the more remarkable when one considers that Carscallen concerns himself wholly with Munro's published works, generally eschewing archival materials and statements of authorial intention.

What Carscallen does do, and overall does very well indeed, is to have us take an entirely different tack toward Munro's work. Instead of theme, character, point-of-view, chronology, disruption, composition or other ways into the fiction, Carscallen sees patterns. By this he means the numerous ways texts reflect, elaborate and echo one another: "single stories seem to me to fit implicitly into a larger one of the same kind as themselves. ... Thus pieces from anywhere in a book may help to illustrate a phase with which those in a particular location are linked in a more special way" (viii). A student of Frye, Carscallen displays that influence here in the ornate and detailed patterns he elaborates in Munro. Offering an account of his own discovery of Munro's patterns, he takes up *Lives of Girls and Women*, noting that "Mrs. McQuade's whorehouse is located next to the B. A. service station. As I myself mused on this unremarkable but included fact, it first occurred to me that, in the world of the chapter, a whorehouse and a service station have somewhat the same function." He then goes from this to King Solomon, who "cultivated wisdom as well as arms and pleasure"—parallels he finds in Del and her mother's pursuit "of enlightenment"—and then goes on to note that there are two allusions to the biblical David. Though fearing that he was engaging in "creative reading," Carscallen ultimately concludes—in a phrase that could be seen as having paradigmatic significance in relation to Munro's fiction—that "once she has established a pattern by putting two worlds in parallel, the pattern assimilates whatever will fit into it" (10–11).

But this is not landmark Munro criticism. *The Other Country* is not a book for a general reader, nor, even, for an interested undergraduate. Nevertheless, it offers a great many insights and bears scrutiny, contemplation, and frequent consultation: Carscallen's is an intricate erudition. At the same time, the book's index of titles and characters, the daunting detail of the discussion—each chapter appears with scores of end notes— are well worth having. I have no quarrel with the approach Carscallen adopts, but I do wonder about the argument's extent and, as well, alternative explanations of what he sees. He takes the Bible as primary referent and, through an analysis of characters' names and a typing of stories—the Apocalypse, the Exodus, the Book of Judges—sees mythopoeic relationships between, throughout, and in great detail. Jumping back and forth between stories and other materials, promising to get into something later, weaving one interpretation of a story into another, and then another, Carscallen offers a view of Munro's fiction like none seen before—though hard to follow, it is often quite worth the trouble.

Even so, a reader finds himself wondering over the degree to which connections are a product of Carscallen's own proclivities—he has also written, one notes, on *The Faerie Queen*—and the degree to which this is a private system of meaning. As well, Carscallen's assertion that Munro thinks through charged images—such as his fine discussion of the story of that title, "Images," in relation to "Monsieur Les Deux Chapeaux" (1985) in terms of their "clear patch" scenes (107–17)—seems relevant, too, especially in light of Cather's point. Although the notion that Munro—not, evidently, an especially religious person—would consistently use the Bible as an analogue seems a bit farfetched, Carscallen's recognition really is an elaboration that her art is rooted in Huron County and in its Scots-Irish culture. That is, the patterns Carscallen finds are derived from the cultural images Munro inherited and has imaginatively dwelled upon and drawn upon for her fiction. These are patterns created by an imagination "teased" for years by her inherited cultural material, "Material," she has returned to repeatedly throughout her career. Part of that material, of course, is the biblical stories Carscallen elaborates, the names, the meaning, and, most especially, the images that demand probing from Munro herself—one "Carried Away" by her "Material," from Huron County, where "Everything … Is Touchable and Mysterious."

Like her colleague Carscallen, Redekop brings another sort of background to her work on Munro; she notes at the beginning of her book that "The Progress of Love" is, both ironically and appropriately, the title of a poem by Jonathan Swift. By using "that phrase as a title, he initiated a satiric questioning and Munro pushes further with those questions." She does so, indeed, in a seriously mocking way, also like Swift: thus Redekop's title, *Mothers and Other Clowns*—"Munro invokes details from her own life not as a traditional autobiographer would do, but as a clown would do" (xiii). Although I wonder what Redekop means by "traditional autobiographer," the notion of clowning, like Carscallen's patterns, is an important one. So is this one:

> The narrator of "Material," herself "pregnant with Clea" reproduces Dotty's litany of complaints. It includes three miscarriages. "My womb," says Dotty, "is in shreds. I use up three packs of Kotex every month." Our laughter cannot take away from the reality of Dotty's suffering, the material conditions of her life in "material" [sic]. The narrator of "Material" tries to write a letter to Hugo about his story. The letter is intercepted by the reader and here is what we read: "This is not enough, Hugo. You think it is, but it isn't. You are mistaken, Hugo." I see Munro's stories as a response to the challenge issued by that jabbing sentence. It is not enough to see madonna and harlot as all dolled up to join the parade. They must be domesticated by being taken up into the family. How may a woman's reproductions act to resist a mimicry that is simply a burlesque, like Del's rag-doll dance? The question will partly turn itself into a question of how the woman can learn to be the clown instead of the rag-doll dummy used by the clown. The answer will lie … in Munro's focus on looking. (15–16)

As this suggests, *Mothers and Other Clowns* approaches Munro's work through an analysis of the female perspective; as such, this book covers much of the same ground as Rasporich's *Dance of the Sexes* (1990). It does so, however, in a far better and more informed way, certainly displacing the earlier book.

What Redekop offers is her own reading of Munro, to some degree an idiosyncratic one, though by no means as much so as Carscallen's. She is, as well, quite critically informed, and goes so far as to suggest that "Munro's stories have a lot to teach theorists writing today." Thus despite Munro's own disavowal of any aesthetic, Redekop has "excavated an aesthetic from Munro's stories" because she wanted to "invert" the premise of feminists "finding a vocabulary to explain what the storytellers are doing" (xii). This she does largely through the "Argument" section, which makes up the first 40 pages of the book. Two quotations encapsulate the approach Redekop takes:

> The result of reading Munro's fiction is not to allow the reader—whether male or female—to be comfortable and smug. It is rather to find ourselves caught in the act of smugness—certainly defined as a part of a group. This is the most subtle of Munro's many tricks, to make us initially unaware of our participation, to lure us into a position where we settle into our own prejudices and stereotypes—then to follow this up by making us excruciatingly aware of our own self-deceptions....
>
> Munro's own tricks do not stop with the thrill of power or even with the moment of ironic understanding. Her clowning offers comfort because it leads to a mutual failure. We read for enlightenment and arrive, repeatedly, at the point of recognized blindness. In this experience, however, we have company: reader and writer share this discovery of mutual foolishness. (30; 34)

Redekop is arriving, in both of these comments, at the point at which the power of Munro's art is most deeply apparent: that is, when reader and writer—alike and together—commingle in empathy. Thus she writes, again with reference to "Material," that "at the deepest level of Munro's writing is her constant awareness that a writer, in the act of writing, is using people" (131).

As in Carscallen's book, there is an idiosyncratic density here. Yet, in contrast to his book, where the connections leading to patterns threaten to envelop a reader, Redekop keeps her readings of Munro's stories balanced, and always in sight of her own argument. At the same time, and again like *The Other Country*, there is a leaping about within Munro's works that at times proves disconcerting: Redekop discusses stories without reference to order of composition and, as well, has no apparent knowledge of the Calgary archives. And given the argument offered here, which has much to say about autobiography both in theory and in Munro's approach to it, about mothers and daughters, and about "The Ottawa Valley" in particular, the omission of any sustained reading of "Home"—despite its inclusion in the bibliography—seems singularly odd.

Not a great book, *Mothers and Other Clowns* is a good one—its "Argument" section is much the best part of the book, theoretically alert and well grounded in Munro's art. Although I would have liked a cleaner rationale for the examination of the fiction—why these stories were chosen, a greater awareness of provenance, and much more critique of other critics in light of her own readings—the one found here is sustained, precise, and convincing. Some of these deficiencies, I recognize, are the same as those I noted above with reference to Heble's and Smythe's books. Yet the difference between the two pairs ought to be clear: the depth of understanding Carscallen and Redekop offer outweigh their books' weaknesses. Theirs are books worth having.

"A fine and lucky benevolence"

Early in *Some Other Reality*, Louis K. MacKendrick makes a point that bears echoing and is, indeed, one already made here; after surveying the various book-length critical studies available to him, he concludes his chapter by writing that "it may be evident that studies of individual stories, not subject to large schematic argument, continue to reveal Alice Munro's truer achievements as a writer. Though this method has not been a consistent practice in Canadian literary criticism, it suits Munro's fictive particularities handsomely" (25). That is, Munro's material—like her "Material," of which more in a moment—best lends itself to close textual treatment on the same more narrow scale she adopts herself. And as this assertion suggests, MacKendrick—followed at only a slight distance by Neil Besner in his *Introducing Alice Munro's* Lives of Girls and Women— is by far the best critic of this group. His knowledge of his subject is clearly as deep and precise as any of the others', and the format he employs—one book sharply focused on, thoroughly contextualized and textualized— yields the best and most useful sustained criticism.

This, I confess, surprised me: I had not expected the books from ECW—of which these are two from its Canadian Fiction Studies series, now numbering over 30 volumes—to be as good as they are. By contrast, and as I have said elsewhere, Catherine Sheldrick Ross's *Alice Munro: A Double Life*—one of the first volumes published in ECW's Canadian Biography series—shows the limitations of the series format (Review). Although she has produced a very good and useful book—one quite effective as a class text—Ross's biography is exceptionally constrained by the series format. In this regard, too, my survey of criticism here has confirmed one particular need in Munro studies: an extended critical biography, one that shapes its material to its construction of Munro's writing life. Ross begins that process, but in her rush to fit into ECW's limitations, this book falls far short of the need.

I want to take up MacKendrick in more detail and with more consideration, so as to conclude this—"with honour, if I possibly can"—with the story that has been a mainstay throughout my own "Munrovian" career, and a leitmotif here, "Material." But before that, a brief note on Besner's book. His introduction to *Lives of Girls and Women* is excellent, thorough, and precise. In keeping with the ECW format, he offers a chronology, addresses "The Importance of the Work," considers its critical reception and stature, and then offers a detailed reading of the book. Besner manages all of this in a balanced way: showing a fine knowledge of the book's provenance and of Munro's intentions and difficulties, and acknowledges with a rare generosity the work of the book's other critics. What is more, he manages to say something original about a book that has received a disproportionate share of critical attention.

Besner is at his very best when he discusses the ending of *Lives of Girls and Women*, particularly when he considers another leitmotif in Munro criticism: the difference between what is real—the title of one of her essays—and what is true. Having rejected Garnet French at the end of "Baptizing," bereft of scholarship, Del confronts "Real Life" (238). Carscallen attempts to meld the two in his final sentence: "Through names and stories, then, Munro offers us true reality: the ordinary made marvellous in its distinctness and the abundance of its life" (*Other* 535). Contrasting the book we have in our hand with the "Halloway novel" that Del writes, Besner asserts:

> The writer's art, regardless of its conventions, creates a reality which, regardless of its own "truth," is both autonomous and related to the world it refers to, however diffuse or symbolic this connection may be. Paradoxically, it is in the Halloway novel that we (along with Del) may be able to see more clearly the relations between the real world and the fictional world. In *Lives of Girls and Women* itself, the relations are more mysterious, for all of realism's supposed mimetic properties; and Del is discovering this mystery at the heart of what will be her art as she sits with Bobby Sheriff, who is himself only the last of the several Jubilee eccentrics who have confronted Del with unknowable and yet alluring realities. (109)[6]

Besner is asking, along with Munro, "What is Real?", and, also along with her, he is acknowledging that in the world, generally, and in Munro's Jubilee, particularly, "Everything Is Touchable and Mysterious." Besner continues, recognizing that *Who Do You Think You Are?* (1978) amounts to Munro's return to many of these same questions; he might have taken the ending of *Lives of Girls and Women*—with its tension between what is real to Del and what is true, what is Munro's fiction and what is Del's—stopped off for a bit at the ending of *Who Do You Think You Are?*, and continued on to "Meneseteung," another of Munro's attempts at the Caroline–Marion problem in *Lives of Girls and Women*.

Early in her celebrity, Munro told an interviewer that "writing is the act of approach and recognition," an act of "just approaching something that is mysterious and important." "I believe that we don't solve these things—in fact our explanations take us further away" (Gardiner Interview 178). Thus Munro may be seen moving from Del to Rose to Almeda, and the mystery continues, as Pam Houston has argued about "Meneseteung," a "clear patch story" par excellence:

> What is true is untrue, what is untrue is true. We have an hysterical bleeding woman inside an admittedly fictitious account, written by a narrator who doesn't even know her name. We have a distortion of reality within a distortion of reality, within a story that is also a poem, and sometimes a river. Nothing here will stay long enough to mean just one thing. (90)

Welcome, one is tempted to say, to Munro where everything is paradoxically touchable and mysterious—that is, not graspable. Explanations do take Munro—and us—"further away," and yet, as Redekop says, this is an author who has much to teach literary theorists: "Also, professors are dumb."

MacKendrick makes substantially the same point when he writes, early in his reading of the text of *Something I've Been Meaning to Tell You*:

> It is quite hopeless and redundant to expect an Alice Munro story to surrender a clear, indisputable, and singular "meaning." The language itself is the prime variable, and it is complicated by an almost predictable complexity of her first-person narrators, few of whom are able to remain disengaged from what they are relating. It is a little surprising, then, that given the possible permutations of language, character, and event, the critical interpretations of her writing should have such an occasional, but interdependent, element of repetition. This is no guarantee, however, that Munro's work will not be used to prove a prescriptive formula of fiction, or a single-minded argumentative philosophy. (26)

Here MacKendrick has provided text to account for the several books reviewed here, plus those that preceeded them. The problem, of course, is in which Munro—by rendering in a long critical form "my" Munro, the authors of such texts are constructing her fiction along the lines of personal proclivities: theoretical, structural, or linguistic. Even MacKendrick, here, tends to privilege "first-person narrators" who, until *Something I've Been Meaning to Tell You*, seemed to be increasing in frequency. Ever at the ready, Munro has since tended more toward third person, folding much of the first-person narrator's uncertainties into the narrative voice—as in "Meneseteung."

As he works his way through the stories in *Something I've Been Meaning to Tell You*, MacKendrick offers readings of each story that are convincing, certainly, but more than that they show him to be ever alert to nuance—and in this Munro volume, which is transitional in several ways, that means looking back to earlier work as well as forward to more recent, and more complex, renderings. Thus

> Munro's stories may have almost cheerful and unapologetic interruptions in any expected narrative line—generally by her preferred voice, a first-person narrator. Very often in reading a Munro story we become pleasantly aware that along with perfectly credible or "realistic" characters and situations we are also variously hearing echoes, reverberations, repetitions, ironies, juxtapositions, contrasts, digressions, interpolations. We are hearing not only a storyteller's tricks but we are hearing them almost as a matter of narrative course. Very often we are hearing a truly oral narrative, a distinctive and personalized voice. (29)

Although his reading of the collection's title story is especially fine—and complex—it is MacKendrick's reading of "Material" that interests me most here. Following on his final point, he concentrates on the oral quality of the narrative, saying that "Material" "is a thorough and consistently revealing self-portrait, with enough ramifications of character that the narrator, ranging through moods and tones, virtually comes to life beyond the confines of this chronicle." What is more, "in the story's present she is marking test papers in history, and Hugo is to be assigned a grade after all the material has been considered—after she has written her history of their relationship." Seeing this narrator's narrative as a "sometimes unflattering self-portrait," one that "is a contest ... between a professional creative writer and his ex-wife, a teacher and corrector, who has nothing to lose and everything to win, for she is the only one aware of the contest" (39).

As MacKendrick notes, "Some of Munro's critics believe the passage [in which she acknowledges Hugo's successful artistry] to be one of [Munro's] personal testaments about her fiction" (43). I have said so myself, and I still believe it is. But I also see the "real truth" of MacKendrick's careful close reading of Munro's text, one that ultimately sees this narrator as a nasty, vituperative person who does, indeed, both "envy and despise" the men in her life, Hugo and Gabriel both, for not being "*at the mercy*" (*Something* 44). Thus "her personal past demons and lingering resentments have once again been dealt with. Gabriel's discovery of Hugo's story has precipitated a farrago of memory, bitterness and self-justification, and an apparent summary confession of spite, jealousy and error. Yet the narrator continues to be a vigorous combatant in her own arena" (45). Writing of the same story, taking a very different tack, Redekop asks, "Has the narrator appropriated some of the power invested in Hugo, the writer? She has, after all, written this story: the story 'Material'" (31). "'Yes,' I said, instead of thank you" (*Lives* 250).

What the critic is asking, in both cases, though most thoroughly in MacKendrick's reading, is "What's 'Material'?" What we have as critics, in the first instance and to use another phrase of MacKendrick's, are Munro's "Narrative Acts." What we do with them, as MacKendrick asserts and I certainly echo based on what I have examined for this review essay, is largely whatever we want. Each of us shapes a Munro to suit—privileging this, downplaying that, exaggerating here, ignoring there—and we emerge (as I certainly do myself, here) having shaped a version of the Munro critique. Perhaps entertaining, perhaps wry, perhaps illuminating, perhaps dry: the answer to all this, again and ever, is the same as before: Go ask Alice, where "Everything Is ... Touchable and Mysterious."

Mapping Munro: Reading the "Clues" (1999)

> My connection was in danger—that was all. Sometimes our connection is frayed, it is in danger, it seems almost lost. Views and streets deny knowledge of us, the air grows thin. Wouldn't we rather have destiny to submit to, then, something that claims us, anything, instead of such flimsy choices, arbitrary days?
> —Alice Munro, *Open Secrets* (127)

This quotation is from "The Albanian Virgin" (1994)—a story in which, perhaps, Alice Munro has strayed as far as she yet has (at least culturally if not geographically) from her "home place," Huron County, Ontario. In that straying, we seem both to have left Munro country and, at the same time, not: here is a narrator's voice, caught in the quintessential Munrovian act: divining, wondering over, articulating, and defining "connection"—connection to the world, connection to various parts of (what she has called "wooing") the self, connection to others. "Connection. That was what it was all about," Munro wrote in "Chaddeleys and Flemings: 1. Connection" (*Moons* 6). As I have been arguing for some time, for Munro *the* most urgent connection has been to her rural southwestern Ontario birthplace in Huron County, Wingham—the "home place," her cultural map, her profound talisman. Flowing through the town, we know, is a mystical and mythic river, the Maitland—called "The Menesetung" by the local Indigenous peoples, as Munro noted in a brief 1974 essay:

> I am still partly convinced that this river—not even the whole river—but this little stretch of it—will provide whatever myths you want, whatever adventures. I name the plants, I name the fish, and every name seems to me triumphant, every leaf and quick fish remarkably valuable. This ordinary place is sufficient, everything here touchable and mysterious. ("Everything" 33)

Yes. "Everything [t]here is touchable and mysterious," as Munro has demonstrated, again and again. But our understanding of those demonstrations falters yet.

Last summer, I wrote an extended review essay focused on the Munro criticism published since 1990; it follows another on work published during the 1980s that appeared in the *Journal of Canadian Studies* in 1991. Munro has had, already, 11 single-author volumes published on her work—itself consisting of, one notes, eight volumes plus the *Selected Stories* (1996). Among the books I looked at, the most spectacular is James Carscallen's almost-600-page tome, *The Other Country: Patterns in the Writing of Alice Munro* (1993). Ironically, given Munro's unwavering attachment to the short story as a form, most of these have posited—in effect—master narratives of putative discursive patterns, à la Carscallen. As well, the journal/article count (via the *MLA International Bibliography*) is now approaching 200.

Given this, I want to suggest another way of "Mapping Munro," one that seems to me to be most needed. First, I am struck by several things having to do with the relationship of Munro's work to its critics. Foremost among these are the ways by which Munro's writing creates what amounts to almost an empathetic union among readers, most especially among critics. We are drawn to her writing not so much by its verisimilitude but by how it makes us feel. This is reality, we think, not artifice. Such a quality in the fiction draws critics to read and critique further. Just as I said in that review essay, the essay preceding this one.

Take as but one instance Munro's early story "The Peace of Utrecht" (1960). In it, the narrator, Helen, returns to Jubilee, enters her childhood home, and looks in the hallway mirror; in it, she sees

> the reflection of a thin, tanned, habitually watchful woman, recognizably a Young Mother, whose hair, pulled into a knot on top of her head, exposed a jawline no longer softly fleshed, a brown neck rising with a look of tension from the little sharp knobs of collarbone—this in the hall mirror that had shown me, last time I looked, a commonplace pretty girl, with a face as smooth and insensitive as an apple, no matter what panic and disorder lay behind it. (*Dance* 197–98)

The processes of self-analysis and self-understanding evident here are symbiotically conjoined in the relationship of each narrator to her home place, and that textual trail is intricate.

The importance of "The Peace of Utrecht" to Munro's *oeuvre* is obvious, as is its demonstration of the fundamentally autobiographical connection the author has to her home place (see Thacker "Connection"; Weaver). Munro has called this her "first really painful autobiographical story," and, more to the point, she has returned to its circumstances again and again (Metcalf Interview 58). The story meditates on the mother–daughter relationship, and that relationship, as any reader of Munro knows, is central to her work: it plays a central role in "The Peace of Utrecht," "Red Dress—1946," "Images," *Lives of Girls and Women*, "Winter Wind," "The Ottawa Valley," "Chaddeleys and Flemings: 1. Connection," "The Progress of Love," and "Friend of My Youth." As Munro writes parenthetically in the uncollected story, "Home" (1974), commenting metafictionally in her own voice in the opening pages of the story: "*Also the bit about Mother, who probably doesn't belong in this at all but I can't come in reach of her without being invaded by her.*" (137, italics in original). The mother's presence is but a single autobiographical instance in Munro's work, but it is one redolent with meaning, and one that confirms Munro's ongoing critique of being human—"being a human being." As well, mainly because she works through the short story, Munro offers what amounts to a persistent, recurrent, and multilayered attempt to articulate the mysteries of being—one that has left multiple traces, or multiple "clues," for the critic.

This latter point needs to be asserted because of what is in the Munro archives at the University of Calgary. The materials there reveal numerous instances in which Munro may be seen trying to find a suitable place for this or that detail or story from her own past and, most often, out of her own home place. The multiple pieces in the archive demonstrate, too, in connection with various single texts, the need for better maps of Munro's work. These resources have been left largely untouched by critics—the most recent group as much as those who published books and articles in the 1980s.

* * *

An example: During the mid-1970s, after her marriage had broken up and she had moved back to Ontario, Munro worked on the text for a book of photographs of Ontario scenes by Peter D'Angelo, which was to have been published by Macmillan. For reasons that are unclear, it never appeared—judging from the archival material, however, Munro spent a good deal of time working on her text. It is made up of short, Sherwood Anderson–like vignettes, few of which are more than a page or so; they are anecdotal, descriptive, and reminiscent. They are also haunting and looming. Among them is one entitled "Clues":

> CLUES
>
> In a little glassed in side-porch, from which people can look out at the street, but not be seen themselves, very easily, the following things can be found, on window-sills or tacked up on the wall:
>
> A calendar picture of a kitten asleep between the legs of a Great Dane, the dates torn off.
>
> A photograph of Princess Anne as a child.
>
> A Blue Mountain pottery vase with three yellow plastic roses.
>
> Six shells from the Pacific coast.

The Lord is My Shepherd, in black cut-out scroll sprinkled with glitter.

An amber glass cream jug, from Woolworth's, with a bunch of wildflowers, drooping. White and orange daisies, white and purple money-musk.

Newspaper photograph of seven coffins in a row. Father, mother, five children. All shot by the father a few years ago in a house about five miles out of town (hard to find but most people have persisted, asking directions at the gas station on the highway and then at a crossroads store; most people have driven past).

[Typed, struck out] A mobile of blue and yellow paper birds, crude and lovely, made by a seven-year-old child at school, bobbing and dancing on undetectable currents of air.

[Replaced with, in Munro's hand] Some blue and yellow paper birds, cut by the wobbly hand of a seven year old child, strung from sticks so they bob delicately on undetectable currents of air. (37.13.11.f27–28)

It is with stark, material images such as these that the author of "Material" (1973) begins, and, indeed, has always begun. During this period, certainly, Huron County material was prominent—her next book was to be *Who Do You Think You Are?* (1978)—but such home-place material is never distant for Munro, though if her characters may be.

A particularly good example of such a crux is "Miles City, Montana" (1985). It ends in the book version with the parents, back in the front seat of their car, yet again heading east toward Ontario from British Columbia, the story's central excitement having ended and their younger daughter, Meg, now quite fine after her brush with drowning in Miles City, Montana. As it ends, Munro refers once more to the image with which she began the story—the drowning of eight-year-old Steve Gauley, his body carried across the field by the narrator's father, though the narrator doubts the veracity of her memory of the event. Munro also develops complicity between the parents and this child's drowning—only Steve's father, who believes life is merely random, is exempt. The book version ends:

So we went on, with the two in the back seat trusting us, because of no choice, and we ourselves trusting to be forgiven, in time, for everything that had first to be seen and condemned by those children: whatever was flippant, arbitrary, careless, callous—all our natural, and particular, mistakes. (*Progress* 105)

Passages like this stand out in Munro's work—they are, in fact, "breathing spaces" (*Progress* 273), and her stories frequently end with them, without really concluding them. Most often, what is valued in Munro's stories is the precision and exactitude of emotion that such passages communicate while also articulating the utter uncertainty and ambivalence of being. Thus among the most interesting—and vexing—questions revealed by the Munro archives are those that have to do with how she got to passages of the sort just quoted. Submerged beneath that paragraph are a welter of emotions, most seemingly contradictory, all of which are made more identifiable by comparing them to, if you will, their earlier selves—that is, reading the "clues," a word redolent with meaning within the context of mapping Munro. Consider a paragraph from the end of a holograph draft of "Miles City, Montana," in which the main action of the story is pretty much as it is in the published versions as she works toward an ending:

> Why wasn't it enough for me, just to have escaped? I didn't believe in escape, that was it. Andrew believed in luck, his luck, would celebrate it like a virtue. If something not lucky happened, he would shove that out of mind, ashamed. That was why he never mentioned the dead baby. And my mentioning it would seem a kind of sickening parade of misfortune, a dishonesty. I understood, I too hated fiercely that reply clinging onto miseries the gloating voices of women saying 'a tragedy['] so how could we understand what we were doing. Who is ready to be a father, a mother, who is fit? I always hated to hear the names of my children called in the streets, I had hated when my own mother called me, in public, as I had hated the name she had chosen: Le-on-a. The names proclaimed the mother's ownership, her creation. I didn't want my own children burdened

like that. What was more, I didn't want them to be crowning products of my life, so I was trying out this less definite, humorous, even tentative, statement of motherhood, thinking we would all be the better for it. (Third accession 7.3)

Though this passage appears to be an early version of the paragraph that now ends the story, it also contains elements of the paragraph that immediately precedes the return to the narrator's memory of Steve Gauley's funeral (103). The dead baby—an autobiographical detail—has also been dropped in the published versions. Yet the question asked here—"Who is ready to be a father, a mother, who is fit?"—and indeed the whole mystery of the narrator's wondering over her "escape," envelopes "Miles City, Montana" and, arguably, the whole of Munro's work. In what is perhaps her first perfect story, "Thanks for the Ride" (1957), Munro describes such moments with the phrase, *"that headlong journey"*; they pose questions of wonder, unanswerable: "To find our same selves, chilled and shaken, who had gone that headlong journey and were here still" (*Dance* 56–57, italics in original).

Implied within such passages, too, are the narrator's recollection of Steve Gauley's drowning and the memory of her ambivalence over his death, her ambivalence toward her former husband, and her feelings for her relatives whom she was about to visit, both her father and her in-laws. Each of these invocations ties the narrator to Munro's home place, to the rural Ontario of her youth, to the years she spent in British Columbia in her 20s and 30s, and to the circumstances of her marriage. They are offered, too, from the perspective of the Ontario native who has returned—though this perspective is largely mute.

The archives also reveal what might be called Munro's recurrences; that is, her repeated returning to an image or incident. From the late 1970s on, for example, she repeatedly tried to find a place for the threatened hanging now at the centre of "The Progress of Love" (1985). A graphic instance of this, and perhaps more interesting, is the recurrence of an industrial decapitation, which first appeared briefly in "Thanks for the Ride"—a story Munro submitted to Robert Weaver at the CBC in 1955—as the cause of Lois's father's death. In the story, the incident is briefly described to Dick by Lois's mother (*Dance* 51). It becomes a major focus in "Carried Away" (1991), in which Louisa's imagined suitor, Jack Agnew, is killed in the same type of accident, described in much more detail—his severed head being "carried away" by the factory owner, Arthur Doud, whom Louisa eventually marries (See Carrington "What's").

What I am suggesting by this too-brief discussion of what is to be found in the Munro archives is that Munro's methods of composition, often readily discernible there, lend themselves to archival analysis. Those methods need to be probed more thoroughly than they have been. This is because Munro's methods are fundamentally organic—that is, as she has written in the introduction to her *Selected Stories*, she often imagines a scene, seeing it as an image, and then tries to write its contexts, to discover what it means. As she both imagines and works through the story, focused on such contexts, she leaves clues throughout her holograph drafts and typescripts. As she works toward the ending, as with "Miles City, Montana," Munro may be seen also discovering the essence, the feelings and meaning, of the story she is telling, based on the connections she is making. Throughout these drafts, such clues abound. And because of this, and especially because Munro's work is in the short story form, hers is an art that demands mapping in ways not yet done. To my mind, all such maps begin in Calgary.

Part Three

Understanding the *Oeuvre*

By 2000, Munro was established as something of a special author. When the title story of *The Love of a Good Woman* was published in the *New Yorker* in late 1996, it was remarked on because of its extraordinary length (more than 70 pages in straight text). In 2004 the magazine's editors made another audacious presentation decision: three stories by Munro—the "Juliet Triptych"—made up the bulk of the *New Yorker*'s summer fiction issue. In between, Munro had published *Hateship, Friendship, Courtship, Loveship, Marriage* (2001), a collection containing stories of great variety and one seen by some as Munro's best single collection. During this time, too, she published a revised version of "Home" (1974), a memoir story that sharply revealed her ongoing feelings about her parents, especially her father, at the time of her return to Ontario in 1973 and redirected herself as a writer at that time. This relationship is a critical one for Munro, permeating the whole of her work. The story's reappearance in the *New Statesman* in late 2001 and, revised further, in 2006 in *The Virginia Quarterly Review*, and its significant place in *The View From Castle Rock* (2006), the "family book" Munro had been thinking about since the late 1970s, revealed her to be experimenting still—using what many saw as the same materials and situations but, however seemingly familiar, able still to render them new, fresh, revealing. Such was the case, too, with *Runaway* (2004), anchored as it was by the "Juliet Triptych," telling us much of the whole of Juliet's life. In these three stories, in succession, she is a young lover, an older daughter, and an abandoned mother. *The View From Castle Rock*, which brought together older published pieces that had never found their way into one of Munro's books, along with some newly written though long-contemplated stories, showed Munro doing something wholly different. Some reviewers blanched at the book's odd shape and uncharacteristic material, but, unperturbed, Munro returned to more characteristic times, situations, and material for *Too Much Happiness* (2009). Even so, the subject of that book's title story is unlike anything Munro had ever done—the life story of a nineteenth-century Russian mathematician—and in this collection, too, is a much-revised and much-improved story, "Wood," first published in 1980.

Given this, the essays and review included in this third section are pieces that take a long view toward Munro's writing, a view borne of long familiarity and study. The first piece, "Alice Munro's Ontario"—written while *Alice Munro: Writing Her Lives* was being contemplated but had not yet taken shape—revised after it was published, uses texts I have long seen as both autobiographically revealing and key to examining Munro's compelling rendering of her parents together: "Home" and, especially, "Working for a Living" (1981). Two other essays, on Munro's Irish heritage and on the story "White Dump" (1986), were derived directly from my readings in the Munro fonds for the biography. Following her genealogical work on her father's Scots side for *The View From Castle Rock*, I realized that Munro wrote her mother's Irish ancestors into "The Ottawa Valley" and that Munro had done research on those people herself in the late 1970s. As this work suggests, Munro has long been a biographer herself. In the essay on "White Dump" I both assert that story's importance within Munro's expanding aesthetic during the 1980s and describe it as a critical story in her numerous renderings of female adultery: "The way the skin of the moment can break open"—indeed, profoundly rendered. The review of *Too Much Happiness* treats that book's effects and jousts with critics who had tired of Munro. The final piece, from a 2013 volume on Munro in a series called "Critical Insights," brings Munro criticism up to date, to the degree that such a thing is possible.

It is not, really. Even before Munro was announced as the winner of the 2013 Nobel Prize in Literature, the pace of published criticism had accelerated. As I wrote my third overview of Munro criticism during the summer of 2011, I knew that Isla Duncan's *Alice Munro's Narrative Art* (2011) was forthcoming but would not appear in time for me to include it. This says nothing of the articles—they have appeared in their dozens since my overview. And then there are the larger volumes, many of which were occasioned by the awarding of the Nobel, but appeared prior to it. In 2012, *Narrative* published a special issue focused on a single story, "Passion" (2004), with a preface, an extended introduction, a summary of the story, five articles, and "dialogues" between the contributors. Since the Nobel, journals in Canada and abroad (China, France, and the United States, at least) have produced special Munro issues, and book publishers are planning critical volumes focused on Munro. At least four such books have appeared from European presses during 2014 to 2015. In May of 2014—unconnected with the Nobel—the University of Ottawa's long-standing annual Canadian Literature Symposium focused on Munro; its university press will produce a volume of essays before long. And while the frequency of attention brought about by the Nobel will doubtless slow as time passes, projects like the special issue of *Narrative* and the others confirm that Munro's critical literary presence is incontrovertible and will continue. I have contributed to some of these publications, and I hope to continue contributing to Munro studies for as long as I can.

Alice Munro's Ontario (2007)

Alice Munro begins "The Love of a Good Woman" (1996) with a list of items to be found in the Walley, Ontario, museum—photos, churns, horse harnesses, and porcelain insulators. The next paragraph adds:

> Also there is a red box, which has the letters D. M. WILLENS, OPTOMETRIST printed on it, and a note beside it, saying, "This box of optometrist's instruments though not very old has considerable local significance, since it belonged to Mr. D. M. Willens, who drowned in the Peregrine River, 1951. It escaped the catastrophe and was found, presumably by the anonymous donor, who dispatched it to be a feature of our collection." (*Love* 3)

"The Love of a Good Woman," extremely long even for the *New Yorker*, where it first appeared, was recognized immediately as a *tour de force*—Munro critics seized on it as a crucial text and several essays have already probed its intricacies (such as Duffy and McCombs). Highlighted in its *New Yorker* presentation by a lurid cover image and subtitled with gothic flourish ("A Murder, a Mystery, a Romance"), "The Love of a Good Woman" constructs Munro as the preeminent writer she is. Margaret Atwood may well be English Canada's leading novelist, but there is little doubt that Munro is its leading storyteller and even, perhaps, its leading writer—she is frequently cited as among the best writers working in the English language.

Although another analysis of "The Love of a Good Woman" might well be justified, I begin with it here only to introduce its subject as my own, "Alice Munro's Ontario." A. S. Byatt has recently written, aptly, that Munro "has learned to depict whole lives from a distance in the same strangely unworked-up and unaccented way [as did American novelist Willa Cather], while also making it entirely new, as her landscape and *moeurs* are new" (53). In the passage just quoted from "The Love of a Good Woman," Munro manages to place the stories of several persons' lives in critical relation to the box of optometrist's instruments now on display in the museum in Walley, Ontario, with which she begins the story. Despite having done so in extended detail (the book version is over 70 pages long), Munro still manages to avoid telling her reader just who was responsible for getting that box of instruments into the Walley museum, and how they managed to get it there. Containing its mystery throughout, the box both opens "The Love of a Good Woman" and stands at its end as a talisman, a trope glowing with meaning yet still withholding an unequivocal explanation. Indeed, "The Love of a Good Woman" both contextualizes Munro's rural Southwestern Ontario home place and demonstrates her ability to render her subjective relationship to a place with more complexity than any other contemporary Canadian writer—Tracy Ware's description of Munro's recent work is apt; he calls it "bewilderingly complex" (Email). That is certainly so in "The Love of a Good Woman."

Beginning in 1950, Munro's published stories have been rooted in her autobiographical home place of Huron County, Ontario. Now, over 50 years later, they still are. As "The Love of a Good Woman" demonstrates, this connection is both detailed and profound. Between 1968 and 2006, Munro published 11 volumes of stories and a putative novel. In those collections are some 51 stories that first appeared in the United States' premier venue for short stories: the *New Yorker*. Complex and detailed, Munro's stories proclaim her connection to Ontario as both a place remembered and one she has lived in and knows well.

Indeed, Munro's Ontario is a complexly rendered fictional territory, one borne in the first part of her career of distance and imaginative return (1951 to 1973), and, since 1973, a place intimately known and long meditated on. As John Weaver has argued, it is possible to read the whole social history of Huron County, and of rural southwestern Ontario generally, by reading Munro's fiction chronologically. This is so because Munro has textured her prose with the surface details of her Ontario place, details at once commonplace and alluring. She has long and freely admitted that she is "excited by what you might call the surface of life," and she has deprecated her writing by saying that she "can't have anybody in a room without describing all the furniture" (Gibson Interview 241, 257). Munro's rendering of fictional contexts in such detail may also be traced through her use of repeated figures; take, as a key example, Munro's use of the Maitland River, which flows through her hometown of Wingham, Ontario, on its way to nearby Lake Huron. In a brief 1974 essay, "Everything Here is Touchable and Mysterious," Munro once wrote:

> There is a short river the Indians called the *Menesetung*, and the first settlers, or surveyors of the Huron Tract, called the Maitland. From the place where the forks join, at Wingham, it winds about 35 miles, to flow into the lake at Goderich, Ont. Just west of Wingham it flows through that straggling, unincorporated, sometimes legendary non-part of town called Lower Town (pronounced Loretown) and past my father's land and Cruikshank's farm, to make a loop called the Big Bend before flowing south under Zetland Bridge, and that is the mile or so I know of it. (33)

Such passages as this are typical of Munro: she knows the details of her home place, and she uses them precisely. Equally, too, those details yield the meaning she seeks, as is evident in the essay's final lines:

> Because I am still partly convinced that this river—not even the whole river, but this little stretch of it—will provide whatever myths you want, whatever adventures. I name the plants, I

name the fish, and every name seems to me triumphant, every leaf and quick fish remarkably valuable. This ordinary place is sufficient, everything here touchable and mysterious. (33)

Munro returned to this river in a story, "Meneseteung" (1988), in which she creates a narrator who is researching the life of a local nineteenth-century "poetess," long dead, an "old maid" named Almeda Joynt Roth. The story is mainly concerned with Roth's near-courtship by a local eligible widower, Jarvis Poulter, as imagined, without any historical provenance, by the narrator. Among Roth's poems is one entitled "Champlain at the Mouth of the Meneseteung" (*Friend* 52). Such a tableau characterizes Roth's old maid's mindset—at one point she thinks of "Champlain and the naked Indians" (70)—but in Munro's creation of Roth, and especially through the narrator's research into the poetess's life, Munro is indeed creating a myth along the Meneseteung. And if the details of Munro's essay demonstrate one central aspect of her writing, the penultimate paragraph of "Meneseteung" offers another. Looking for Roth's gravestone, wondering over a reference in one of the published poems, the narrator finds the name Meda written on a gravestone, and reflects that she is perhaps not the last person to make the connection between the poet and the poem, for people do "put things together ... in the hope of ... making a connection, rescuing one thing from the rubbish." The last paragraph continues:

> And they may get it wrong, after all. I may have got it wrong. I don't know if she took laudanum. Many ladies did. I don't know if she made grape jelly. (*Friend* 73)

These last questions refer to incidents in the story proper, but their exact meaning is less important than the effect of the final paragraph, which Munro reinstated after the story's first publication in the *New Yorker*. This paragraph compromises the narrator's authority if not dashing it altogether and welcomes us to Munro's world, where everything is both "touchable and mysterious," a world in which each character, especially those who narrate or serve as vehicles for Munro's wonderings, is keenly aware of the myriad difficulties in the way of "seeing this trickle in time," or "making a connection" (Thacker "Writing 'Home'").

Focusing on this same story, Pam Houston discusses the relationship between Munro's narrator and the character she describes, Almeda Roth, and asks, "'Does the landscape, then, exist separately from the way these women see it?' And neither woman can answer. The two women have momentarily become one voice, bound together by the metonymic qualities of language, and by the inability of metaphor to speak to them" (89). The metonymy Houston deduces here is crucial to the defining of Munro's Ontario, although I would argue that her notion of "two women becoming one voice" is better applied to Munro herself and the speaking voice in her stories—sometimes a first-person narrator but more often not, because third-person narration has predominated in recent years.

What I mean by this is that Munro's Ontario is constructed along the line—if a line it is—between fiction and memoir. It is a world rooted in the times and the touchable surfaces and characters of Huron County, Ontario, a place inhabited since the early 1850s by Munro's ancestors (a time she has been taking up more and more, first signaled by "Meneseteung"), a place she has imagined fully and deeply (Thacker "Writing 'Home'"). "A place that ever was lived in is like a fire that never goes out," Eudora Welty wrote in "Some Notes on River Country" (*Eye* 286) and Munro's focus on the area around "this little stretch" of the Meneseteung/Maitland River has certainly proved her assertion that it is an "ordinary place sufficient" for her work, one that she is probing even yet, as "The Love of a Good Woman" demonstrates.[1]

* * *

Given these contexts, I wish here to look at what I take to be a key aspect of Munro's method: a memoir she published in 1981 entitled "Working for a Living." Because it began as a fiction but—for various reasons—became a memoir, the piece is apt for demonstrating Munro's method and her Ontario-rooted art. As such a transformation suggests, what Munro has done in her stories has been to define and probe factual complexities, wondering over what she has called "the rest of the story" (Introduction, *Selected* xvi). Before I take up the memoir, however, I need to contextualize it with some brief discussion of Munro's methods and some brief mention of other works.

As in "Everything Here is Touchable and Mysterious," Munro has several times addressed the relationship between the factual and the imaginative in her fiction. In another essay, "What is Real?" (1982), she asserts her unshakable conviction that "every final draft, every published story, is still only an attempt, an approach, to the story." To illustrate, Munro cites her story, "Royal Beatings," from *Who Do You Think You Are?* (1978); rejecting any pretense of using an incident "to show anything," she says rather that she "put this story at the heart of my story because I need it there and it belongs there. It is the black room at the centre of the house with all the rooms leading to and away from it. That is all." She continues:

> Who told me to write [the character, Hat Nettleton's] story? Who feels any need of it before it is written? I do. I do, so that I might grab off this piece of horrid reality and install it where I see fit, even if Hat Nettleton and his friends are still around to make me sorry.
>
> The answer seems to be as confusing as ever. Lots of true answers are. Yes and no. Yes, I use bits of what is real, in the sense of being really there and really happening, in my story. No, I am not concerned with using what is real to make any sort of record to prove any sort of point, and I am not concerned with any methods of selection but my own, which I can't fully explain. (36)

Trying to explain, though, Munro rejects the notion that a story is "a road, taking me somewhere. ... It's more like a house. ... I go into it, and move back and forth and settle here and there, and stay in it for a while" (5).

By speaking of "the black room at the centre of the house," Munro posits not so much an essentialist approach as a core mystery informing each story. In "The Love of a Good Woman," it is Mr. Willens' talismanic box of optometrist's instruments: how did it get into the Walley museum, yes, but more significantly, what human interactions took place to result it Willens's death? In "Meneseteung," it is the inferred actions of Almeda Roth during a Saturday night and Sunday morning, a moment transfixed in the story, that might have brought about a connection, and with it, transformation. It does not. As these examples suggest, Munro places a crucial fact at the core of her stories—these facts are, like Mr. Willens' instruments, both evident and mysterious, leaving us aware of them but also leaving us wondering. "It's the fact you cherish," Munro wrote in a 1994 essay entitled "What Do You Want to Know For?" (208). For her, such cherished facts are the beginning of the story, the wonderings that produce the imaginative wanderings—about the imagined house—that create the story at hand.

* * *

For Munro, no house has been the site of more imaginative wondering, and more imaginative wandering, than her family home in Wingham, Ontario. It was there that she grew up, living in the house from 1931 to 1949, when she moved away to attend university and then, in 1951, to live in Vancouver with her first husband, James Munro. Although the next 22 years were spent nearly a continent away from Ontario, her "Home," Munro was ever beckoned imaginatively back to Wingham, and especially to her family home where her mother fought the debilitations of Parkinson's disease until her death in 1959. A direct result of her mother's death was "The Peace of Utrecht" (1960), a story that Munro once called "her first really painful autobiographical story ... the first time I wrote a story that tore me up." (Metcalf Interview 58). In it the narrator, Helen, visits her home in Jubilee to see her sister, Maddy, after their mother has finally died from a long, lingering illness. Helen is the sister who got away to a life of her own while Maddy stayed behind to nurse their "Gothic Mother." The story's details are less important here than its parallels to Munro's own life, as well as a passage in which Helen remembers the feelings she had on earlier trips home, seeing once more the town's familiar details: "feeling as I recognized these signs a queer kind of oppression and release, as I exchanged the whole holiday world of school, of friends and, later on, of love, for the dim world of continuing disaster, of home" (*Dance* 200, 191).

The circumstances of this story suggest that Munro got away from her "home place," Ontario, only to return repeatedly in her imagination; more than this, Munro literally returned home to stay in 1973, long after her mother's death but before her father's death in 1976. This return to Ontario and to Huron County from British Columbia, where she had lived since 1952, occasioned a perceptible shift in Munro's work. It could be seen initially in the circumstances surrounding *Who Do You Think You Are?* (1978; see Hoy "Rose"), which might well be described in Munro's own phrase, "the dim world of continuing disaster, of home." Munro has, certainly, returned repeatedly to the circumstances surrounding her mother's lingering death—"The Ottawa Valley" (1974), "Home" (1974), "The Progress of Love" (1985), "Friend of My Youth" (1990)—but since her return to Ontario a deepened analysis of the cultural history of her home place has been predominant—seeing her own family's history as derived from, and connected to, the larger history of Huron County, a place first settled in the earlier nineteenth century as the Huron Tract (see Thacker "Connection"; "Writing 'Home'"). The "continuing disaster" Munro has drawn upon in her fiction since *Who Do You Think You Are?* has been less a matter of literal disaster than a sense of, again in Munro's own phrasing, "a devouring muddle"—that is, a recognition that any understanding is contingent, its clarity apparent only, and apt to disappear on further reflection into "sudden holes and impromptu tricks and radiant vanishing consolations" (*Open* 50).

This sense may be seen developing in "Home," Munro's rendering of a trip she made to Wingham in 1973, just after her return to Ontario from British Columbia, to visit her father who was then living with his second wife and suffering from the heart disease to which he succumbed in 1976. One of a handful of pieces Munro published individually but has chosen not to include in a collection, "Home" may be reasonably paired with "The Ottawa Valley," also first published in 1974.[2] It also takes up Munro's mother's illness and in it, like "Home," Munro herself breaks into the narrative to comment metafictionally. At the conclusion to "The Ottawa Valley" she steps back and writes, "If I had been making a proper story out of this, I would have ended it, I think, with my mother not answering and going ahead of me across the pasture." This is the moment when her mother does not respond to the narrator's question, "'Is your arm going to stop shaking?'" "For the first time she held out altogether against me. She went on as if she had not heard, her familiar bulk ahead of me turning strange, indifferent" (*Something* 246, 244).

Throughout "Home," however, Munro is more venturesome with her authorial interjection, punctuating the narrative with italicized authorial second thoughts: "*A problem of the voices, the way people talk, how can it be handled? It sounds like parody if you take it straight, as out of a tape-recorder. My own attitude, too; complicated and unresolved*" (142). Yet these interjections confirm that the memories offered as fiction from the home place are real—that it is actually memoir. Munro's final paragraphs suggest this: "*There was something else I could have worked into an ending*," the narrator writes, "*the setting of the first scene I can establish as a true memory in my life*." Particular details follow: a flight of steps, a black and white cow in 1935, warm clothes, a three-legged milking stool. Then she adds:

> *You can see this scene, can't you, you can see it quietly made, that magic and prosaic safety briefly held for us, the camera moving out and out, that spot shrinking, darkness. Yes. That is effective.*
>
> *I don't want any more effects, I tell you, lying. I don't know what I want. I want to do this with honour, if I possibly can.*
> (152–53, italics in original)

The tension here is palpable. Munro's decision not to collect this story until 2006 owes to her rejection of such metafictional techniques and also because she used the "characters" and situation in "Home" as a basis for Flo and her husband in *Who Do You Think You Are?*, as well as another rendering of her father in "The Moons of Jupiter" (1978). Finally revised and included in a book, *The View From Castle Rock* (2006), "Home" reappears without its metafictional commentary.

This crux, and the evident tension between memory and fiction in "Home," can also be found in "Working for a Living," a memoir about her parents, especially her father, that Munro published in 1981. Its provenance is also indicative of Munro's method, because it was written by Munro just at the point of what might be called her "deep empathy" with her home place, with its well of memories. Munro began "Working for a Living" as a story but, as I have indicated, it became a memoir. In the story version—which exists in a variety of drafts in Munro's papers at the University of Calgary, and which was rejected by the *New Yorker*—the character Janet has an argument with the bursar at the beginning of her final year at university, and rather than compromise as she had in previous years, she leaves school and goes home. Arriving there, she sees it differently through her now-educated eyes, as a place from *Winesburg, Ohio* or a Russian village from Chekhov. Such illusions fade fast, as Janet says:

> I saw my parents' life as a tragedy. I saw it finished off, hopeless. When I read Death of a Salesman, I thought yes, they're like that, they're worse off, if anything. My tragic view of life, and particularly of their life, had an arrogance, a satisfaction about it, that I was quite unable to see. I did not actually back off the hope of improvement (my father getting out of debt, my mother having a miraculous remission); such hopes, such possibilities, never even occurred to me. But when I came home this time I threw myself into that part of life you never see in stage tragedies, rarely read about. While the speeches are being made, the emotions twisted, the truth laid bare, who is keeping the background in order, washing the sheets and towels and sweeping the floor? It seemed essential to me that the tragedy be played out in cleanliness, in comfort, that the piled-up mess disappear from the porch and the torn, dusty plastic curtains be taken down. I housecleaned ferociously and impatiently, kept the incinerator smoking all day, scrubbed down to the bedrock of poverty, which was the torn linoleum and the sheets worn out in the middle. (38.10.36.f8)

Here is Munro, as she has consistently for some time, creating fictional "effects" out of her own experience, and out of her parents' experience. The draft continues with the returned, housecleaning Janet settling back into life in Dalgleish, taking charge at home in view of her mother's illness, getting work, and at one point visiting her father, who was then working in a local foundry.

In the published version of "Working for a Living," Janet is gone. She is replaced by Munro, speaking as herself, matter-of-factly and analytically, beginning: "In the first years of this century there was a notable difference between people who lived on farms and people who lived in country towns and villages" (*Grand Street* 9). Taking up her parents' lives—there is no mistaking here that she is describing her father, Robert E. Laidlaw (1901–1976) and her mother, Anne Chamney Laidlaw (1898–1959)—Munro places them within the social history of early-twentieth-century Huron County and, retrospectively, dissects their lives through representative, though not minute, detail. In transforming "Working for a Living," Munro made something of a "glorious leap" from fiction to memoir, a leap that if not characteristic, seems nevertheless to have been demanded by the facts she presents in the story, facts that accord with the personal family history Munro has told through her fiction: "Connection. That was what it was all about" ("Author's" 125; *Moons* 6). Here, however, a reversal of her usual practice asserts that connection.

Munro places her father within both social and family contexts—there is a great deal of detail about his parents, some of which echoes material seen in such stories as "Chaddeleys and Flemings" (1978–79) and "The Progress of Love"—describing his education through "the Continuation School in Blyth": these were "small high schools, without the final fifth form, now Grade Thirteen; you would have to go to a larger town for that" (10). Her father had, Munro writes,

> a streak of pride posing as humility, making him scared and touchy, ready to bow out, never ask questions. I know it very well. He made a mystery there, a hostile structure of rules and secrets, far beyond anything that really existed. He felt a danger too, of competition, of ridicule. The family wisdom came to him then. Stay out of it. (10–11)

Although he might have gone on in school, Robert Laidlaw did not; instead, during high school "he began to spend more and more days in the bush," and when the time to decide came, "he turned his back on education and advancement. They had the farm; he was the only son, the only child" (11). Even so, he read, and "would certainly have read Fenimore Cooper. So he would have absorbed the myths and half-myths about the wilderness that most country boys did not know" (12). Munro continues, detailing her father's path imaginatively and practically, accounting for his life:

> My father being a Huron County farm boy with the extra, Fenimore-Cooper perception, a cultivated hunger, did not turn aside from the these boyish interests at the age of eighteen, nineteen, twenty. Instead of giving up the bush he took to it more steadily and seriously. He began to be talked about more as a trapper than as a young farmer, and as an odd and lonely character, though not somebody that anyone feared or disliked. He was edging away from the life of a farmer, just as he had edged away earlier from the idea of getting an education and becoming a professional man. He was edging towards a life he probably could not clearly visualize, since he would know what he didn't want so much better than what he wanted. The life in the bush, on the edge of the farms, away from the towns; how could it be managed? (13)

Here Munro is wondering over the same question that informs her meditation on the American novelist Willa Cather in "Dulse," a story she wrote concurrent with "Working." In it, her narrator, Lydia, wonders about Cather: "But was she lucky or was she not, and was it all right with that woman? How did she live?" (*Moons* 58). As with the fictional Lydia's questions about Cather, here, too, Munro is focused on facts: her parents, especially her father, were actual people, not characters. In this way she details her father's move from trapping into fox farming, and the subsequent visit of a

> young woman, ... a cousin on the Irish side, from Eastern Ontario. She was school-teacher, lively, importunate, good-looking, and a couple of years older than he. She was interested in

> the foxes, and not, as his mother thought, pretending to be interested in order to entice him. ... She looked at the foxes and did not see their connection with the wilderness; she saw a new industry, the possibility of riches. She had a little money saved, to help buy a place where all this could get started. She became my mother. (17)

Adept as she is at describing salient human characteristics, Munro's meditation on her parents' characteristics and motives, and her own understanding of each, over time, is detailed, tentative, and ultimately profound. She imagines them as youthful, "helpless, marvelously deceived"—but realizes that she does so as much to imagine herself as a child born out of real rather than "sting" or "half-hearted" affection (17–18). As part of a detailed accounting of her parents' characteristics, Munro focuses on two memories of her own, indicative of each of them, in the balance of "Working for a Living." The first is of her mother's triumph at retailing their best furs at a hotel in Muskoka—Munro and her father drove her there in a rickety automobile that should not have been on the highway, so, she later inferred, her father took back roads as a precaution. He had little money to take on the trip, so they all depended on Munro's mother's success. Through the "gifts she had," Anne Chamney Laidlaw made the money they needed (27). In "those later years" after she had died, Robert Laidlaw

> would speak of my mother's salesmanship, and how she had saved the day, and say that he didn't know what he was going to do, that time, if she hadn't had the money when he got there. 'But she had it,' he said, and the tone in which he said this made me wonder about the reservations [about her mother] I had assumed he shared. Such shame now seems shameful. It would be a relief to me to think he hadn't shared it. (28)

As this episode suggests, things were tight in Laidlaw's fox-farming business, and in 1947 it failed. Munro writes:

> When my father went looking for a job he had to find a night job, because he had to work all day going out of business. He had to pelt all the stock and sell the skins for what he could get, he had to tear down the pens. ... He got a job as a night-watchman at the Foundry, covering the hours from five in the afternoon till ten in the evening. (28, 29)

One evening in 1949, while he is working there, "the last spring, in fact the last whole season, I lived at home, I was riding my old bicycle ... to give a message to my father" at the foundry (28). This visit is the central incident shared by both the fictional and memoir versions of "Working for a Living." In it, Laidlaw gives Munro a tour of the foundry—where she has never been—and she, for her part, realizes the nature of his job there (he mops the floor, for example, something he would never have done at home). Munro moves from this to an account of a practical joke the supervisor played on a worker there, and from that to her father's account of his enjoyment of his work at the foundry: one night, gathered in the caretaker's room, the men discussed the question, "what is the best time in a man's life? When is a person the happiest?" A variety of views were offered. "Then my father said, 'I don't know, I think maybe right now'" (36).

Munro's father also told her about how, when leaving the foundry one night at midnight, he found "a great snowstorm in progress." Leaving his car where it was, he began to walk the two miles home, and when nearly there was stopped by the storm:

> He thought of his death. He would die leaving a sick crippled wife who could not take care of herself, an old mother full of disappointment, a younger daughter whose health had always been delicate, an older girl who was often self-centered and mysteriously incompetent, a son who seemed to be bright and reliable but who was still only a little boy. He would die in debt, and before he had even finished pulling down the [fox] pens; they would be there to show the ruin of his enterprise.

"Was that all you thought about?" I said when he told me this.

"Wasn't that enough?" he said, and went on to tell how he ... had got home.

But I had meant, didn't he think of himself, of the boy who had trapped along the Blyth Creek, and asked for Sign's Snow Paper; the young man about to be married who had cut cedar poles in the swamp to build the first fox-pens; the forty-year-old man who had thought of joining the army? I meant, was his life now something that only other people had a use for? (36–37)

Munro then breaks from the text, and when she takes it up again she unites her parents in a final paragraph to mark them "off, to describe, to illumine" but not at all "to *get rid*" of them (*Something* 246):

> My father always said that he didn't really grow up until he went to work in the Foundry. He never wanted to talk much about the fox-farm, until he was old and could talk easily about anything that had happened. But my mother, as she was being walled in by the increasing paralysis, often wanted to talk about her three weeks at the Pine Tree Hotel, the friend and money she had made there. (37)

Robert Laidlaw and Anne Chamney Laidlaw are here, together, in "Working for a Living." They have been textualized, their daughter's words having caught something of their lives, having imprisoned the essence of who they are—even though they are gone and wondered over yet—in her text.

And yet, as Munro's changes to "Working for a Living" demonstrate, a fictional persona such as Janet is a mask sustained at cost: the illusion that none of this happened, that all of it is fiction, made up—or if portions did happen, they did not occur in just the way invoked by the author. As Munro wrote in "Dulse," "that is what she said to the doctor. But is it the truth?" (*Moons* 55). Around the same time Munro was working on "Dulse," pondering versions of "truth"—fictional, factual, and (given Cather's presence in the story) biographical—she was also working on "Working for a Living." That piece, by collapsing into fact, and by eliding fictional persona, defines the deep empathy at the heart of Munro's fictions, an empathy derived from her intimacy with and long contemplation of her own home place, Huron County, Ontario. Technically, too, "Working for a Living," like "Dulse," shows Munro moving across the putative line between memory and imagination, recreating on the page our connections to people, to places, to memory, to the present moment: that is, the very nexus of identity. Those connections are "what it was all about" in the work of Munro (*Moons* 6); in her words, "this ordinary place is sufficient, everything here touchable and mysterious." For Munro, "here" is "Home," "Home" is Huron County, Ontario.

* * *

A final quotation, one that encapsulates this whole imaginative process. Connection is "what it was all about" in Munro's story by that title: "Chaddeleys and Flemings: 1. Connection." And as she ends that story before taking up her father's side of the family in its second part, "Chaddeleys and Flemings: 2. The Stone in the Field," Munro returns to the image of long-gone people singing—"a mould in which to imprison for a moment the shining, elusive element which is life itself" (Cather, *Song* 254). In the story, the narrator remembers her younger self hearing her mother's visiting cousins, singing together as sleep draws near, "*Row, row, row your boat / Gently down the stream.*" The song, the voices, the people singing in such high spirits: all are clear—until memory fades out like the song itself, like life. "To my surprise—for I am surprised, even through I know the pattern of the rounds—the song is thinning out, you can hear the two voices striving, 'merrily' turning into 'dream,' and then only "one voice alone ... singing on, gamely, to the finish ... *Life is*. Wait. *But a*. Now, wait. *Dream*" (*Moons* 18).

A "Booming Tender Sadness": Alice Munro's Irish (2008)

> But what if the cows in my story were actually cows in Edna O'Brien's rainy fields in County Clair? That is the sort of thing that can happen.
>
> —Alice Munro, "Good Woman in Ireland" (2003)

The August 29, 2005, issue of the *New Yorker* included Alice Munro's piece called "The View From Castle Rock." It was accompanied, as is that magazine's practice, by an apt photograph: in this case, a period image of a group of people, obviously European immigrants, crowded tightly and uncomfortably on the deck of a ship. At the centre of the photograph, a man wearing a bowler hat and suit lies awkwardly on his side, partially wrapped in a blanket, looking away from the camera. Ringed behind him, each staring at the camera, are three young women with shawls over their heads; behind them, also staring our way, are another woman and another man—she also with a shawl, he also with a bowler and a suit. But for the first man looking away, the image looks rather like a family portrait. Perhaps it is, though no one looks formal, or happy. As it was meant to do, this photograph asserts a single, overarching historical context:

immigration.¹ Coming to America, coming to Canada. I'll return to this image.

"The View From Castle Rock" begins with the incident referred to by its title: accompanying his father along with a group of men, a 10-year-old boy named Andrew who is visiting Edinburgh looks out from Castle Rock. This is how Munro describes it:

> It had just stopped raining, the sun is shining on a silvery stretch of water far ahead of them, and beyond that is a pale green and grayish-blue land, a land as light as mist, sucked into the sky.
>
> 'America,' his father tells them, and one of the men says that you would never have known it was so near.

Ignoring comments made by the others, the father continues, "'So there you are, my lad'—he turns to Andrew—'and God grant that one day you will live to see it closer, and I will myself, if I live.'" Munro ends this scene with a characteristic narrative corrective before heading her reader into the story proper:

> Andrew has an idea that there is something wrong with what his father is saying, but he is not well enough acquainted with geography to know that they are looking at Fife. He does not know if the men are mocking his father or if his father is playing a trick on them. Or if it is a trick at all.
>
> Some years later, in the harbor of Leith, on the fourth of June, 1818, Andrew and his father—whom I must call Old James, because there is a James in every generation—and Andrew's pregnant wife, Agnes, his brother Walter, his sister Mary, and also his son James, who is not yet two years old, set foot on board a ship for the first time in their lives. ("View" 65)

The family name of these people is Laidlaw, and so, although the *New Yorker* ran "The View From Castle Rock" as fiction, in it Munro is narrating the story of her Scots ancestors who left Ettrick in 1818 to immigrate to Canada. She has surviving letters to guide her, but, typically, she has imagined much of the detail of the voyage across.

This was not the first time Munro had written about the emigration of her father's people from Scotland to America. She is herself descended from another Laidlaw brother, William, who remained in Scotland when the others left in 1818 and did not immigrate until 1836, and then to Illinois. She tells this story in "Changing Places," an essay she published in 1997. She has also used parts of it in her fiction, in "Chaddeleys and Flemings: 2. The Stone in the Field," for instance, and in "A Wilderness Station." Nor will it be the last time she takes up this subject, given that *The View from Castle Rock* is the projected title (it used to be *The Power in the Blood*) of her next book, due to be published in the fall of 2006. Along with "The View From Castle Rock," that book is to include two of Munro's most powerful meditations on her family connections, "Home" (1974) and "Working for a Living" (1981). Though published some time ago and little known, neither has been included in one of Munro's books. *The View from Castle Rock* is the book about her family she has been thinking of doing since the late 1970s—and I am one who is glad that these older fugitive family pieces will be included in one of Munro's books.

Munro's maternal ancestors, the Chamneys and the Codes, immigrated to eastern Ontario—then Upper Canada—about the same time as the Laidlaws left Scotland, around 1820. Irish-Protestant farmers from County Wicklow, they settled in an area called, ironically, Scotch Corners. They farmed marginal land between the Canadian Shield and the St. Lawrence River, raised their families, and lived among a larger extended family. They were poor, poorer than the Laidlaws in Huron County that Munro's mother married into, and Munro has said that they respected themselves (see Thacker, *Writing* 19–25, 32–36).

The immigrant voyage across the Atlantic in "The View From Castle Rock" was also not the first time Munro imagined such a voyage. She did so in "1847: The Irish," a story she was commissioned to research and write as part of a CBC-TV series called *The Newcomers/Les arrivants*. The film based on Munro's script was broadcast in January 1978, and the next year it appeared in narrative form as a story—now called "A Better Place Than Home"—in a collection based on the whole series. But unlike "Changing Places" or "The View From Castle Rock," Munro's first version of an immigrant story does not appear to be based on her own family's story. Rather, it is very much a part of the shift in subject matter that characterized Munro's work after she returned to Ontario from British Columbia in the fall of 1973. This shift was brought about by Munro's imaginative confrontation with the legacies of her family inheritances, seen in a new light brought about by her return to Ontario, a recognized writer in her early 40s. The shift can be seen especially in three family-focused stories she wrote in late 1973, when she was living in London and visiting Wingham with some regularity, owing to her father's declining health. "Home" and "Winter Wind" focus on her father, his mother, and his aunt, but "The Ottawa Valley"—arguably one of the most critical stories, if not *the* critical story, in Munro's *oeuvre*—focuses on Munro's maternal relatives and on her recollections of the onset of her mother's Parkinson's disease. That story is based on a long visit she made, with her mother and sister during the summer of 1943, to her Irish-Protestant relatives in Lanark County; there, during that visit, the 11- or 12-year-old Alice Laidlaw first realized the import of the symptoms of the disease that would eventually kill her mother, after a near 20-year struggle.

She also recalls some of the characteristics of these relatives living in Scotch Corners near Carleton Place in the Ottawa Valley. In the story, there is a character named Uncle James who, the narrator notes, had "kept the Irish accent my mother had lost and [her cousin] had halfway lost. His voice was lovely, saying the children's names. Mar-ie, Ron-ald, Ru-thie. So tenderly, comfortingly, reproachfully he said their names, as if the names, or the children themselves, were jokes played on him." This character is based on her mother's brother John, who would have had five of his six children by the summer of 1943. Coming home in a car from some event with this family, the narrator reports that

> unexpectedly, Uncle James began to sing. He had a fine voice of course, a fine sad, lingering voice. I can remember perfectly well the tune of the song he sang, and the sound of his voice rolling out the black windows [of the car], but I can remember only bits of the words, here and there, though I have often tried to remember more, because I liked the song so well. *As I was a-goen over Kil-i-kenny Mountain* ... I think that was the way it

started. Then further along something about *pearly*, or *early* and *Some take delight in*—various things, and finally the strong but sad-sounding line: *But I take delight in the water of the barley.*

As Uncle James sings, all in the car listen: "nobody broke the singing, its booming tender sadness" (*Something* 233, 237–38).

Uncle James's singing is but an image in "The Ottawa Valley," a story that is focused sharply on the mother and her illness: "it is to reach her that this whole journey has been undertaken," Munro writes in her well-known metafictional critique, the coda that ends the story. And so Uncle James with the Irish accent, the Irish lilt to his voice, the Irish songs he sings, is, in the end, like one of "the brownish snapshots with fancy borders that my parents' old camera used to take" (246). Yet by describing him in a succession of images—speaking, singing, and reciting a poem just before the story ends—his character lives on with its "booming tender sadness," his presence an imagistic detail within the imagined recollection that is "The Ottawa Valley."

These images of Uncle James take me back to the *New Yorker*'s image of shipboard immigrants looking variously away or toward the camera as their snapshot was taken. Although the magazine's editors were merely finding an appropriate image to accompany Munro's "The View From Castle Rock," they were also (probably knowingly) following her own aesthetic—this is a writer who very often begins with an image that has caught her eye and then strives to figure out what that image means, working out "the rest of the story." Such an image begins "The View From Castle Rock," with Andrew, his father, and the others looking out at Fife. These images strike Munro at her heart, as she wrote in her introduction to the paperback edition of her *Selected Stories* (1997), and thus are at the centre of her art. In that introduction, she describes an image she saw from the window of the Wingham Public Library when she was about 15—a man with his horses in swirling snow "carelessly revealed." Munro describes this scene as giving her "something like a blow to the chest." Once the moment had passed "it was more a torment than a comfort to think about this [scene] because I couldn't get hold of it at all" (Introduction xvi–xvii).

Having defined these contexts for understanding Munro's Irish heritage, I want now to take up "A Better Place Than Home," the narrative version of Munro's television script, "1847: The Irish." The television script was shot during the summer of 1977 and broadcast early in 1978, which means Munro would have been researching and writing the script around 1975 and 1976 (according to W. Paterson Ferns in a letter to Munro dated January 4, 1977; 37.2.31). What interests me most about this project is that Munro accepted it and worked on it just as she had returned not only to Ontario, but also to Huron County; she had moved to Clinton from London by September 1975. This was the same time during which she was working on "Places at Home" and, after that project was abandoned, on the stories that were published in *Who Do You Think You Are?*, as well as the three family-related stories held out of that book and published in *The Moons of Jupiter* (1982): "Chaddeleys and Flemings" (two parts) and "The Moons of Jupiter" (see Thacker, *Writing* Chapter 6, *passim*). What this means, both biographically and in relation to Munro's development as a writer, is that her return to Ontario and Huron County saw her confronting, after over 20 years away, the facts of her home place, the absences of relatives and others who had been there when she left in 1951 (though her recollection of them was strong), and, with her research for "1847: The Irish," the historical contexts of her mother's ancestors. As I have argued elsewhere, when Munro returned to Ontario she was, quite truthfully, unsure about just what she would write, or even if she would write (Thacker, *Writing* 265). Seen this way, the research for her Irish project confirmed a new, research-based direction she would subsequently take in some of her stories. "Dulse" (1980) required her to research the life of Willa Cather, and in "Meneseteung" (1988) the narrator is researching the life and circumstances of Almeda Roth, putatively an historical figure. Indeed, it is quite possible to see that narrator as Munro herself as she researched "1847: The Irish."

In an undated Munro typescript called "Notes on treatment" in Munro's papers at the University of Calgary, she offers an overview of what she was researching and writing:

> I see this story as paralleling pretty well the experiences of the
> Irish immigrants of that time—the traumatic beginning, the

bewildering and difficult struggles, the nearly paralyzing disappointments (James' death), then the slow prosaic adjustment and absorption into the country's life. There can't be any spectacular 'making it' in the new land because the Irish usually didn't get that far. They remained mostly working class, lower middle-class, or self-sufficient farmers. (Never mind Timothy Eaton)[.] But this woman, speaking in 1900, would see her family's survival, their modest occupations, as a source of great pride and satisfaction.

Here, too, she gives us a glimpse of her methods. She has been reading emigrant letters, writing that "all the letters are quite sufficiently changed from the originals, all place names, names, times, factual details are changed, but the outline, the whole development of the story is not changed." Earlier, explaining the details and events she uses in her description of the Atlantic crossing, Munro writes:

> Uneatable ship's stores, unseaworthy ship, desperate, ill-prepared, sickly passengers, the familiarity with death, terrifying inroads of the fever, the despair of those taken to the quarantine sheds on Grosse Isle. The details such as the showing of the tongue, the dead baby, are true. (37.20.4.2.f1–2)

The story Munro tells is that of James and Mary, a young married couple with two small children in Ireland. (They are Catholic—Munro has told me that the board of historians who vetted the script for the CBC insisted that the characters be Roman Catholic, another detail at variance with Munro's circumstances.) Having failed in business there, James books passage to Quebec, leaving Mary and the children with her father, an Irish merchant whose fortunes have not slipped. Mary wants to follow James to Upper Canada as soon as possible but her father, against that plan, takes some time before he relents and allows her to go. James, meanwhile, has a rough passage alongside other immigrants, seeing horrific poverty, near-starvation, and many deaths from cholera among his fellow passengers. Not ill himself, he is allowed ashore and travels to Brantford, where, as fate has it, he arrives to find that the sponsor he was seeking has just died. He attends the man's wake, drinks and eats a great deal, and leaves to find a job working on a gang building a road between Brantford and London. Receiving word that Mary and the children are coming, he heads east to meet their ship at Quebec, stopping in Montreal to pick up some work before the ship arrives. Mary arrives but James never appears, so she travels to her sister's near Chatham and waits. It takes some time, but eventually she learns that James has died in Montreal of the cholera before she travelled through Montreal herself. Unable to face a return voyage back home, she stays and ends up marrying a bachelor neighbour of her sister and brother-in-law's in Chatham, remaining there for the rest of her life.

So far as I know, Munro's script has not survived, but there are drafts of her transformation of "1847: The Irish" into "A Better Place Than Home," including two that are reasonably complete. In the first, Munro appears to be ending the story with James just off the ship, wondering how to come to terms with the horrible scenes that he's just seen aboard the ship:

> He would carry the memory under his daily life, not speaking of it, but always knowing it was there, just as he knew what was under the boards of the this deck. But even as he thought this he thought he might forget[,] and that might be how people managed, passing from dreams to waking and waking to dreams, and life to death, forgetting. (37.20.11.f19)

The second draft contains the ending Munro opted for, focusing on Mary after she's learned and digested the news of James's death, and after the neighbour has begun to indicate his interest in her and his intentions:

> Over at the wood pile, Henry Norris was splitting logs, with Elsie's husband. Mary took the sheet [she was folding] away from her face and looked at him. He was strong still, with the axe. He was gentle with her children. He would be good to them even when he had his own children, because he was a just

man. The wedding ring she wore had been loose on her finger for a long time. It was easy to slide it off, into her apron pocket.

Her name would be Mary Norris. She would stay here, she would die here. She would change from the person she was into someone she could not imagine, another man's wife, and would put those letters [from James] away where she could not look at them until she was old, so old they couldn't trouble her, and with so much life between her and them she would read them like a story. ("Better" 124, see 37.20.12.f19)

As Munro indicated in her treatment notes for the script, in the film this scene was explicitly placed in 1900, as Mary looks back on her life in Canada and at her family's successes there. Here in the printed version—"she would read" James's letters "like a story"—Munro may be seen doing what would become a characteristic technique once she returned to Ontario: telescoping a character's life, often at the end of a story, though not always just there, into a few sentences or a paragraph. This technique can be seen throughout *Who Do You Think You Are?* In "The Beggar Maid," for instance, Munro tells the reader everything about Rose and Patrick— their meeting, romance, marriage, life together, divorce—in a short space. In "Accident," she writes as the story ends of Frances, whose whole life was defined by the central accident of the title: "She's had her love, her scandal, her man, her children. But inside she's ticking away, all by herself, the same Frances who was there before any of it. Not altogether the same, surely. The same" (*Moons* 109). In "Miles City, Montana," in the midst of the recollection of the family vacation that makes up most of the story, the narrator abruptly announces that she hasn't seen Andrew, the husband with whom she had just been quarrelling, "for years, don't know if he is still thin, has gone completely gray, insists on lettuce, tells the truth, or is hearty and disappointed" (*Progress* 92). One reviewer called this a "single sentence, lacerating paragraph" (Thacker, *Writing* 438), and it is, so abrupt is its effect in piercing the moment Munro has so carefully constructed.

To conclude, though I am not ultimately claiming a great deal for Munro's treatment of her Irish inheritances, as I said at the beginning and as "The View From Castle Rock" again demonstrates, Munro has treated her Scots ancestors in greater detail and in a most sustained fashion. That conceded, "1847: The Irish" and "A Better Place Than Home," coming as they did at a critical moment in Munro's career, played a part in the transformation of Munro's art as she returned to Ontario, and to Huron County, after over 20 years in British Columbia. Though not focused on her own Irish ancestors, Munro's research into the mid-nineteenth-century Irish exodus from Ireland helped contextualize the images she was happening upon in Ontario in the 1970s and that she subsequently fashioned into stories. Her research was also a template for that researching narrator in "Meneseteung," who in researching Almeda Roth is "reading microfilm, just in the hope of seeing this trickle in time, making a connection, rescuing one thing from the rubbish" (*Friend* 73). This image was borne, I am sure, from Munro's experiences researching "1847: The Irish" and "A Better Place Than Home," and, as here, its effects are felt throughout the balance of her work.

A final, final word: speaking of rubbish, there may be reason to hope that Munro will return more explicitly to her Irish ancestry: In a recent essay, "Good Woman in Ireland," Munro recounts the circumstances in which she discarded a version of "The Love of a Good Woman" (1996) when she was staying in Carrigadrohid, on the River Lee, in County Cork. Her dissatisfaction with that version of the story derived, she writes, from changes she had made to it while she was staying in Ireland: the problems

> had all to do with something I would have to call tone. Something unmistakable but hard to define. And yet I knew now where that had come from. It had come from Irish stories, from William Trevor and Edna O'Brien and Frank O'Connor and Mary Lavin, all of whom I had read for decades, long before I went to Ireland, and whom I was not reading during that particular time in their country. I was not reading them but I was seeing through them, through their eyes and their words.

Munro discarded her story and, once home, found an earlier version of it, written before the changes, and so she decided, she wrote, to "fetch everything back" (Good Woman 30). Munro did, and it has made all the difference, Munro being no one but Munro.

No Problem Here: A Review of *Too Much Happiness* (2009)

Munro's Latest Continues, Extends, Returns, Surprises

Too Much Happiness
Alice Munro
McClelland & Stewart
A Douglas Gibson Book, 2009.

When Alice Munro's recent collection, *The View From Castle Rock*, appeared in 2006, some of its reviews contained an intriguing echo of the critique Willa Cather received from Granville Hicks and Lionel Trilling in the 1930s. These two titans aimed gloves-off assessments at Cather, even though she was arguably the leading American novelist of the 1920s. Hicks accused her of having "fallen into supine romanticism because of a refusal to examine life as it is" (147). Trilling wrote that it "has always been a personal failure of [Cather's] talent that prevented her from involving her people in truly dramatic relations with each other" (155). Cather's response, a feisty and pointed collection of essays titled *Not Under Forty*, did not prevent Hicks' and Trilling's critiques from having staying power: Cather's art was familiar in the public mind and not, emphatically, what they felt was needed then.

This is similar to the reception given to *The View from Castle Rock*. Wrongly assuming that this would be Munro's last book, Stephen

Henighan, writing in the *Times Literary Supplement*, surveys Munro's career, damns with faint praise, and niggles over Canadian references, and concludes, sadly, that the collection's two "best" stories are "not the ending for which Alice Munro would have wished." Likewise, in a 2007 essay entitled "The Problem with Alice Munro," Philip Marchand asserts that Munro's "problem" is that "she has been so true to the world she has chosen to depict." He writes, "The horizons ... are uniformly low, due partly to the absence of characters whose education, experience and character might enable them to expand those horizons." Noting "the sad paltriness of her world," Marchand wonders if "the limitations of her world have to correlate so closely to the limitations of her art" (13–14).

Munro's recent Man Booker International Prize—now foremost among the many attentions she has garnered abroad—makes such Canadian considerations seem, well, so provincial. That these critics feel free to complain of Munro's limitations—however tentatively—is another indication of the strides Canadian writing has made during Munro's career. Her life as a writer in this country is in many ways an allegory of Canadian publishing since the Second World War—exposure on the CBC, publication in small and commercial Canadian magazines in the 1950s and 1960s, a first book with Ryerson Press in 1968, second and third books with McGraw-Hill Ryerson, and a move to Macmillan to work with Douglas Gibson and then, following him, to McClelland and Stewart for *The Progress of Love* and the many books since. As well, her publication during the late 1970s in the *New Yorker* and with Alfred A. Knopf brought significant international attention. "She's our Chekhov," the American writer Cynthia Ozick famously proclaimed. "Ours," you say? Her writing is too familiar, however seamless. Nothing surprising here. Quite naturally, they want to move on.

Too Much Happiness is Munro's thirteenth collection. All of its 10 stories have been published previously in either the *New Yorker* or *Harper's*. The long title story, "Too Much Happiness"—stunning and shining—appeared in the August 2009 edition of *Harper's*. Consistent with her practice, all have been revised for *Too Much Happiness*, and one, "Wood," her fifth *New Yorker* story, published there in 1980 and uncollected until now, has been added to and reshaped—which is unsurprising for an intuitive artist who never feels her stories are complete.

Throughout *Too Much Happiness*, echoes of earlier stories abound, and there is darkness everywhere: a horrific violence occurs in the first pages; there are random, accidental, and premeditated injuries and deaths; a husband dies suddenly, collapsing in front of a hardware store; an adolescent child disappears, never to be found; while another narrator recounts the effects of his facial birthmark on his life. Munro never repeats earlier stories; she extends, she probes, she develops. She does so now from the perspective of a person who has thought deeply about what she has seen and felt. "I am amazed sometimes to think how old I am," she begins the story "Some Women." In "Fiction," one of the *Harper's* stories and one that is reminiscent of Munro's important early "Material," a young— perhaps too young—writer, a woman whom the protagonist knew and taught music to as a child, publishes a book of short stories called "How Are We to Live." That title, abounding with irony, could well describe Munro's entire *oeuvre*. How, indeed? Through fiction and through personal fictions—what we know, what we remember, what we choose to believe, what we think we know.

The answer, for Munro, lies in writing stories. As she has asserted, she wants to discover "the rest of the story" herself. Meditating on such matters, in "Fiction" Munro records her narrator realizing: "here was where the writer would graft her ugly invention onto the people and the situation she had got out of real life, being too lazy to invent but not to malign" (*Too* 56). The core incident in the story happened years ago—marriages and lives have come and gone—but there it still is, glowing with meaning through both memory and being fictionalized. Tellingly, Munro's protagonist notes that "How Are We to Live" is a "collection of stories, not a novel." This "seems to diminish the book's authority, making the author seem like somebody who is just hanging on to the gates of Literature, rather than safely settled inside" (*Too* 49–50). So, too, has Munro been seen throughout her career. Just short stories. Like Chekhov.

In "Face," one of the several stories in the collection capturing an entire life, the narrator returns to his childhood home, which appears to be in Goderich, Ontario, intending to clean the place up and sell it, then return to Toronto. He recounts the critical childhood events that animated his family relationships—the reactions of friends and family members to his prominent facial birthmark—and describes a recent and especially vivid dream in which part of a poem by Walter de la Mare, a poem he does not know, is recited to him by an unknown person who may be a long-gone childhood playmate. This confirms his decision to change his plans and stay in the old place. He thinks: "Something happened here. In your life there are a few places, or maybe only the one place, where something happened, and then there are all the other places" (*Too* 162).

Munro knows this well, having herself returned to Huron County in 1975 to start a new life at home. That return in many ways made her art, as she acknowledges. But as if to invert present expectations—that she offers "only" the Huron County culture, about which Marchand complains—Munro closes her new book with "Too Much Happiness." As with Cather turning to a different historical era, Munro, too, turns toward something utterly new: a detailed telling of the final weeks—in 1891—in the life of the well-known mathematician Sophia Kovalevsky. It is stunning and shining, but it contains no mention of Canada or Huron County, nor has it any of the character types we have come to expect from Munro. Instead, toward the story's end we see Kovalevsky—little more than 40, ill, and taken to her deathbed—murmuring "too much happiness" and thinking about a story she planned to write: "Her hope was that in this piece of writing she would discover what went on. Something underlying. Invented, but not" (*Too* 301). Exactly. The discovery of lives inside an inner place. Like Munro's, like Chekhov's. There is never too much happiness in such writing. After all these years, Munro still surprises. No problem here.

"The Way the Skin of the Moment Can Break Open": Reading Alice Munro's "White Dump" (2010)

On November 1, 1977—after Alice Munro had published two stories in the *New Yorker*, "Royal Beatings" and "The Beggar Maid"—her editor at the magazine, Charles McGrath, wrote to tell her that they had decided against "Chaddeleys and Flemings." It was a long, two-part story that ultimately became the opening of Munro's *The Moons of Jupiter* (1982). William Shawn—the longest-serving editor of the *New Yorker* and still the least understood person to hold that position—had overruled McGrath and the other fiction editors, who were in favour of printing the story. Shawn believed, McGrath wrote, that "we should publish less reminiscence and less autobiographical fiction," and Shawn felt the piece "read more like straight reminiscence than a story." Distancing himself from the decision, McGrath continued, writing, "I don't know whether it's autobiographical or not, but it's my feeling that you've taken the material of reminiscence and turned it into something much stronger—a moving, complicated work of fiction" (37.2.30.5). So saying, McGrath perceived and defined *the* great critical fact of Munro's writing at a critical moment (and perhaps *the* critical moment) of her career: that her stories' most powerful effects derive, in some sense, from a reader's sense that this is too real to be fiction, that this is real life. Reading her stories, we sense that all this may have happened.

Though certainly not overly concerned about her fiction's autobiographical underpinnings—she has long admitted that "there is always a starting point in reality" and once published an essay entitled "What is Real?"—Munro is herself well aware of this issue. In *The View From Castle Rock* (2006) she decided to include three patently autobiographical pieces that she had published before but had held from including in any book of hers. Perhaps as a consequence, Munro directly addressed the question of reminiscence versus fiction in a foreword for the book, explaining her hesitation about the three pieces—"Home" (1974), "Working for a Living" (1981), and "Hired Girl" (1994):

> In other first-person stories I had drawn on personal material, but then I did anything I wanted to do with this material. Because the chief thing I was doing was making a story. In the stories I hadn't collected I was not doing exactly that. I was doing something closer to what a memoir does—exploring a life, my own life, but not in an austere or rigorously factual way. I put myself in the center and wrote about that self, as searchingly as I could. But the figures around this self took on their own life and color and did things they had not done in reality.

Munro concludes by asserting that, considerations of autobiography and memoir notwithstanding, "these are *stories*" (*View* x).

Well, yes. But it is not so simple as that, as I have argued in *Alice Munro: Writing Her Lives*. I wish to continue those considerations here by looking at the two stories that bookend *The Progress of Love* (1986)—the title story, briefly, and, at greater length, "White Dump" (1986), because the two together are indicative of the direction in which Munro was moving in the 1980s. Just as McGrath wrote when he rejected "Chaddeleys and Flemings," she was creating "moving, complicated work[s] of fiction" from what she calls "personal material." But however Munro's argument in the foreword of *The View From Castle Rock* is understood after so long a career drawing upon her own life for the purposes of her fiction, hers are stories daunting in their verisimilitude. Well aware that in Munro he had "discovered"—for American and British audiences, at least—a genuinely special writer, McGrath wrote to Virginia Barber, Munro's agent, on December 13, 1984, telling Barber that "she is simply one of the finest short story writers alive, and it's a great honor and privilege for us to be able to publish her" (396/87.3.2a.1). To Munro herself—who has frequently produced finished stories in clumps, with great productivity followed by empty spells—McGrath had written a few months earlier that "you're sending in these stories faster than I can edit them, and each one is more dazzling than the last. I feel the way Rilke's editor must have felt—if he had one" (October 15, 1984: 396/87.3.2.13).

The stories McGrath was dealing with then became *The Progress of Love*, Munro's strongest collection. Of its 11 stories, the *New Yorker* first published five—the others were placed elsewhere after McGrath and his colleagues had declined them. In his letter to Munro, he refers to three of those they had decided on: "Lichen" (1985), "Miles City, Montana" (1985), and "The Moon in the Orange Street Skating Rink" (1986). The final two they took—"The Progress of Love" (1985) and "White Dump"—became, respectively, the opening and closing stories of *The Progress of Love*, anchoring the volume. Each of these stories takes up a trio of women—daughter, mother, and grandmother—as a way of examining "the progress of love" through the generations. Paired together, these two stories both look back at what Munro had done in her previous work and look forward toward the works she would produce during the 1990s and after. When McGrath wrote Barber in June of 1985 to accept "White Dump," he called it "one of Alice's very best. The writing is stunning throughout, and the story performs something like a little miracle there at the end when it pulls all those different threads so beautifully together" (June 25, 1985: 396/87.3.2a.1).

"The Progress of Love"—a story whose title, Magdalene Redekop has noted, both echoes that of a poem by Swift ("Phillis, Or, The Progress of Love") and offers the image of life as a parade (*Mothers* 175)—is among Munro's most caustic examinations of familial inheritance, passed down through the generations. It begins with the narrator—who goes by the nickname "Fame," from her given name, Euphemia—recalling a phone call from her father telling her the news of her mother's death. The story becomes a meditation on mothers and daughters, and a comparison of the lives of three women—including Fame. Fame's mother, Marietta, was fervently religious ("My mother prayed on her knees at midday, at night, and first thing in the morning. Every day opened up to her to have God's will done in it. Every night she totted up what she'd done and said and thought, to see how it squared with Him" [*Progress* 4]). Marietta carried a deep hatred for her father, a womanizer and gadabout who mistreated her mother. Justification for Marietta's hatred derives from a central scene— serious but also comic—in which her mother prepares to hang herself because of her husband's behaviour. The young Marietta awakens one sunny Saturday morning to discover her mother out in the barn, standing on a chair, a noose around her neck; Marietta's mother tells her to "go and get your father." ("That was what her mother told her to do, and Marietta obeyed. With terror in her legs, she ran. In her nightgown, in the middle of a Saturday morning, she ran" [*Progress* 11].) Marietta never forgot this, especially not the reasons why her mother thought it necessary to threaten suicide, so when her father dies she not only refuses his bequest to her, she converts it to cash and burns it in the family stove. ("'That's a lot of hate,'" one of Fame's friends comments when she tells him about it [*Progress* 26].)

For years, Fame saw this act—the burning of the inherited money— as something her parents did together as an act of mutual support ("A solemn scene, but not crazy" [*Progress* 30]). But over the course of the story she realizes that her mother had gotten the money, taken it home, and burned it herself, alone, as a proprietary act; that is, without her father's knowledge, presumably fearing his objection. Fame not only realizes—just as her own mother has died—that she had it wrong all these years, but also that neither her parents burning the money together, an image that had comforted her, nor her mother burning the money alone are things she approves of herself. Later, Munro telescopes a moment of shared understanding that Fame has with a former lover onto the relationship between her parents and, implicitly, between her grandparents, writing at the end of "The Progress of Love":

> Moments of kindness and reconciliation are worth having, even
> if the parting has to come sooner or later. I wonder if those

moments aren't more valued, and deliberately gone after, in the setups some people like myself have now, than they were in those old marriages, where love and grudges could be growing underground, so confused and stubborn, it must have seemed they had forever. (*Progress* 30–31)

"The Progress of Love" is a *tour de force* for its multigenerational cast and its explicit use of an autobiographical context. Fame's situation is modelled, with some adaptations, on Munro's relationship to her mother, but more significantly the story echoes the experiences of Munro's maternal grandmother and great-grandmother in the Ottawa Valley—the womanizing great-grandfather and his religious daughter were among Munro's ancestors. Arguably, such probing of family-based relationships has been a constant in Munro's work from the beginning—each of her previous books contains stories that use autobiographical and ancestral material. Yet with "The Progress of Love"—both the story and the entire collection of the same name—there is a new-found distancing and shaping, what McGrath apprehended as heading toward "a moving, complicated work of fiction."

* * *

Less frequently noted than the title story, "White Dump" is an equally powerful rendering that includes autobiographical touches without explicit personal prototype and is an apt pairing to "The Progress of Love" with its daughter-mother-grandmother comparison. Prior to writing it, Munro had published stories in which adultery was central, but with "White Dump" she signals that the subject would become of particular significance in her subsequent writing—at one point in the putting together of *The Progress of Love* she suggested "White Dump" as the book's title, and subsequently included it in her *Selected Stories* (1996). Its situation and concerns anticipate such other stories as "The Children Stay" (1997), "The Love of a Good Woman" (1996), and "My Mother's Dream" (1998). As McGrath wrote to Barber when accepting it, "White Dump" ends with "something like a little miracle," as its threads are brought together in the story's conclusion. As well, more than other of Munro stories, "White

Dump" is replete with phrases that, in context, strike to the heart of her characters and their most important concerns.

The story focuses on a late summer visit by Denise to her father and stepmother at their cottage in the Ottawa Valley. Denise runs a Women's Centre in Toronto: "She gets beaten women into shelters, finds doctors and lawyers for them, goes after private and public money, makes speeches, hold meetings, deals with varied and sometimes dangerous mix-ups of life. She makes less money than a clerk in a government liquor store" (*Progress* 276). Denise has steeled herself for this visit—listening to Mozart in the car on the way up—to avoid arguing with her father, Laurence, who "owns a small factory," and baits her over issues that highlight their contrasting politics. On this day, however, Denise's "resolve has held. She has caught the twinkle of the bait but has been able to slip past, a clever innocent-seeming fish." (*Progress* 275, 277). Instead, when his wife and daughter are discussing "various details of house renovation," Laurence "speaks abruptly to Denise," asking "'How is your mother?'" "'Fine,' says Denise. 'As far as I know, fine.' Isabel lives far away, in the Comox Valley, in British Columbia" (277).

With this question and this answer, Munro moves from the visit and the frictions between Denise and Laurence over politics to her real subject: the moment when, years before, while Denise and her brother were children, their mother resolved to act on the sudden attraction she felt for a man she happened to meet. She did, with cataclysmic consequences for the family, subsequently sundered because of her act. Munro focuses not on the affair or the breakup but rather on the moment when Isabel first knew she would step out of her marriage. She does this by recalling another visit to this same cottage during the summer of 1969, "the year of the moon shot. The moon shot was actually just a couple days after" Denise gave her father a plane ride for his fortieth birthday. She had heard her father say that he wished he could look at "this country from a thousand feet up" (278). But for one, the whole family went up in the plane, including Laurence's mother, Sophie, who was still alive then. Isabel, however, did not go up. The plane was a five-seater, and "'somebody had to bow out, so she did,'" Laurence explains; he also told the pilot that day that "'sitting by herself is my wife's greatest pleasure'" (303).

Isabel does, of course, ultimately "bow out" "by herself" as a consequence of this incident—the affair she entered into was with the pilot of the plane that day in 1969, just before the moon shot, a person Isabel would never have met had Denise not decided to give her father the flight as a gift. Munro recreates the personalities and circumstances of each family member that day in 1969, detailing the day's events as all were engaged in preparations for the celebration of Laurence's fortieth birthday. In particular, Munro details the history of Sophie who, 40 years before, had borne Laurence out of wedlock, impregnated by a married professor when she was a graduate student. Munro also has Sophie suddenly appearing before her family, stark naked, as the birthday celebrations begin that morning. She wishes her son, who is shocked and appalled at this sight, a happy birthday and then explains that some hippies had come along during her morning swim and destroyed her bathrobe while she was in the lake.

However, any recounting of plot and character details from "White Dump" misses its most powerful effects, which derive from the way Munro constructs the story, its sense of time, its pacing. That construction, and also a succession of startling, otherworldly images, directly evoked, lend the story its especial power. Each image captures the sense of wonder that is, ultimately, Munro's actual subject—in this case, in the "miracle" that is the "White Dump." With the moon shot, Munro conveys people's sense of wonder as they witness a never-before-seen event—Munro develops this sense of wonder within the family through this event. Analogous to this event, smaller but perhaps equally important in the family, is the plane ride down the Rideau Lakes where, among other things, they see a "glint lake"—that is, a lake that straddles the geologic transition from the St. Lawrence Lowlands to the Canadian Shield (*Progress* 304). A "glint," of course, is also something seen in someone's eye as she looks amorously toward a promising lover. Such a glint is part the critical moment in this story. The "white dump" is first referred to toward the end of the story, once Isabel has resolved to connect with the pilot. During dinner on his birthday, Laurence tells Isabel that they "'saw the silica quarry from the air ... It was like a snowfield.'" Isabel replies that when she went to school "we used to have the White Dump" where, because the school property backed onto that of a biscuit factory, every now and then, they'd sweep up these quantities of vanilla icing and nuts and hardened marshmellow globs and they'd bring it in barrels and dump it back there and it would shine. It would shine like a pure white mountain. Over at the school, somebody would see it and yell, "White Dump!" and after school we'd all climb over the fence or run around. We'd all be over there, scrabbing away at that enormous pile of white candy. ... It was like a kid's dream—the most wonderful promising thing you could ever see. (*Progress* 306)

Munro is likening the sweetness Isabel saw in the White Dump to the sweetness she feels in her attraction to the pilot. However, other than telling us that Isabel has remarried and is far away in British Columbia, and that Laurence has also remarried, Munro's focus remains largely on the family's activities on Laurence's fortieth birthday in 1969. Mid-story, she shifts to an incident that occurred late the next summer, 1970, recalled from Denise's point of view. While Denise, her brother, and their father were making lunch, a woman came to the door asking for Isabel; after being told that Isabel was not there, the woman agrees to see Laurence, who takes her into a private room. The woman, who runs a catering business and had made Laurence's birthday cake the year before, is the wife of the pilot who took the family—except for Isabel—up in his plane. The interview proved to be a long one, and while Denise and her brother wait for their father to return to their lunch preparations, they listen to "the terrible sound of a stranger crying in their house" (287). Having offered this fact, Munro immediately flashes back to the cockpit of the plane when the pilot, conversationally, tells of a time when, flying, he reached out toward the plane's windshield and "flames came shooting out of my fingers. ... Little blue flames. One time in a thunderstorm. That's what they call St. Elmo's fire." Listening, a year later, to "the spurts of sound coming out of the dining room made her [Denise] remember ... the pilot with cold blue fire shooting out of his fingertips, and that seemed a sign of pain, though he had said he didn't feel anything" (*Progress* 287–88).

Ending a book entitled *The Progress of Love*, Munro's "White Dump" recreates both the inevitability of passion and the psychological effects of deep and longtime intimacy. Running through the text are numerous details of Isabel and Laurence's intimate life—they make love the morning of Laurence's birthday before the children troop into the room to begin the celebrations; there are details regarding Laurence's proprietary tending of Isabel's body and particularly her tan, in which he relishes. As the story moves toward its conclusion, Munro shifts the chronology to intertwine both Isabel's impending affair and her ongoing sexual connection to Laurence. As these considerations swirl in the reader's mind, Munro writes of Isabel's feelings after the group thanks the pilot and says goodbye:

> When they were walking toward the car, she had to make an effort not to turn around. She imagined that [she and the pilot] turned at the same time, they looked at each other, just as in some romantic movie, operatic story, high-school fantasy. They turned at the same time, they looked at each other, they exchanged a promise that was no less real though they might never meet again. And the promise hit her like lightning, though she moved on smoothly, intact.

Munro follows this with: "But, it isn't like lightening, it isn't a blow from outside. We only pretend that it is" (*Progress* 305). With this, Isabel has committed to taking actions that will end her marriage to Laurence. And knows she will take them—as is made clear here, she feels the inevitability of it.

After this, the family returns home to the birthday dinner that Isabel has laboriously prepared—including the caterer's cake—to be just so. It is over this dinner that they discuss the glint lake and Isabel tells of the White Dump of her childhood, to which Laurence responds:

> "White Dump!" said Laurence—who, at another time, to such a story might have said something like "Simple pleasures of the poor!" "White Dump," he said, with a mixture of pleasure and

irony, a natural appreciation that seemed to be exactly what Isabel wanted.

She shouldn't have been surprised. She knew about Laurence's delicacy and kindness, as well as she knew about his bullying and bluffing. She knew the turns of his mind, his changes of heart, the little shifts and noises of his body. They were intimate. They had found out so much about each other that everything had got cancelled out by something else. That was why the sex between them could seem so shamefaced, merely and drearily lustful, like sex between siblings. Love could survive that—had survived that. Look how she loved him at this moment. Isabel found herself newly, and boundlessly, resourceful. (*Progress* 307)

Munro offers this thumbnail summation of the intimacy between husband and wife just before describing Isabel, the next day, returning to the airport to connect with the pilot and begin their affair. With this passage, in its precise phrasings, Munro captures the crucial moment:

In the years ahead, she would learn to read the signs, both at the beginning and at the end of a love affair. She wouldn't be so astonished at the way the skin of the moment can break open. But astonished enough that she would say one day to her grownup daughter Denise, when they were drinking wine and talking about some things, "I think the best part is always right at the beginning. At the beginning. That's the only pure part. Perhaps even before the beginning," she said. "Perhaps just when it flashes on you what's possible. That may be the best. (*Progress* 307–08)

The flash of this moment is just like St. Elmo's fire—one of the draft titles of this story. What Munro creates here is the sense of astonishment at, as she says, "the way the skin of the moment can break open." Munro does this, here and elsewhere, with both immediacy and perspective, the two intertwined. At the core of this writing—just as with St. Elmo's fire, the striking quality of a glint lake, the sweetness of a "White Dump"—is a sense of mystery over the very process of being, and of being human. It is the progress of love, recreated and understood, standing on a page.

* * *

Stories like this, published in the *New Yorker* throughout the 1980s, 1990s, and into this century, have made Munro a "writer's writer" in the United States and Britain. Oddly, and somewhat perversely, Munro seems to be approached abroad as an ongoing discovery and source of wonderment, especially for other writers who long to achieve similar effects themselves. Reviewing *Runaway* (2004) in the *New York Times Book Review*, for instance, Jonathan Franzen dissects the probable reasons for her putative neglect—mostly owing to Munro's devotion to the form of the short story—and makes one crucial, though over-the-top, request, which he calls a "simple instruction": "Read Munro! Read Munro!" (16). Francine Prose asserts in *Reading Like a Writer* (2006) that "Alice Munro writes with the simplicity and beauty of a Shaker box. Everything about her style is meant to attract *no* notice, to make you *not* pay attention" (23). In something of the same fashion, though infused with her long familiarity, Margaret Atwood introduces Munro in a new selection of stories, *Carried Away*, first published in 2006 in the United States in Knopf's Everyman's Library series (and in 2008 in Britain with the same title and in Canada as *Munro's Best*). Atwood writes:

> In Munro's work, grace abounds, but it is strangely disguised: nothing can be predicted. Emotions erupt. Preconceptions crumble. Surprises proliferate. Astonishments leap out. Malicious acts can have positive consequences. Salvation arrives when least expected, and in peculiar forms. But as soon as you make such a pronouncement about Munro's writing—or any other such analysis, inference, or generalization about it—you're aware of that mocking commentator so often present in a Munro story—the one who says, in essence, *Who do you think you are? What gives you the right to think you know anything*

about me, or about anyone else for that matter? (Introduction xiv, italics in original)

Atwood might well have been writing here about "the progress of love" in the parade of stories from "The Progress of Love" to "White Dump," stories in which we readers all stand back and wonder over "the way the skin of the moment can break open" in our lives, "so confused and stubborn," as if we "had forever." As Munro well knows, and communicates profoundly in all of her stories—though especially well in these—we don't have "forever." Melding the personal with the imaginative, Munro makes her complex, caring art. As Charles McGrath understood in June 1985 as he accepted "White Dump" for publication in the *New Yorker*, it *is* "something like a little miracle."

Critical Interlude:

Alice Munro: Critical Reception (2013)

Early in 2008, while reviewing William Trevor's *Cheating at Canasta* in the *New York Review of Books*, Claire Messud made an apt observation. She noted that Trevor's books had been praised in the same pages by a long list of "distinguished" reviewers, whom she names, and then asks, "But when did William Trevor—or, for that matter, his fellow contemporary master of the short story form, Alice Munro, the pair of them sharing of the laurels of Chekhov … —last spark a controversy, let alone incite a debate?" (20). As regards Munro, Messud's point is ultimately fair enough, although it is possible to counter it by citing attempts to ban her putative novel *Lives of Girls and Women* (1971) in parts of Ontario in the 1970s for being controversial; or her decisions to pull *Who Do You Think You Are?* (1978) from the press for restructuring just before publication, and later to follow her editor to a new publisher with an almost-finished book in hand. More recently, Munro criticized and refused to give permission to quote from archived letters to a particular critic, who, for her part, published her book without the quotations, with wounded protest. Munro also recently caused small stirs when, in 2006, she announced that she might well give up writing altogether, and when, in 2009, she announced that she had had cancer (see Thacker, *Writing* 333–36, 348–50, 418–22, 532, 549–50; McCaig, *Reading* ix–xiv).

That these small controversies escaped Messud's notice is no surprise, given that Munro herself has largely stayed out of the limelight since the beginning of her career. Instead, she just writes. Munro has written out of her own life and her own place; she writes of being alive, of just being human, of wondering, of trying to understand, of trying to maintain. She avoids politics, personalities, lessons—the stuff of controversy. And she has gained her reputation—a large one, as befits a winner of the 2009 Man Booker International Prize—by writing only short stories. As such, Munro's critical reception has been one of steady, persistent growth since she published her first book, *Dance of the Happy Shades*, in 1968. Made up of stories written over a 15-year span, that book won Canada's highest literary award; it was followed in 1971 by *Lives of Girls and Women*, a book that quickly became something of a feminist *cri de coeur*. After another collection of stories appeared in 1974, Munro hired a New York agent, Virginia Barber, who both placed her stories in commercial magazines—most notably the *New Yorker*—and brought Munro's next book, *Who Do You Think You Are?* (published as *The Beggar Maid* in the United States) (1979), to Alfred A. Knopf. There have been nine collections since, with another announced for the fall of 2012. Her *Selected Stories* appeared in 1996; *Carried Away*, an Everyman's Library selection, was published in 2006; and stories in the *New Yorker* and in *Harper's* have continued to appear. Munro writes on, reviewers' superlatives abound, and critical analyses have increased to a level befitting Munro's major-author status. In 2005, my extended biography written with Munro's cooperation, *Alice Munro: Writing Her Lives*, was published, and an updated paperback appeared in 2011. And in 2007, Carol Mazur and Cathy Moulder released their massive *Alice Munro: An Annotated Bibliography of Works and Criticism*, supplanting earlier attempts at bibliography. The MLA International Bibliography lists almost 200 entries on Munro's work published since the mid-1990s.

Throughout the growth of Munro's reputation, reviewers and critics have consistently struggled to define and articulate just how Munro does what she does in her stories. E. D. Blodgett writes that Munro is a writer whom readers see "endeavoring to locate the meaning that unifies, and yet is always wary of it"; hers is an art of "accommodating contradictions" (*Alice* 68, 126). Ildikó de Papp Carrington sees Munro in the same fashion, an author who tries to "control the uncontrollable." Louis K. MacKendrick maintains that it "is quite hopeless and redundant to expect an Alice Munro story to surrender a clear, indisputable, and singular 'meaning'" (26). Katherine J. Mayberry asserts that for Munro, "to tell is at best to revise, but never to perfectly revive" and that a Munro story "virtually defies plot summary" (540, 532). And Helen Hoy quotes a 1987 interview with Munro in which she said that in each story she is seeking "'an admission of chaos'" because "'a belief in progress is unfounded'"; as she told another interviewer, "'It doesn't make much difference ... how [a heroine] ends up at all. Because we finally end up dead.'" Thus Hoy asserts that "Munro both captures life's capriciousness and requires a simultaneous acceptance of conflicting perspectives on reality" ("Alice" 17, 18, 20). That said, Magdalene Redekop offers what is perhaps the great fact of Munro's most effective and affective art: that each of us as readers perceives "the story Alice Munro is telling *me*," that the "pleasure of reading Alice Munro is, in the final analysis, that we catch ourselves in the act of looking" (*Mothers* x, 3). She looks at the way life is and, at the same time, recognizes in postmodern ways the impossibility of any narrative to truly reconstruct a central event in someone's life. Again and again in her stories, as with "White Dump," Munro shows us how "the way the skin of the moment can break open" (*Progress* 308).

* * *

Although Munro began publishing stories and having them read on the Canadian Broadcasting Corporation (CBC) during the 1950s, and made several appearances in the *Montrealer* in the early 1960s, her critical reception really began with the publication of *Dance of the Happy Shades*. The collection, and the singular nature and quality of the praise it received (one reviewer spoke of "the breadth and depth of humanity in the woman herself, and the beauty—the almost terrifying beauty—she commands in expressing it"), vaulted Munro to the forefront of Canada's leading writers (Thacker, *Writing* 193). Such reaction not only continued but became amplified and more acute with the publication of *Lives of Girls and Women* in 1971 in Canada and with its appearance the next year from McGraw-Hill in the United States. Taken together, the reviews that these and subsequent books received mark the beginning of Munro's critical reception (summary overviews of these reviews, gauged to Munro's biography, are available throughout my *Alice Munro: Writing Her Lives*).

Separate from newspaper and broadcast reviews, and from various pieces with broader treatment in the literary press, the first critical article on Munro's fiction was a thematic study of "unconsummated relationships," which appeared in early 1972 in *World Literature Written in English* (Dahlie). It was followed in 1975 by two pieces published in 1975 by J. R. (Tim) Struthers, one on Munro and the American South, the other on Munro and James Joyce in *Lives of Girls and Women*. These two critics were the vanguard, and were followed by others throughout the 1970s, with increasing critical attention on Munro as the decade passed. Articles appeared in such journals as *Canadian Literature* (Conron, Bailey), the *Journal of Canadian Fiction* (Martin, "Joyce"), *Modern Fiction Studies* (Macdonald, "Madman"), *Mosaic* (Dawson), *Open Letter* (New), *Studies in Canadian Literature* (Macdonald, "Structures"), and *Studies in Short Fiction* (Monaghan). At the same time, Munro was considered very much a part of book-length studies examining Canadian fiction as an entity (Blodgett, "Prisms"; Moss, Packer). During the 1970s as well, much critical work was being done in graduate theses. The initial critical impetus was one of identification and connection, of examining central matters in the fiction, and of making connections between Munro and other writers; it also focused on her work amid what were then seen as "Canadian" considerations, given the nationalist fervor of the decade in English-speaking Canada and its concomitant concern with the growth of a definable Canadian literature. In keeping with this, Dahlie returned to Munro in 1978 with an overview essay, "The Fiction of Alice Munro," published in the American magazine *Ploughshares* to accompany one of Munro's stories, "Characters" (never republished in a collection). There he writes, accurately and presciently, that Munro's "fiction is rooted tangibly in the social realism of the rural and small town world of her own experience, but it insistently explores what lies beyond the bounds of empirical reality" (56–57). So it was then with Munro, and so it is still.

By this time Munro had made her first appearances in the *New Yorker*, and the interest that the editors of that publication and those of *Ploughshares* had in her—along with the editors of *Modern Fiction Studies* and *Studies in Short Fiction*, already noted, from the 1970s—suggests that the growth of Munro's critical reputation during that decade was a two-tracked affair. Although certainly seen at home as primarily, even quintessentially, a *Canadian* writer, Munro has from the early 1970s on attracted her critics irrespective of nationalist considerations, and perhaps even despite them. Munro writes of life, not nations, and because she is a Canadian writer, the ways she is read abroad—most especially in the United States—has proven to be at times a bit vexing for her critics at home.

Early in 1980, Helen Hoy published "'Dull, Simple, Amazing and Unfathomable': Paradox and Double Vision in Alice Munro's Fiction," a singular essay that directed critical attention away from thematics and toward language, structure, and style in Munro's stories. "Verbal paradox ... particularly cryptic oxymoron, remains a more distinctive feature of Munro's style, and ... functions particularly as a means of definition, of zeroing in on the individual qualities of an emotion or moment" (106). Frequently cited since, Hoy's essay proved prescient in directing critical attention into the textures of Munro's well-wrought stories, which critics began exploring in earnest during the 1980s. The first book devoted to Munro, *Probable Fictions: Alice Munro's Narrative Acts* (1983), edited by Louis K. MacKendrick, offered nine essays by various hands (and an interview with Munro by Struthers); each one, seen now, proved influential in shaping subsequent scholarship—frequently noted and responded to as they have been since.

In 1984, three more publications appeared: another collection of essays devoted to Munro, *The Art of Alice Munro: Saying the Unsayable*, edited by Judith Miller; the first single-authored book-length study, B. Pfaus's *Alice Munro*; and my own annotated bibliography of Munro in the fifth volume of *The Annotated Bibliography of Canada's Major Authors*. Taken together, following after *Probable Fictions* and with the recently published *The Moons of Jupiter* (1982) showing Munro to still be ascendant, these demonstrate an accelerating critical interest in Munro's work. The Miller volume, a collection of presentations (and an interview) from the first Alice Munro conference held at the University of Waterloo in 1982, especially demonstrates this (see Thacker "Conferring").

Although Pfaus's book is technically the first single-authored critical book to have been published on Munro, its brevity and many weaknesses are such that it has exerted almost no influence in Munro studies. Nothing of the sort can be said of the *10* such volumes published between 1987, when W. R. Martin's *Alice Munro: Paradox and Parallel* was published, and 1994, when Ajay Heble's *The Tumble of Reason: Alice Munro's Discourse of Absence* appeared. More than this, during the same period, essays continued to be published, a brief though very fine biography by Catherine Sheldrick Ross appeared, and Coral Ann Howells, who would later publish what is still perhaps the best single-authored book on Munro, offered an extended consideration of Munro in her *Private and Fictional Words: Canadian Women Novelists of the 1970s and 1980s* (1987). Looking back at this outpouring now, the critical books of sustaining influence have been Carrington's *Controlling the Uncontrollable* (1989), Redekop's *Mothers and Other Clowns* (1992), and, largely because of its theoretical inflections (which engage and extend Blodgett's in his *Alice Munro* [1988]), Heble's *The Tumble of Reason* (1994). Yet two of the books published among the 10 appearing between 1987 and 1994, Neil K. Besner's *Introducing Alice Munro's* Lives of Girls and Women (1990) and Louis K. MacKendrick's *Some Other Reality: Alice Munro's* Something I've Been Meaning to Tell You (1993), demonstrate abundantly that Munro's art, one of always pushing the limitations of the short story, is not well served by the critical form of the single-author extended critical overview. On the contrary, Besner and MacKendrick's books, as short (about 100 pages) critical volumes focused sharply on the aesthetic and biographical contexts defined by a single Munro collection, demonstrate that Munro is an artist whose variegated stories elude broad overview. In fact, Munro's critical reception has demonstrated that her work is best understood at the level of the single story or by considering a small group of stories.[1]

As it happened, in 1991 and again in 1998, I surveyed Munro criticism in two omnibus review essays published in the *Journal of Canadian Studies* (Thacker "Go Ask Alice", "What's 'Material'?"). In these I considered the 10 critical books noted above, along with others that treated Munro as one of several authors in other contexts, and in the 1998 essay I also surveyed the critical articles. Given the availability of these essays, there seems little point in reiterating my assessments here, so I refer readers to them. That said, I would also point readers toward Coral Ann Howells' final chapter in her *Alice Munro*, also published in 1998, in which she offers differing views on much of the same critical writing (137–53).

In 1998 as well, I edited a special issue of *Essays on Canadian Writing* devoted to Munro, entitled "Alice Munro, Writing On…" A year later it was republished as a book, retitled *The Rest of the Story: Critical Essays on Alice Munro*; it is in the later form that it is most often noted. Following *Probable Fictions* and *The Art of Alice Munro*, *The Rest of the Story* again demonstrates that the best critical approach to Munro's art is by way of the single story, and more than that it demonstrates, too, that individual stories in each collection seem to draw repeated critical analyses. "Royal Beatings" (1977), "The Moons of Jupiter" (1978), "The Progress of Love" (1985), "Meneseteung" (1988), "Carried Away" (1991), "Vandals" (1993), "The Love of a Good Woman" (1996), "The Children Stay" (1997), and "Save the Reaper" (1998) have continued to garner the most attention, most especially "Meneseteung" and "The Love of a Good Woman."

* * *

Throughout the 1990s and leading up to the publication of *The Rest of the Story*, individual critics—some with previous writing on Munro, some not—published essays that were broadly general in analyzing the bases of Munro's art and, as well, sharply focused on a single telling story. Katherine J. Mayberry did this in 1992 by focusing on "Hard-Luck Stories" (1982) from *The Moons of Jupiter*, while in the same year Pam Houston offered an early and almost immediately influential reading of "Meneseteung." Taking that story into her classroom, Houston contextualizes it within the work of numerous other renowned short story writers, and within narrative theory, and asserts that

> what is true is untrue, what is untrue is true. We have an hysterical bleeding woman inside an admittedly fictitious account, written by a narrator who doesn't even know her name. We have a distortion of reality within a distortion of reality, within a story that is also a poem, and sometimes a river. Nothing here will stay still long enough to mean just one thing. (90)

Keeping close to Munro's latest stories, too, was Ildikó de Papp Carrington, who followed her 1989 book with several articles on stories from Munro's most recent works during the next decade; well grounded in Munro's techniques, always attuned to telling details, Carrington's essays persuade by their precision and well-informed research.

The work of these critics, and others, during the 1990s demonstrates that critical analysis of Munro's stories was being driven in part by her own publications; beginning with *Friend of My Youth* (1990) and continuing through the increasingly complex stories in *Open Secrets* (1994) and *The Love of a Good Woman* (1998), her status well established, Munro seemed to immediately draw critics intent on discerning the complexities of her work and on probing new directions in it. Nathalie Foy, for instance, wrote that the "stories in *Open Secrets* hang together precisely because they are not continuous but layered. Some layers remain forever parallel, and some intersect in the weird geometry of this collection" (153). This notion of layering in Munro's work—spatially, geographically, historically, and especially chronologically—has drawn and continues to draw critical analysis. Writing about the same time as Foy, Charles Forceville and Coral Ann Howells ("Intimate") examined Munro's layering in persuasive ways that both acknowledge and extend our understanding of the relationship between space and time in her stories. In the same way, critics turned their attention to previously unexamined aspects of Munro's art: Robert Lecker extended John Weaver's earlier examination of Munro's telling of Ontario's history by looking at the economic and social history told in "Carried Away," while Magdelene Redekop ("Scottish Nostalgic") and Christopher E. Gittings began the discussion of Munro's use of her Scots ancestors that has continued through to the present, especially with Munro's *The View From Castle Rock* (2006) (see also Karl Miller).

During the 1990s, too, articles began appearing that, whatever their interest in Munro, seemed much more intent on demonstrating ways in which her stories confirmed the writings of various literary theorists (see for example Garson "Synecdoche"). Much less a matter of Munro's stories confirming secondary writing on theory, some critics demonstrated that her stories are themselves inherently theoretical, that they demonstrate the limitations of narrative completeness. Mark Nunes, for instance, writes in "Postmodern 'Piercing': Alice Munro's Contingent Ontologies," an important essay, that Munro "defies [the] margins of 'Postmodernism' while raising the same challenges of adetermination, overflow, and the denial of totalizing narrative. Her writing, she has noted, captures the 'funny jumps' of living: bumps that unsettle the narrative frame" (11). Complementing this view, Mark Levene writes in a powerful essay that has much to say about Munro's writing generally, but *The Progress of Love* through to *The Love of a Good Woman* especially, that "in the most obvious sense, Munro is a regional writer, but her regionalism, like her overt realism, is densely ambiguous not because she is really writing about covert biblical or Freudian realms, but because no world is intact, or can be assumed to be whole or predictable, to be knowable" (845).

From the early years of her critical reception, Munro has attracted commentators who have written in more personal terms about her work, with an eye toward the intimate communion they feel when reading Munro's stories (see Wallace). Avowedly nonacademic, such writers are bent on defining, as Redekop wrote, "the story Alice Munro is telling me." In 1998, Judith Maclean Miller, who edited *The Art of Alice Munro*, published the first of three such essays in the *Antigonish Review*; they are singular and complementary pieces. The first of these, "An Inner Bell that Rings: The Craft of Alice Munro," looks closely at published interviews with Munro and connects her work to the Canadian photographer Freeman Patterson's reverence for, and understanding of, the surfaces he photographed. In the same way, Munro

> shows us not a pre-chosen, fixed, un-changing way of writing or seeing, but a deep integrity which insists on finding its way into whatever is interesting, especially what is not well understood, or talked about, to find the angle of vision from which it can be experiences, and then to find a way to construct that. (175–76)

The second essay, largely a review of *Friend of My Youth*, bears attention also, but the third, "Deconstructing Silence: The Mystery of Alice Munro," offers a sharp and precise reading of "Save the Reaper" that wholly demonstrates Munro's construction of mystery in that story. Miller writes: "these are stories about strange deaths, sinister people, darkness, and also about story, about mystery, creating without ever saying so a new genre, another way to write about the unsolved, the unspoken. About what is said. Or not said" (51). Miller's impulse here, and in the creative non-fiction form she uses to express that impulse, has become frequent in the past decade or so: it has turned up in issues of the *Writer's Chronicle*—published by and for those involved in creative writing programs—in which there have been articles titled "How to Write Like Alice Munro" and "Rhyming Action In Alice Munro's Stories" (Aubrey, Bucholt), as well as a "how to" essay. Younger writers have come to Munro for inspiration and the fellowship of being writers together (Strayed), while others, also fiction writers, have sharply probed her stories out of a deep sense of shared endeavour (Glover).

As this suggests, it is possible to see Munro's critical reception at the end of the century as engaged in several separate fields. She was inspiring fellow writers, both at home and abroad. Equally, Munro was still important to questions regarding Canadian literature—in 2001, for instance, Gerald Lynch writes in his excellent *The One and the Many: English-Canadian Short Story Cycles* that "the masterful *Who Do You Think You Are?*" is central in "the continuum of Canadian short story cycles" (159). As well, owing largely to her work's ongoing presence in the *New Yorker*—by the end of 2001 she had published 40 stories there, and in 2004 its editors would publish three Munro stories in a single issue—Munro was established as a looming literary presence. As such, during the past decade, criticism and single volumes devoted to Munro have increased in both frequency and extent.

In June 2000, the Canadian writer John Metcalf published an essay in the *National Post* entitled "Canada's Successful Writers Must Count on Blessings from the U.S. First," a piece that he had originally called "Who Reads Alice Munro?" Intended to be contentious, Metcalf's point was that Munro's reputation was determined outside of Canada, not within. He hit his mark at home. Its publication brought a flurry of letters to the editor, including one from Munro herself and another from her editor at McClelland & Stewart, Douglas Gibson. She disputed the interpretations of one of the essayists Metcalf mentions, JoAnn McCaig, who had published an article in *The Rest of the Story* on her correspondence with Virginia Barber, Munro's agent, found in the Munro archive at the University of Calgary (see Thacker "Canadian Literature's"). For her part, McCaig also wrote to defend what she was doing, and after some delay caused by Munro's refusal to allow her to quote from her letters in the Calgary archive, McCaig published *Writing In: Alice Munro's Archives* (2002). Focused on what is available in the archive—rather than on Munro's fiction—the book is more a meditation on the uses of evidence than a critical or biographical analysis. Infused with inappropriate theoretical analyses, avoiding historical and biographical contexts, and defiantly iconoclastic in its cultural studies approach to the Munro archive, *Writing In* is simply not a very good book. Even so, McCaig has at least done what only a very few Munro critics have: she has read and used the available archival sources. My own essays and biography have attempted to demonstrate this ongoing necessity in critical work on Munro, but there remains a great deal yet to do. Would that more critics stir themselves to actually use this invaluable resource (see Thacker "Mapping").

* * *

The frequency and number of critical articles on Munro published since 2000 certainly suggest that interest in her work not only continues but shows no sign of abating. Of particular note have been several influential studies in which critics have focused on a wide range of classical and mythological allusions (Stich), on *Sir Gawain and the Green Knight* (Luft), on Charlotte Brontë and Henry James (Garson "Alice"), and on Virginia Woolf (Lilianfeld). These analyses have been offered through detailed and often compelling arguments. Munro's relationship to the short story as a form—what Adrian Hunter in a masterful analysis called a "minor literature"—has received close attention; recognizing that Munro is writing within a generic continuum and that her use of history has played a critical role in her work's development, Hunter argues that her "interrogative stories dramatise an interdiction against all kinds of summary statement" ("Story" 237; see also May). Each of Hunter's essays on Munro have been significant, including another published in 2010 on Munro's use of her ancestor James Hogg's *The Private Memoirs and Confessions of a Justified Sinner* (1824) in "A Wilderness Station" (1992). In it she argues that Hogg and Munro both write "stories that refuse to take possession of their subjects" ("Taking" 127).

Another notable Munro critic who has emerged during the past decade is Robert McGill, who has published a succession of essays on "Vandals," "Something I've Been Meaning to Tell You" (1974), "Material" (1973), and Sarah Polley's adaptation of "The Bear Came Over the Mountain" (1999–2000) for her feature film, *Away From Her* (2007). The latter two articles are especially good, with "'Daringly Out in the Public Eye': Alice Munro and the Ethics of Writing Back" of special note. In it, McGill offers what is probably the best analysis of the oft-analyzed story "Material," which he calls "a metafiction about the ethics of writing fiction. ... [it] considers the relationship between ethical writing and ethical living and what the criteria for each might be" (875).[2] With his essay on adaptation, McGill positions Polley's film both in relation to dominant discourses on Canadian writing and, more effectively, to the effects of Munro's story and especially her overall aesthetic of indeterminacy.

The last decade has also seen publication of a succession of Munro tribute volumes. In 2003/04, *Open Letter* published papers from an Alice Munro conference held in May 2003 at the University of Orléans, France, "L'écriture du secret/Writings Secrets." Similarly, *Reading Alice Munro in Italy* (2008) is based on another gathering held in May 2007 in Siena, Italy, "Alice Munro—the Art of the Short Story." Each volume is a valuable record of how Munro's work is seen in Europe, although each includes North American critics. In *Open Letter*, Coral Ann Howells, in one of the strongest essays in the volume, concludes by wondering if Munro's stories "are like houses that we enter, as she once suggested, or are they like floating bridges, unstable spaces thrown out over dark spaces where we can see stars reflected from above, but not the secrets hidden beneath the surface of the water?" (52). Another singular piece is the dialogue—two interwoven papers presented together at the conference in a back-and-forth style—between Donna Bennett and Russell Morton Brown. While discussing Munro's use of time in "Save the Reaper," Bennett asserts that "perhaps no other Canadian writer so often makes use of counterfactual statements and of past perfect and conditional perfect tenses" (192). Concluding a discussion of "The Love of a Good Woman," and discussing the character Enid at the end of that mysterious story, Brown says, "It is no longer guilty secrets that intrigue her; she is now preoccupied with those secrets that open one heart to another. Munro does not permit the readers to do more than speculate on how that plot will unfold" (206). Like most conference volumes, this one is uneven, but together its essays reveal the broad and extremely high critical stature accorded Munro's art. Again and again, its critics confirm an assertion made by coeditor Héliane Ventura: "To look at a Munro landscape or to read a Munro text is not to participate in the decoding of photographic realism. It is to take part in an archaeological process which consists of recovering traces that have been destroyed" (256). In the same way, *Reading Alice Munro in Italy* offers a succession of readings on individual stories, with forays into broader matters; there is also an especially good piece by Susanna Basso on translating Munro's work into Italian.

Five more recent Munro volumes are notable: Ailsa Cox's *Alice Munro* is a brief introduction published in a British "Writers and Their Works" series in 2004. It is current on both Munro's fiction and its criticism, and offers a sharply focused and detailed appreciation that displays eminent good sense throughout. Munro's work demonstrates, Cox writes, that "nothing defeats mortality, but fiction can suspend time for a while. ... But in every story, finally, words fail. There is always something which has to be left out, and can only be approximated through imagery and paradox" (85, 97). Another brief single-authored book appeared in 2009, *Daughters and Mothers in Alice Munro's Later Stories* by Deborah Heller, who had an excellent essay on *Friend of My Youth* in *The Rest of the Story*. In this book, not much more than an essay, Heller considers Munro's recent use of the perennial mother–daughter relationship in "My Mother's Dream" (1998), "Family Furnishings" (2001), and the Juliet Triptych in *Runaway* (2004). Another tribute from various hands, in 2006 the *Virginia Quarterly Review* published "Ordinary Outsiders: A Symposium on Alice Munro." It includes a biographical critical overview by Marcela Valdes and appreciations by Munro's editors, her agent, and other writers and friends. It also includes the revised version of Munro's memoir story, "Home" (1974), which was included in *The View From Castle Rock*. Also in 2006, a special issue of *Eureka Studies in Teaching Short Fiction* was devoted to Munro's work—it demonstrates a wide range of interest in teaching Munro's stories, and in their broad appeal. In 2009, Harold Bloom included Munro in his "Bloom's Modern Critical Views" series, republishing 10 critical essays and sections from books (most mentioned here). In his brief introduction, Bloom says he only managed to read Munro's *Selected Stories* himself, but from that he places Munro in the second tier of "major artists of short fiction of the twentieth century"; she does not, however, make his top 10, which includes James, Chekhov, Kafka, Joyce, Hemingway, and others: all men (1).

* * *

In an important though contentious recent article, "The Problem with Alice Munro," Philip Marchand argues that Munro's "problem"

> is that she has been so true to the world she has chosen to depict.... The horizons in this world are uniformly low, due partly to the absence of characters whose education, experience and character might enable them to expand those horizons. Instead, it's a standoff between her hicks and her smarties. Her intellectuals have no heft and are riddled with egotism; her men of God are pale reflections of their Victorian predecessors. Her heroines, who are a combination of hick and smarty, who only want to be allowed to go off somewhere and study Greek, like Del Jordan's mother and Juliet Henderson, are as passive and helpless in the face of the world's unfriendliness as Munro's adolescent girls are helpless in the face of sexual urgency.

Munro's great talent notwithstanding, we critics should not "shirk the issue of the sad paltriness of her world," according to Marchand. He also asks, "Did the limitations of her world have to correlate so closely to the limitations of her art?" (13–14). Marchand's essay is less compelling than it is indicative of just where Munro criticism is now: in trying to approach Munro's *oeuvre* as a whole, he offers salient and broad commentary on her material, some of it quite good, but he ultimately fails to convince that his objections are any more than niggling preference. The essay may also indicate, at least in Canada, some weariness over Munro's familiar material, her approaches to it, and, especially, her dominating presence. Here, too, "niggling" seems an apt description.

By contrast, and certainly consistently enough to see a trend, Munro's critics during the last half dozen years have narrowed their focus, limiting their treatment most often to a single story and, more specifically, to questions of narrative structure within that story. Caitlin J. Charman does this in her examination of "Fits" (1986), Ryan Melsom on "Labor Day Dinner" (1981), and, most impressively, Tim McIntyre on "The Moons of Jupiter," offering an extremely close, detailed, and thorough analysis. Each critic synthesizes previous commentary, too, in ways that suggest that their reading is fairly complete. Two other stories, "Meneseteung" and "The Love of a Good Woman," have continued to draw detailed and extensive analysis. Taking up the latter story in the *Journal of Narrative Theory*, John Gerlach builds on the work of previous critics to argue that the story's open ending is a

> charged incompleteness [that is] particularly tantalizing and distinctive among open endings ... In this story, ultimate issues, good and evil, confession and repression are stunningly irresolvable. Secondly, Munro has teased us with very traditional expectation: she has written in the mode of realism, not as a self-conscious, mocking postmodern. She has teased us with variable types of closure in the various sections of the story.

Detailing this in the story, Gerlach almost exclaims, "we've been teased in every way possible; the rhythm of delay with stunning penultimate climaxes surely must resolve itself. But it doesn't" (154–55; see also Carrington, "Don't"; Duffy, "Dark"; McCombs; and Ross, "Too").

But if "The Love of a Good Woman" has attracted considerable and sustained analysis, then "Meneseteung" continues to be a paradigmatic text, given the sustained attention it has drawn. Two essays published in 2010—by Tracy Ware and Dennis Duffy, included in the same critical book on historical fiction, *National Plots*—demonstrate this unequivocally, and Ware and Duffy's work is supplemented by another essay by Douglas Glover. Ware, a critic who reads criticism carefully, completely, and thoughtfully, creates what might be called a deep synthesis of criticism already published on "Meneseteung" and links it to broader theories on the uses of historical fact in fiction. Ware writes that at one point, "Munro is less skeptical of history than of the ethics of 'historical metafiction.' What right does she have to supplement history with concerns of a later day? How can she know she is not doing that, despite her best intentions?" (76). Drawing on these distinctions and especially on his sharp synthesis of other critics' analyses, Ware convincingly argues that with the story, Munro "aligned her resistance to any ideological program with the skepticism at the core of much historical fiction" (77). Duffy, for his part, locates "Meneseteung" deeply in what he calls "the Munro Tract"— her home place in Huron County, Ontario—and draws persuasively on Munro's biography and on her use of prototypes for the protagonist, Almeda Roth. He argues that the "story's fictional weight rests instead on the foundations that its narrative mode composes, a way of storytelling reminiscent of the devices of orality." In so doing, Munro "has produced a story that appears to follow the agenda set by the traditional, continuous, and pointed historical novel but which finally slams through those guardrails, crosses the median, and drives away in the other direction of the postmodern, de-centred, and diffuse fiction familiar to us now" (210–11).³

But if Ware's and Duffy's essays are impressive in their deep and scholarly syntheses—and they very much are—Douglas Glover reminds critics in his "The Mind of Alice Munro" that in "Meneseteung" it is all about the primary text itself:

> She uses resonating structures so that various parts of the text echo off each other. She uses a complex point of view structure to create variety and contrast in the types of text threaded through the narrative (and thus a variety of perspectives). She dances with time. She creates action, conflict, and emotion even in those parts of the story that are not directly relating plot. ... Munro seems to realize that the inner life of a man or a woman is also a text, that in our secret hearts we are talking to ourselves, muttering, declaiming; at its deepest point this is our experience of experience. (31, 35)

Concluding, Glover cites what is perhaps the most quoted line from "Meneseteung," its penultimate image of the narrator—and by extension Munro herself—engaged in research "in the hope of seeing this trickle in time, making a connection, rescuing one thing from the rubbish" (73). He then asserts that there "is this allegorical element in everything Alice Munro writes; she is always teaching readers how to read her stories as she writes them; there are always connections to be made" (37). So there are, always, as we read her stories and hear the stories Munro is telling each of us—so we, her critics, have realized from our first readings, and so we continue to realize now. Not controversial; human. Profound. Alice Munro, "our Chekhov." Better still, our Alice Munro.

Afterword:

"A Wonderful Stroke of Good Fortune for Me": Reading Alice Munro, 1973–2013

Having just met Alice Munro when they shared a program of readings at a New York City bookstore on March 1, 1983, Cynthia Ozick wrote Munro's editor at Knopf, Ann Close, telling her that when she met Munro, "Alice said, 'This isn't the *real* me.'" Having thought this comment over, Ozick says: "I guess she meant the lectern-person, the one who Appears in Public. In the train going home I thought and thought about that, and felt so much of the 'real' Alice was there: I liked her instantly and completely. She struck me as 'real' all through, as artist and human being." Ozick then concludes, writing, "It was a wonderful stroke of good fortune for me to be able to share an evening with her" (396/87.2.1.3).

As it happened, I attended those readings at Books & Company that night, for I had come down from Burlington where I was teaching at the University of Vermont to meet Munro myself—as I said in the introduction here, I was then at work on my annotated bibliography and I had some questions to ask her. She, for her part, was in New York to launch *The Moons of Jupiter* in the United States. After the readings, as I also said at the outset, I told Munro that when we had talked about Willa Cather at lunch I had not yet read "Dulse," her considered biographical meditation on Cather, on the writer's persona, and on the writer's egotism. "'This isn't the *real* me,'" she told Ozick. Even so, Ozick found the real Munro that night, an "artist and human being" who she liked "instantly and completely." So did I.

The book Munro was launching on Knopf's spring list, *The Moons of Jupiter*, had already been published by Macmillan of Canada the previous autumn. Three of its stories—the title story, "Dulse," and "The Turkey Season"—had already appeared in the *New Yorker*, as had another story, "Wood" (1980), which would not be included in one of Munro's books until 2009, when a revised version appeared in *Too Much Happiness*. Three more stories in the *Moons of Jupiter* had been published in Canadian magazines. By 1983, too, critical interest in Munro's work was well established—there had been an Alice Munro symposium at the University of Waterloo, and *Probable Fictions*, the first book-length critical examination of her work, was published. "Clear Jelly," the first of my essays included here, was in that volume and just then, too, I was at work on "Chaddeleys and Flemings: 1. Connection" from *The Moons of Jupiter*, work that would result in the second essay here, "Connection: Alice Munro and Ontario." The third essay, a review, focused on the proceedings of that first Munro symposium. Also in 1983 I moved from Vermont to St. Lawrence University, a place that has fostered and facilitated my readings and writings about Munro ever since.

Although I certainly am not going to offer here a more detailed account of my trajectory as a Munro critic (and, later, biographer), my point about these parallels between Munro's career—and most especially her emergent international career—and my own ought to be evident. As Ozick wrote and as I have said, I consider my connection with Munro to have been "a wonderful stroke of good fortune for me": it has been a constant throughout, from my first reading of "Material" in the fall of 1973 through to my reading of *Dear Life*—as she has said, probably her last book—when it appeared in 2012. From that first meeting in New York in February 1983, I have found Munro to be just as Ozick described: "'real' all through, as artist and human being." For many years, that first meeting, a solitary telephone interview, and some time together at a 1988 conference were my only personal contacts with Munro—as a critic, I took the view that writers should be left alone to write. And given the infrequency with which *this* writer appeared in public as a writer—not very often, mostly only when she was publishing a new book, or to accept an award for her work, or in pursuit of some personal interest—that seemed the best approach. This would change in early 2000 when Munro agreed to cooperate on the literary biography that became *Alice Munro: Writing Her Lives*, but even then our connections have not been frequent, only regular and focused—little more than half a dozen meetings in all, with some correspondence and phone conversations, too.

My hope as I conclude this collection is that the essays reprinted here in their original form offer what I hope is a cogent record of the emergence of one of the major literary figures of the twentieth and early twenty-first centuries, as I saw that emergence and understood it. Although I am too close to claim any real perspective, Munro certainly seems to me to be one of the greatest writers to have lived. And because I noticed her work fairly early and, more than notice, have persisted in my analyses of that work as something of an obsession—let us call it what it is—the record I offer here of a life in Munro criticism is unique. In June 2003 when I was working on my biography I was able to spend an afternoon driving Munro around Wingham and Huron County, Ontario, with the tape recorder rolling on the seat between us. Accounting this experience to others, I have often said it was like driving William Faulkner around Oxford, Mississippi: that is, around Yoknapatawpha County. Truly, it was "a wonderful stroke of good fortune for me."

* * *

The September 19, 2011, issue of the *New Yorker* contained Munro's "Dear Life," a piece identified there as "personal history" and one that later provided the title for her 14th book, *Dear Life*. In that collection it is the last of the "four works" that conclude the "Finale" section, which in turn ends *Dear Life*—a grouping that, Munro writes in a descriptive coda, "are not quite stories" but are "the first and last—and the closest—things I have to say about my own life" (*Dear* 255). In its magazine version it is illustrated by a photograph of baby Alice Ann Laidlaw when she was between two and three years old. Among other things, "Dear Life" reveals a good deal about Munro's knowledge and memories of her mother, Anne Chamney

Laidlaw (1898–1959), and also about her father, Robert Eric Laidlaw (1901–1976), from the time when Munro was in school and growing up on the family's fox farm in Lower Town, Wingham, Ontario. It is a period stretching from the years just before Munro's birth in July 1931 until she left for the University of Western Ontario in the fall of 1949. Describing the location of her family's home as a way of building up the small mystery she structures the piece around, Munro writes that their house "turned its back on the village, facing west across slightly downsloping fields to the hidden curve where the river made what was called the Big Bend. Beyond the river was a patch of dark evergreen trees, probably cedar but too far away to tell." As she had before in "Working for a Living," Munro tells us that "even farther away, on another hillside, was another house, quite small at that distance, facing ours, that we would never visit or know and that was like a dwarf's house in a story." She and her family knew only the name of the person who lived in that house, "Roly Grain, his name was, and he does not have any further part in what I'm writing now, in spite of his troll's name, because this is not a story, only life" (*Dear* 307).

Not a story, only life.

This phrase—this putative distinction—resonates throughout the whole of Munro's work. When she wrote her foreword to *The View From Castle Rock* (2006), a volume she had long envisioned as a "family book," Munro comments on that book's second group of stories, which drew on "personal material" and which she had previously published but until then had kept out of her books. With them she says that she was "doing something closer to what memoir does—exploring a life, my own life, but not in an austere or rigorously factual way." She continues, saying, "Some of these characters have moved so far from their beginnings that I cannot remember who they were to start with." Even so, and given this process, she asserts emphatically, "These are *stories*" (Foreword x; see Thacker, *Writing* 526–49). They are indeed, but appearing as they do in *The View from Castle Rock*, just after that book's first section of pieces drawn from Munro's own family history and her own memoir "Working for a Living," it is fair to wonder. With the "works" offered as the "Finale" to *Dear Life*—which Munro says are all based on things that happened—she seems now to have backed off from her previous assertion. Not a story, only life. Or life made into a story.

As I mentioned in the introduction to this book and have also noted in other essays here, when I reviewed *The Progress of Love* for *Canadian Literature* in the fall of 1986, I noted that Munro once told an interviewer that "'writing is the art of approach and recognition. I believe that we don't solve these things—in fact our explanations take us further away'". Applying this to *The Progress of Love*—a breakthrough volume in her *oeuvre*—I commented then that that "these stories offer a complex wonder at the strangeness of it all" (*Reading Alice Munro* 73, 76).

"Dear Life" was followed in the *New Yorker* by Munro's sixtieth publication there, "Leaving Maverley," a story set just after the Second World War, as is usual for her, in a Wingham-like town in Ontario. It begins seeming to focus on a man who runs the Capital theatre in Maverley, Ontario, a man named Morgan Holly; it then shifts and seems to be focusing on a teenaged girl he hires as a ticket taker, but ultimately it alights on Ray Elliot, the town's "night policeman." He "had taken the job so that he would be able to help his wife manage for at least some part of the daytime." His wife, Isabel, is chronically ill with "something called pericarditis. It was serious and she had ignored it to her peril. It was something she would not be cured of but could manage, with difficulty." Isabel and Ray "had no children and could get talking anytime about anything. He brought her the news of the town, which often made her laugh, and she told him about the books she was reading" (*Dear* 69, 70–71). Munro follows these two while also following the girl hired to take tickets, Leah, who first seems to be just the eldest child of a strangely religious family dominated by the father. Ray and Isabel wonder over her personality and characteristics. But then she elopes with the visiting son of the United Church minister, moves away and has two children with him, and sometime later returns to Maverley with her children, estranged from her husband. She has an affair with the new United Church minister—and a scandal, too, because the minister confesses their liaison from the pulpit. There is, as Munro commented parenthetically in "Images" (1968), "all this life going on" (*Dance* 31).

Reading "Leaving Maverley," we follow Leah's disappearance and elopement, and like Ray and Isabel, who talk together about what happened, we wonder what will happen next. Munro stays with Ray and his sick wife: Isabel takes a turn for the worse, is moved to a hospital in the city, and eventually goes into a coma. Ray stays with her, taking a job in the hospital in order to do so after she lapses into the coma. While working there after a long period in which Isabel's situation remains unchanged, Ray meets Leah again. She, too, now happens to work in the same hospital. Leah tells him the rest of her story in a happenstance meeting just before Ray discovers that "Isabel was finally gone. They said 'gone,' as if she had got up and left. When someone had checked on her about an hour ago, she had been the same as ever, and now she was gone" (89).

Here is Munro's "approach and recognition" to life itself. Just after this passage—which, incidentally, echoes the opening of "The Progress of Love"—she offers three critical, brief paragraphs, the first two each a single sentence: "He had often wondered what difference it would make," and, "But the emptiness in place of her was astounding." And then, after a paragraph of detail describing Ray adjusting to this new fact while a nurse speaks to him, is this sentence: "He'd thought that it had happened long before with Isabel, but it hadn't. Not until now." The story's title, "Leaving Maverley," illuminates layers of meaning as we read. Munro concludes the story with Ray making arrangements "for the remains":

> And before long he found himself outside, pretending that he had as ordinary and good a reason as anybody else to put one foot ahead of the other.
>
> What he carried with him, all he carried with him, was a lack, something like a lack of air, of proper behavior in his lungs, a difficulty that he supposed would go on forever.
>
> The girl he'd been talking to, whom he'd once known—she had spoken of her children. The loss of her children. Getting used to that. A problem at suppertime.
>
> An expert at losing, she might be called—himself a novice by comparison. And now he could not remember her name. Had lost her name, though he'd known it well. Losing, lost. A joke on him, if you wanted one.
>
> He was going up his own steps when it came to him.
> Leah.
> A relief out of all proportion, to remember her. (89–90)

When I reviewed *The Progress of Love*, I noticed a passage in "Circle of Prayer" (1986) in which Munro asks, "What are those times that stand out, clear patches in your life—what do they have to do with it? They aren't exactly promises. Breathing spaces. Is that all?" (*Progress* 273). Here yet again as she concludes "Leaving Maverley," Munro offers us these passages and wonders over the "breathing space" that is a "clear patch" in Ray's life as he realizes the "lack" that Isabel's absence is for him, just as he "loses" her, as we say—"losing, lost," as Munro writes. Or, as she wrote before in "Images," "all this life going on." Recovering Leah's lost name, despite the lack created by Isabel's death, keeps Ray connected to life. Partially because of this, he will go on living: "They aren't exactly promises. Breathing spaces. Is that all?"

Yes, we answer, it is. In the penultimate sentence of my review of *The Progress of Love*, I wrote: "In these stories we approach the mystery of being, follow the narrative wooing of the self and, in the end, even if we don't come to an understanding, we emphatically recognize life—as it is lived, experienced, and wondered about" (*Reading Alice Munro* 77). As Munro wrote in "Material"—as it happened, as I mentioned in the introduction here, my own first Munro story—Ray is another person "lifted out of life and held in light, suspended in the marvelous clear jelly that [Munro] has spent all [her] life learning how to make. It is an act of magic, there is no getting around it; it is an act, you might say, of a special, unsparing, unsentimental love. A fine and lucky benevolence" (*Something* 43).[1] "Because this is not a story, only life." Judging from "Dear Life" and "Leaving Maverley"—and from the whole of *Dear Life*, which with its "Finale" may turn out to be her last book, as she has said it will be—Munro has continued to wonder as she has written on into her ninth decade, still creating her own "clear jelly," and defining and detailing her own, and our own, breathing spaces. It is a fine and lucky benevolence, in fact.

* * *

After 14 books, 62 contributions to the *New Yorker*, a raft of literary prizes, interviews and personality pieces too numerous to count, two biographies, and critical books and articles and bibliographic studies also too numerous to count, Munro was awoken before dawn on the morning of October 10, 2013, by a reporter seeking her reaction to the news that she had been awarded the 2013 Nobel Prize in Literature. Reflecting on this some weeks later, just as her daughter Jenny was planning to go to Stockholm to accept the prize on her behalf, Munro was quoted in a piece in the *Globe and Mail* titled "Vindication for a Lifetime of Short Stories" saying, "Nothing in the world could make me so happy as this."[2] She also explains her 2012 decision to stop writing, saying "I wanted to behave like the rest of the world.… When you're a writer, you're doing a job people don't know you're doing and you really can't talk about, and you're always finding your way in this secret world. I guess I was a little tired of that." In the article she also calls the hoopla surrounding the news of the Nobel "bewildering," as it most certainly was for her, but maintains that, in the reporter's words, "the prize is an acknowledgment of the importance of the arts, and that it is a vindication for the short story, the smaller cousin of the novels that usually dominate literary awards" (Perreaux).

Although this is but a single newspaper article chosen from among the mass coverage that welcomed the news of Munro's Nobel Prize—and welcome is the correct word here, with many literary commentators noting the universal joy with which the news was met—Perreaux captures what it is about Munro that has made her achievements both so remarkable and so edifying to her readers and critics. Munro is a writer who—from the late 1940s on—has spent much of her working time "finding [her] way in this secret world," the world of her writing, and the world of the short story, in which, as has long been said of both the genre and her practice of it, insights are momentary, fleeting, contingent. Episodic, just as life itself, the short story keeps a reader wondering and doubting. We wonder with Munro, who is irrefutably "a master of the contemporary short story," as the Nobel committee asserted. But she is also, more importantly, an artist who, in her secret world, has articulated in her stories the very feelings of being alive, and of being human. We critics are always hearing and being affected by the stories she is telling us as we read through her stories toward the impeccable "Finale," to what she has said is her last book, *Dear Life*.

There, with those "first and last—and the closest—things" she has to say about her own life (*Dear* 255), she returns again to her childhood in the final four autobiographical pieces. In "The Eye," "Voices," and "Dear Life," she is back in the thrall of her assertive and domineering mother, aware of being the eldest child (and for a time seeming the special only child), during those years before Anne Chamney Laidlaw was struck by Parkinson's disease and the Laidlaw's family life was transformed. In "Night," we find a companionable Alice Laidlaw wondering over some sleeping troubles with her father, Robert Eric Laidlaw, a fox farmer whose business was failing. Finding her out of bed early one morning, troubled by dreams when she is normally asleep, he gives her good advice. As she writes, "on that breaking morning he gave me just what I needed to hear and what I was to forget about soon enough." She then wonders about the uncharacteristically formal clothes he is wearing that morning, and why he might be wearing them. Her wondering takes us to the end of "Night":

> I have thought that he was maybe in in his better work clothes because he had a morning appointment to go to the bank, to learn, not to his surprise, that there was no extension on his loan. He had worked as hard as he could but the market was not going to turn around and he had to find a new way of supporting us and paying off what we owed at the same time. Or he may have found out that there was a name for my mother's shakiness and that it was not going to stop. Or that he was in love with an impossible woman.
> Never mind. From then on I could sleep. (*Dear* 284–85)

Munro goes from this to "Voices," where she depicts her mother as sociable, imperious, and moralistic—suddenly dragging her fascinated 10-year-old daughter away from a festive house dance when she discovered a local madam was there, too.

But then she turns to "Dear Life," another—and perhaps final—visitation with her mother. The central incident is of her mother, needlessly worrying over a baby Alice and holding on to the infant "for dear life," keeping her safe from an apparently threatening neighbor. The story also focuses on Munro's own recent discovery of what was most likely actually going on. But as she ends "Dear Life," Munro returns, as she has so many times before, to her mother in the final throes of her illness, finally succumbing after almost 20 years to her Parkinson's disease. In the *New Yorker* version, Munro ends the story with these two paragraphs, following a line break:

> I did not go home for my mother's last illness or for her funeral. I had two small children and nobody in Vancouver to leave them with. We could barely have afforded the trip, and my husband had a contempt for formal behavior, but why blame it on him? I felt the same. We say of some things that they can't be forgiven, or that we will never forgive ourselves. But we do—we do it all the time.
>
> When my mother was dying, she got out of the hospital somehow, at night, and wandered around town until someone who didn't know her at all spotted her and took her in. If this were fiction, as I said, it would be too much, but it is true. (47)

When "Dear Life" appeared in the collection *Dear Life*, this final paragraph had been deleted. When I asked her about this omission, Munro replied that she judged it too late in "Dear Life" to introduce this harrowing fact about her mother (September 6, 2013). True enough.

And yet I wonder. Here Munro is in the last and title piece of the "Finale" of what she says is her last book, again having returned home, again having returned to the details of her mother's death in early 1959. "Home"—she has returned again to the circumstances of "Home," the story-memoir that begins by elaborating on the heart condition that led to her father's death. In the penultimate paragraph of "Soon" (2004), another story drawing on her mother's death, Munro writes, tellingly: "Because it's what happens at home that you try to protect, as best you can, for as long as you can" (*Runaway* 125). Reading Munro, we see her as one who has always returned "Home": "The problem, the only problem, is my mother," she wrote in another critical and well-known coda, ending "The Ottawa Valley" and her third book. "And she is of course the one I am trying to get; it is to reach her that this whole journey has been undertaken" (*Something* 246). Not a story, only life.

Notes

"Clear Jelly": Alice Munro's Narrative Dialectics (1983)

1 These critics alone attempt to define the workings of Munro's narrative art. Others writing on Munro have emphasized themes, her similarities to other writers, and her "vision"; they appear to have been under the influence of the egregious prevailing thematic approach taken by critics of Canadian literature over the past decade. The inapplicability of this approach to a stylist like Munro illustrates its very limited usefulness.

2 Munro uses the father's clothing here subjectively as a symbol of the man. This is a technique that she uses often in the later stories included in *Dance of the Happy Shades*, such as "Images" (36). In this, the most recently composed story to be included in the volume, the narrator's consideration of her father's boots as an extension of his personality corresponds to this earlier instance.

3 Gardiner's interview with Munro is included as an appendix to the thesis.

4 See Schorer. At one point, talking about the "cultivated sensitivity" of the styles of Welty, Katherine Anne Porter, and Jean Stafford, Schorer states that the values in each writer's style lies "in the subtle means by which sensuous details become symbols, and in the way the symbols provide a network which is the story, and which at the same time provides the writer and us with a refined moral insight by means of which to test it" (106). Munro's style is of the same sort because the "network which is the story" in Munro's case is an aggregate of setting, character, and theme, strung together by her retrospective narrative technique, which provides perspective.

5 The first parenthetical insertion is mine, the second is Gardiner's.

6 Of the 13 stories written after "Good-by Myra" and included in *Dance of the Happy Shades*, only three—"Sunday Afternoon," "The Shining Houses," and "A Trip to the Coast"—employ a detached

third-person narrator; the other 10 use the remembering first-person narrator, as does the whole of *Lives of Girls and Women*.

7. In both "The Time of Death" and "A Trip to the Coast"—each story published alone and then included in *Dance of the Happy Shades*—Munro uses setting symbolically, in the former story by the way in which she handles the first snowfall of winter and in the latter by the way she handles the first few droplets of rain.

8. It is worth noting that Munro did not revise this story prior to its publication in *Dance of the Happy Shades*, as was the case with the other stories published originally in the 1950s and included there.

9. This order of composition, as with that used throughout, reflects the one given by Munro in her 1972 interview with John Metcalf. This order is corroborated by Gardiner (xii). For those stories not mentioned by Munro, I have adopted date of first publication to establish order of composition.

Connection: Alice Munro and Ontario (1984)

1. To underscore my point of the myth of the Ontario small town, see Germaine Warkentin's 1974 anthology, *Stories from Ontario*. Although her scholarly introduction defines and describes various types of Ontario fiction—from the bush of Susanna Moodie to the urban stories of Morley Callaghan, and Hugh Garner—Warkentin selects Leacock's nostalgic evocation of the small town in "The Marine Excursion of the Knights of Pythias" as her "prologue." Such editorial emphasis, which suggests Leacock's vision is the most apt, confirms a sense of the small town ethos in Ontario as the preferred myth.

2. Regarding my use of the term "epiphany," one of the best books on the short story as a genre is Frank O'Connor's *The Lonely Voice* (1962).

3. See Lorna Irvine's "Changing Is the Word I Want" in *Probable Fictions*. I cite Irvine's word, "jerky," in complete agreement with its context: "Furthermore, the peculiarly jerky, I might even say breathless, pace of a Munro narrative reflects the kaleidoscope of moods that are the stories' contents." "Moods," however, is not the word I would use, since the jerky quality of which Irvine speaks is produced, most often, by shifts in memory triggered by past association. A useful article in this regard is W. H. New's "Every Now and Then: Voice and Language in Laurence's *The Stone Angel*."

4. Regarding Munro and American southern writers, see J. R. (Tim) Struthers, "Alice Munro and the American South." Munro has also discussed this in her interviews.

5. See Struther's interview for Munro's use of "holding pattern" versus "the real material." Regarding Munro's use of setting to define inarticulate characters, and in particular Lois in "Thanks for the Ride," see my "Clear Jelly: Alice Munro's Narrative Dialectics," the previous article here.

6. The ellipses here are Gardiner's but the parenthetical insertions are mine.

Conferring Munro (1987)

1. For a contemporary review of B. Pfaus's *Alice Munro* see Lorraine M. York, "Joyless in Jubilee?" Beverly Rasporich's "The Art of Alice Munro," and Miriam Packer's "Beyond

the Garrison: A Critical Study of Munro, Atwood, and Laurence," were scheduled to be published by Quadrant Editions. Lorna Irvine's *Sub/version: Canadian Fictions by Women* has recently been published by ECW Press. And W. R. Martin has a book on Munro forthcoming from the University of Alberta Press.

2   The reader would have hoped for strong editing—either through blue pencil or by exclusion—but the editorial weaknesses here extend to the minute: Miller does not bother to tell us when the conference was held, beginning her brief introduction, "Here is the collection of critical papers on Alice Munro presented at the Waterloo Conference on Munro. Finally" (iii), as if we all knew about the conference and had been anticipating its proceedings. As it happens, I did know and I had been looking for the papers, but doubtlessly many readers will not have, and what is more, would like to have such details included. Similarly, the contents page offers us "table of contents" twice, for some reason, and, after she lists the editions of Munro's works "consistently" referred to in the volume, Miller allows the authors to offer—repeatedly—full bibliographic citations for Munro's works.

3   In addition, Munro discusses her appreciation of American southern writers as early as 1971 in "Alice Munro Talks to Mari Stainsby." Her most well known discussion of the subject is with John Metcalf in "A Conversation with Alice Munro."

4   Such a grand generalization as this requires support, certainly. What I have in mind are, essentially, two types of articles common during the late 1970s, and I exclude biographical-overview pieces in the popular press. The first sort is exemplified by Rae McCarthy Macdonald's "A Madman Loose in the World: The Vision of Alice Munro." Macdonald, egregiously under the (in my view) influence of Frye's "garrison mentality," blithely applies it to Munro because—so it seems—the author is Canadian, and then offers a thematic discussion of some of Munro's work. Such an approach is not only too simple, it is simple-minded. The other type of article, of the same ilk, but more troubling because editors have persisted in publishing them, is Miriam Packer's "*Lives of Girls and Women:* A Creative Search for Completion." In these articles authors offer only their own reading, making no attempt to avail themselves to what others have published, nor any attempt to engage in critical debate. Packer shares Macdonald's view of Frye's garrisons, which is bad enough, but she writes as if no one had previously published a thing on *Lives of Girls and Women*, citing only Munro's book. J. R. (Tim) Struthers made something of this same point in "Some Highly Subversive Activities."

"So Shocking a Verdict in Real Life"

1   With the exception of the title of "Material," Munro has discussed these alternate titles in interviews. As a preliminary, I should like to note that this essay was written before I had the opportunity look at the Munro papers held by the University of Calgary's Special Collections. My examination, however, confirmed in a multitude of additional ways the nature of the relationship between Munro's life and her fiction examined here.

2   This phrase, of course, is Nebraska novelist Wright Morris', whose phototext/novel *The Home Place* was published in 1948. Morris' affinities

with his Nebraska boyhood are analogous to Munro's with Huron County, Ontario.

3   In connection with another essay, I recently asked Munro during a telephone conversation about her use of Willa Cather in "Dulse." She replied that she had visited Grand Manan Island—the actual New Brunswick island where Cather summered for years—with a friend, and there she met a man very much like Mr. Stanley, a person she described as "a Cather fanatic." She had been working on Lydia's story before her visit and, afterwards, brought the two events together. During the same conversation, she confirmed a personal visit to the Royal Ontario Museum's planetarium as described in "The Moons of Jupiter," though the visit took place about a year after her father's death.

4   Though these doubts have come to the fore in more recent work, they have been in evidence from *Dance of the Happy Shades* on. "The Office," for example, a story first published in 1962 and one which Munro says simply happened to her (Metcalf Interview 58), concludes: "While I arrange words, and think it is my right to rid of" Mr. Malley, the narrator's landlord who will not leave her alone in her office to write and who, patently, does not believe that she is writing in there. Osachoff discusses this point in relation to Munro's narrative voice.

Review Essay: Go Ask Alice

1   Taken together, these essays offer a reasonable summary of the critical contexts and something of the dynamics of canon formation, and note published criticism on Canadian literature writ large. Regarding the latter, a comprehensive treatment is *Literary History of Canada: Canadian Literature in English* (1990).

2   The notion of Munro's reception by critics as being something of a paradigmatic case was the point of departure in my "Alice Munro and the Critics: A Paradigm," a paper presented to the Association for Canadian Studies in the United States, in October 1979; this part of the paper was dropped and the revised balance was published as "'Clear Jelly': Alice Munro's Narrative Dialectics," in *Probable Fictions* (see the first essay in this volume). Some years later, I updated this discussion in "Conferring Munro," a review of *The Art of Alice Munor: Saying the Unsayable*, edited by Judith Miller (see the third essay here). I note these activities not to toot my own horn but by way of preparing for my comments on scholarship, below.

3   The first book-length collection on Munro's writing was *Probable Fictions* (1983); it was followed the next year by another collection—made up of papers presented at a conference on Munro held at the University of Waterloo in 1982—*The Art of Alice Munro: Saying the Unsayable*, edited by Judith Miller. My "Alice Munro: An Annotated Bibliography," in *The Annotated Bibliography of Canada's Major Authors, Volume 5*, was published in 1984 as well, as was the first "critical" book on Munro by a single author, B. Pfaus's *Alice Munro*. The latter is so bad as to make any serious scholar-critic shudder. Though technically not the first, then, W. R. Martin's *Alice Munro: Paradox and Parallel* ought to be considered so. Throughout this period, too, articles and book chapters on Munro's work appeared with increasing frequency.

The point here, of course, is that just as Munro's work gained reputation,

4   Redekop's book, putatively entitled *Alice Munro and Our Mock Mothers: Reading the Signs of Invasion*, according to Hutcheon, has not appeared in late October 1990 as I write. This time lag seems strange in view of Hutcheon's acknowledgement, which was probably written over two years ago. Perhaps ironically, this situation is reminiscent of a Rasporich volume, entitled *The Art of Alice Munro* and announced as forthcoming by Quandrant Editions in 1985 but never published (along with one by Miriam Packer, also never published); that book doubtless bears some relation to the volume at hand here.

5   Other titles in the series include children's books, English-Canadian theatre, film, and folklore (in print); as well as Indigenous literature, Jewish writers, science fiction and fantasy, diaries and journals, literary criticism, the press, and photography (forthcoming).

6   The very existence of this book, or that of any other relevant criticism on the subject, is ignored by Gadpaille. Indeed, her book is reminiscent of the short introduction to this or that Canadian author that was often the only extended critical piece available during the 1960s and early 1970s—Michael Ondaatje's book on Leonard Cohen, cited by Hutcheon (43), from McClelland and Stewart, is the sort of work I have in mind. Such volumes may be making a comeback, judging from ECW's newest series, "Introducing..."; see for example, George Woodcock, *Introducing Margaret Laurence's* The Stone Angel: *A Reader's Guide*. Published initially in hardback by ECW, these are short introductory readings of often-taught novels designed for the student market; they at least have the advantage of focusing on a single work.

7   Besides *Controlling the Uncontrollable*, two volumes were published recently by Southern Illinois University Press: *Margaret Atwood: Vision and Forms* (1988), edited by Kathryn VanSpanckeren and Jan Garden Castro; and Karen Gould's *Writing in the Feminine: Feminism and Experimental Writing in Quebec* (1989). My own *The Great Prairie Fact and Literary Imagination* was published by the University of New Mexico Press in 1989; it followed Yale University Press' *Prairie Women* by Carol Fairbanks. Similarly, in 1988 the University of Wisconsin published *Nationalism and Politics of Culture in Quebec* by Richard Handler; this is less remarkable, though, since there are fields—anthropology, history, political science—where American presses publishing on Canadian topics is unremarkable; that these presses are noticeably more receptive to manuscripts on Canadian literary topics, however, seems a relatively new phenomenon.

In passing, too, I wonder if the subvention policies of the granting agencies, which largely ensure that only books by Canadians or landed immigrants receive subventions, have not played a role here as well. Scholarly presses in Canada normally do not publish without a subvention, so it is conceivable that manuscripts on Canadian topics by Americans (of whom, I should say, I am one) might be denied publication solely for the absence of such grant support. Books by non-Canadians or non-landed immigrants must pass an additional hurdle for subvention

8   J. R. (Tim) Struthers made this same point in "Some Highly Subversive Activities" in 1981 and I echoed him in "Conferring Munro." This remains a fundamental critical problem, to my mind. Too many "critics" fashion themselves as only that—not scholars—and editors and publishers aid and abet them.

9   This is not to suggest that Howells cites every discussion of *Lives of Girls and Women* and *Who Do You Think You Are* in print; on the contrary, there are several pieces on each that she might well have mentioned, and I would have preferred that she had. But—and this is the point about scholarship I am making here—Howells draws upon published scholarship in a way consistent with her topic, focus, scope, and audience; clearly, she knows what the critics have written, and cites those directly relevant to her own argument. This, it seems to me, is a long way from Oxford's arrogant decision to omit all critical apparatus from Gadpaille's book; a list of cited works would not have added appreciably to that book's length.

10 Rasporich is quoting Sandra Gilbert and Susan Gubar's *The Madwoman in the Attic: The Woman Writer and the Nineteenth-Century Literary Imagination* (1979).

11 Rasporich makes an honest attempt to use scholarship, but there are some curious gaps; some of this may owe to the book's gestation, for at times Rasporich is right up to date while at others she is well behind. For example, given her feminist approach, I am surprised that Smaro Kamboureli's "The Body as Audience and Performance in the Writing of Alice Munro" (1986) or Constance Rooke's "Munro's Food" are not mentioned, although the timing may have been off. Similarly, while she discusses the gothic elements in Munro, and cites some scholarship on the subject, Rasporich does not directly mention Macdonald's "A Madman Loose in the World," although she does list it in her bibliography. On a personal note, despite her discussion of Ontario as place, Rasporich makes no mention of my "Connection: Alice Munro and Ontario" (1984), a piece that is directly relevant to her subject. This sort of casualness in an otherwise scholarly book is problematic, for it affects the author's authority. Its presence can be noted in smaller matters, too: Rasporich gets the years of first publication wrong for both *Dance of the Happy Shades* and *The Moons of Jupiter* and consistently refers to a story entitled "Chaddeleys and Flemings 1. Connection" as "Connection." These are not big things, but they are bothersome.

12 Neither Blodgett nor Carrington is especially convincing in discussing Munro's use of Cather here, although Carrington consults suitable scholarly sources (see Stich "Cather").

13 Carrington is quoting from an interview with Beverley Slopen conducted with Munro and published in *Publisher's Weekly*.

14 Martin discusses Yeats in connection with Munro on several points, but he does not deal specifically with this story. Gold also suggests the parallel. Carrington sees "The Wild Swans at Coole" and "Leda and the Swan" as the primary analogues, but, especially in light of Blodgett's discussion of Bobby Sheriff's pirouette at the end of *Lives of Girls and Women*, I would see "Among School Children" as in some ways the better

match. The point of all this—beyond display of erudition and proving the postmodern notion that texts are made of other texts—is that Munro is clearly a much more literary writer than she has traditionally been seen. In the same fashion, see Lorraine York's "The Rival Bards." All of these lines of enquiry—including that of Cather—warrant further critical investigation.

Alice Munro's Willa Cather (1992)

1. The Cather–Lewis companionship has received considerable attention; the two met by 1903, and five years later, when each was working at *McClure's*, they began sharing an apartment. This living arrangement continued until Cather's death in 1947, after which time Lewis guarded her friend's reputation as executor until her own death in 1972. For a judicious overview of the relationship, see Marilyn Arnold's foreword to the most recent edition of *Willa Cather Living*. As well, O'Brien's discussion of it—though perhaps overstated—recognizes its importance in Cather's life (*Emerging* 353–57).

2. Although "Dulse" offers the most discrete indication of the influence of Cather's fiction on Munro, numerous other echoes are worth pursuing. Not the least of these is the structural symmetry between Cather's "Old Mrs. Harris" (1932) and Munro's "The Progress of Love" (1985). Both stories focus on three women—grandmother, daughter, and granddaughter—and probe the paramount values of each; that is, how each woman lives with dignity, given the social mores of the time and her own personal values. Munro, moreover, has called "Old Mrs. Harris" her favourite Cather story (Telephone interview). Similarly, this comparison could be extended further throughout both writers' works in that relationships between women of different generations, and especially mother–daughter relationships, is a shared central theme.

3. Thus when Munro published *Who Do You Think You Are?* (1978), some reviewers complained that it was a revisiting of her earlier material in *Lives of Girls and Women* (1971). Carrington, however, has recently refuted these claims, arguing convincingly that Munro does not "repeat herself," but rather that she "demonstrates the validity of her own aesthetic: by returning to the same theme, she clarifies her misconception of what she thought was happening and sees what she had not understood in the earlier attempt" (98).

4. Jewett's influence on Cather—coming as it did at a propitious time, when the younger woman was struggling to free herself from her duties at *McClure's* in order to write—has been seen as critical to her development. See Woodress (201–06); O'Brien (*Emerging* 334–52 and *passim*).

5. Unless indicated otherwise, parenthetical page references from "Dulse" are from its final form, that in *The Moons of Jupiter*; all quotations from Munro's papers are from the second accession; the identification numbers are from the published catalogue.

6. Of those in print, Carrington's reading of "Dulse" is much the best. "With the paradigmatic clarity of a psychiatric case history," she writes, the story "dramatizes self-destructive ambivalence" (146). Carrington relates the story well to the rest of Munro's work, applies Karen Horney's work on neurosis to Lydia's situation, and sees Cather as "an alter ego of the writer-protagonist"

(148), but she makes no real attempt to probe Munro's Cather for its full meaning, nor does she suggest Cather's influence on "Dulse" more broadly.

7   Munro may have been aware that what Lydia envisions here for Cather's cottage is exactly what Edith Lewis allowed to happen to it after Cather's death, and this despite pleas from Grand Manan residents to see to repairs, according to Brown and Crone (129–36). Munro may have heard this history through the same sorts of oral sources.

8   As regards Cather after her reputation was established, this description of her behaviour is accurate. What is more, a vital part of Cather's persona was her great determination to succeed, a quality she evinced from her university years onward, and which is treated autobiographically in *The Song of the Lark* (1915). In 1922 when she arrived at Grand Manan for the first time, however, her reputation was established and was in the process of being cemented. Brown and Crone, in their study of Cather in the northeast, offer a version of Cather on Grand Manan that accords with Mr. Stanley's (36–43); this book, which O'Brien has rightly called "maddeningly undocumented" (*Willa Cather* 244 n47), could probably not have been a source for Munro because it was published in the same year as "Dulse." The more likely source for Mr. Stanley's version of Willa Cather is the person whom Munro met on Grand Manan; it conforms to the folklore surrounding Cather on Grand Manan as presented by Brown and Crone.

9   Though known primarily for fiction, each wrote and published poetry. Cather's first published book was a collection of poems, *April Twilights*

(1903), and Munro, for her part, wrote poetry, although the extent of its publication has not yet been established. An untitled poem of hers, signed Anne Chamney (her mother's maiden name), appeared in 1967 in the *Canadian Forum*. I should like to thank Jean Moore, of the University of Calgary Special Collections staff, for bringing this to my attention.

10 Gardiner's article is particularly useful as regards the workings of the autobiographical in Cather and Munro. There, drawing upon the identity theories of Erikson and, especially, Choderow, and arguing that "female identity is a process," Gardiner looks at "typical narrative strategies of women writers—the manipulation of identifications between narrator, author, and reader and the representation of memory" in order to suggest ways that an author's text relates to her own identity. Following this, Gardiner asserts that "novels by women often shift through first, second, and third persons and into reverse. Thus the author may define herself through the text while creating her female hero" (349, 357).

11 This reading of the story is one that I have heard in discussions of "Dulse" but have not seen in print; it was also put to Munro herself in a letter she received just after "Dulse" appeared in the *New Yorker* (38.1.82).

12 Lorenz was Conrad Aiken's second wife; Olney is reviewing her *Lorelei Two: My Life with Conrad Aiken*.

Alice Munro and the Anxiety of American Influence (1994)

1   The Struthers interview is Munro's most detailed discussion of influences, though the matter comes up in virtually all her interviews.

2. Critics have noticed and speculated on Munro's use of the word "connection," and one has gone so far as to count its usage: none in *Dance of the Happy Shades*; 14 times in *Lives of Girls and Women*; four times in *Something I've Been Meaning to Tell You*, five in *Who Do You Think You Are?*; and a full 19 times in *The Moons of Jupiter*, which features a story with "Connection" as its subtitle. Counts are not in yet for either *The Progress of Love* or *Friend of My Youth* (York, "Gulfs" 145). Somewhat peevishly, and owing to a long-held view that Munro critics generally do not read relevant criticism as closely as scholarship dictates, nor, apparently, do the editors who publish essays with insufficient critical bases, I must note than an essay of mine was the first to discuss Munro's use of "connection": see my "Connection: Alice Munro and Ontario." Blodgett's, Martin's, and, especially, Carrington's book, however, are all exempt from this criticism. Counting aside, "connection," as both a word and a concept, continues to figure in Munro's most recent stories. During the tribute to Margaret Laurence held at Trent University in March 1988, I raised the frequent use of the term with Munro herself—she claimed not to have noticed it, but upon reading her story "Meneseteung" (*Friend of My Youth*) as a part of the tribute, both of us noticed its appearance in the final paragraph of that story.

3. The story was first published in the *New Yorker*—told from the first-person point of view. It was revised (to third-person, with other changes) and included in *The Moons of Jupiter*. Although all of the authors of the full-length books on Munro mentioned here nod toward the Cather connection, only Carrington treats it seriously. More troubling, Blodgett quotes a questionable source, offering what amounts to disinformation on Cather (167 n5).

4. Beverly J. Rasporich seems to be moving in this direction in *Dance of the Sexes*, especially in her chapters on Munro as "Folk Artist and Ironist" and "Regionalist."

5. One should add in passing that W. R. Martin, to take but one example, came to Munro from a background in modern British literature.

6. The relationship between *Lives of Girls and Women* and *Who Do You Think You Are?* is a good case in point; upon the latter's publication, many reviewers complained of Munro's revisiting the same material a second time. Yet, as Carrington has recently demonstrated, Munro did not repeat herself: though in some ways similar, these two books are radically different, the former growing out of its author's youth, the latter out of her return to Huron County in the seventies after years away (98).

7. In the 1986 interview quoted at the outset, Munro rejects her metafictional comments in "The Ottawa Valley" and "Home," saying that now she is "disillusioned with the disillusionment. I'm not going to make those pronouncements anymore." Now, she says, she would "like to rewrite ['Home'] just as a simple story like I would have done when I was 25, and get rid of that stuff about backing off and commenting on the story—which got me all sorts of praise at the time" (Freake Interview 8).

8. Munro has attempted nonfictional work. Her "A Better Place Than Home," a documentary script for CBC-TV, deals with the Irish emigration to Canada. She also did

considerable work writing the text to accompany a book of Ontario photographs by Peter D'Angelo; the text was never published, although it bears some relation to *Who Do You Think You Are?* See Alice Munro Papers, Special Collections Division, University of Calgary Library, MSC 37.13.7–14; *The Alice Munro Papers: First Accession* 132–35.

9   The final quotation is from *The Golden Apples.*

10 "Prickly" is a word used by James Woodress to describe Cather in later life; see his *Willa Cather: A Literary Life*, which promises to be the standard biography.

11 See, for example, Munro's introduction to the Penguin edition of *The Moons of Jupiter* (xiii–xvi).

12 In *Willa Cather: The Emerging Voice*, Sharon O'Brien inserts "[sic]" after Cather's use of the male pronoun as she quotes the "gift of sympathy" passage (347). Though contemporary convention must be acknowledged, I am sympathetic to O'Brien's objection.

13 See my "Alice Munro's Willa Cather," above.

14 See Alice Munro Papers, MsC 38.8.20; *The Alice Munro Papers: Second Accession* 161.

15 Although there has been an explosion in critical materials on Cather during the past decade, there were enough reminiscences, biographies, and other pieces extant to have been the basis of Munro's depiction of Cather. There is also the possibility that the "fanatic" whom Munro met was sufficiently informative. For those interested in a good discussion of the Cather–Edith Lewis bond—the basis of Munro's characterization—see O'Brien, *Emerging* 352–59.

16 For example, what might be called the "geological dimension" of "Before Breakfast"—Grenfell meets a geologist who has set up a temporary research camp on his island; the man tells him about the geological history of the island, an episode which puts Grenfell out of sorts—has its parallel in Munro's title story, with its meditations on the moons of Jupiter; they, too, represent a deepness, like geological time, that the human imagination can only dimly understand. Another parallel, though more tentative, is between Mr. Black, the mysterious man of European extraction who dies in the corner of the field and is buried there, beneath the stone, in the second "Chaddeleys and Flemings" story, and Cather's Mr. Shimerda in *My Ántonia*, a suicide victim who lies buried in a similar place. There are other such parallels.

17 Munro's use of photography has been the focus of considerable comment, beginning with Struthers' article on the American South. See, in particular, York, "'The Other Side of Dailiness.'"

What's "Material": The Progress of Munro Criticism, Part 2 (1998)

1   Both Klaus P. Stich and I have examined the Munro–Cather relation in some detail. What it reveals, like other parallels between Munro and numerous other writers, particularly Eudora Welty, is that Munro has a deep understanding of the writer's position vis-à-vis herself, her family, her society, and her critics. As I suggest throughout this essay, Munro quite reasonably now puts critics at the end of this line, whatever her attitude was years ago in Victoria.

2 Although my focus here is on critical books on Munro's work published since 1990, I want to comment briefly on journal articles that, as I say, have appeared with increasing frequency. While doing the work for this review, I read my way through those articles that appeared during the same period, as well as some from the 1980s I had missed.

One is struck that hand in hand with her international celebrity, Munro has received attention from foreign critics—American and European alike. Much of this is of little worth, owing largely to the perspective of the critics or the peculiar approach they take—far too many critics, still, discover Munro and rush to print without doing the necessary scholarship; their insights are mundane, their arguments commonplace (Sturgess, Ventura, Seyersted). Equally, too, editors have discovered Munro and commissioned overview pieces that—though probably of some use to those who have never read any of her work—would be better off left to reference books (Ditsky). One of these, by Georgeann Murphy, is particularly troubling in that it includes a full bibliography of Munro's work without any acknowledgement of the various published bibliographical sources that, doubtless, were consulted in the compilation. Other foreign critics have contributed articles that have derived from reading and teaching individual stories, and are offered without reference to Canadian literature as a subfield (Cam, Clark, Elliot, Goodman, Houston, Mayberry). At the same time, foreign critics who have established themselves as scholars of Canadian literature have continued to contribute; one, Carrington, has done so with her usual detail and zeal (see also Gilbert and Irvine). Canadian critics, in the same vein, have continued to offer examinations of Munro that extend the theoretical and nationalist discourse with regard to her work (Canitz, Garson, Goldman, Hoy, McCarthy, Rooke, Seaman, Sellwood, Smythe, Stubbs). Others, most notably John Weaver, have approached Munro's work from an altogether new vantage point. As will become evident below, my own view is that given that Munro's form is the short story, articles are much the better format for criticism of her work than books. Indeed, since she published *Controlling the Uncontrollable*, Carrington's work has abundantly demonstrated the efficacy of the critical article to Munro; would that Smythe and Heble had done as much. And while some critics have availed themselves to the wealth of information available in the Calgary archives (Hoy, Tausky), this remains a largely untapped resource.

3 Even with this fine insight, Mayberry offers an example of the sort of blinkered scholarship I bemoan. In an excellent article she manages to discuss Munro's use of paradox without citing Helen Hoy's work in this area; though she does cite critics who acknowledge Hoy—Blodgett and Carrington—that hardly seems enough.

4 A most graphic instance of this is the recurrence of an industrial decapitation that first appeared in "Thanks for the Ride" (1957)—a story Munro submitted to Robert Weaver at the CBC in 1955—as the cause of Lois's father's death. There the incident is a brief description offered to Dick by Lois's mother (*Dance* 51). It is a major focus in "Carried Away" (1991), where Louisa's imagined suitor, Jack Agnew, is killed in the same accident, his severed head being "carried away" by the factory

owner, Arthur Doud, whom Louisa eventually marries. Such recurrent incidents seem more worth analysis than many, if not most, of the patterns Carscallen elaborates.

5   These two books, ironically, derive from dissertations submitted in 1990 to the University of Toronto's Department of English, the same department among whose members are Carscallen and Redekop. Largely regarded as the pre-eminent department in the country—at least by those associated with it—Toronto has been slow in establishing a hospitable environment for the critical study of Canadian writing; that history may enter into the phenomenon such books as these represent, since each author aspires to tie the argument to some discourse other than Canadian literature. However seen, such an assertion needs to be defended, certainly, especially when a reasonable response to it would be the three words "Frye," "Atwood," and "Davies." See my "Gazing Through the One-Way Mirror" for a discussion of the historical contexts of Canadian writing in the Canadian academy generally, and in the English Department at Toronto particularly.

6   It may be worth noting that here, in 1990, Besner is critiquing mimesis in Munro, à la Canitz, without recourse to the current jargon used by Heble. It goes without saying, too, that Besner's "sophistication" outstrips Heble's and Carscallen's in my view.

ALICE MUNRO'S ONTARIO (2007)

1   Munro's relationship to her Ontario home place is of major consideration in my *Alice Munro: Writing Her Lives: A Biography,* a book that was written subsequent to this essay.

2   In 1980, Munro corresponded with Douglas Gibson, her editor, about "a kind of family book I want to do someday" (see Thacker, *Writing* 367–68). That book is *The View From Castle Rock* (2006), which among other pieces includes "Home"—without its metafictional commentary (285–315)—"Working for a Living" (also revised, 127–70) and "What Do You Want to Know For?" (also revised, 316–40).

A "BOOMING TENDER SADNESS": ALICE MUNRO'S IRISH (2008)

1   This image is in the collection of the Library of Congress, item LC-USZ62-7307.

ALICE MUNRO: CRITICAL RECEPTION (2013)

1   This is a point I first asserted in "What's 'Material'" (208). There have been no single-authored volumes focused on the fiction since Howells' save a faulty "appreciation" by an ill-informed American reader, Brad Hooper, and a fine small book by Ailsa Cox in a British series that introduces writers to students. Another scholarly volume, by Isla Duncan, has been announced for November 2011.

2   Despite its many strengths, I nonetheless notice an important weakness in McGill's essay: he entirely neglects to mention Louis K. MacKendrick's *Some Other Reality*, which covers many of the same considerations of this important story; this is hardly justified.

3   Another essay that might have been mentioned regarding "Meneseteung" is Naomi Morgenstern's "The Baby or the Violin?"—it considers the story in concert with "My Mother's Dream" (1998), concentrating on the ethics of feminism, and paying special attention to Almeda's dream in the story. Driven by an apparent desire to demonstrate that Munro actualizes literary theory in her stories, Morgenstern offers readings of Munro's stories that are ultimately unsatisfactory.

Afterword

1   I am aware that many critics, owing to their analysis of the narrator's character in "Material," see this phrasing as ironic. Whatever the animus this narrator feels toward Hugo, her former husband, I take this "fine and lucky benevolence" as genuine appreciation.

2   This video interview, held in November 2013 after the Nobel Prize was announced, is available on the Nobel Prize website (accessed December 18, 2013): http://www.nobelprize.org/nobel_prizes/literature/laureates/2013/munro-lecture.html.

Works Cited

A. Primary Works by Alice Munro (By Publication Date)

1. BOOKS

Dance of the Happy Shades. Foreword Hugh Garner. Toronto: Ryerson, 1968.

Lives of Girls and Women. Toronto: McGraw-Hill Ryerson, 1971.

Something I've Been Meaning to Tell You: Thirteen Stories. Toronto: McGraw-Hill Ryerson, 1974.

Who Do You Think You Are? Toronto: Macmillan, 1978.

The Beggar Maid. New York: Knopf, 1979.

The Moons of Jupiter. Toronto: Macmillan, 1982.

The Progress of Love. Toronto: McClelland and Stewart, 1986.

Friend of My Youth. Toronto: McClelland and Stewart, 1990.

Open Secrets. Toronto: McClelland and Stewart, 1994.

Selected Stories. Toronto: McClelland and Stewart, 1996.

The Love of a Good Woman. Toronto: McClelland and Stewart, 1998.

Hateship, Friendship, Courtship, Loveship, Marriage. Toronto: McClelland and Stewart, 2001.

No Love Lost. Selected with an Afterword by Jane Urquhart. Toronto: McClelland and Stewart / New Canadian Library, 2003.

Runaway. Toronto: McClelland and Stewart, 2004.

Carried Away: A Selection of Stories. Intro. Margaret Atwood. New York: Knopf/Everyman, 2006.

The View from Castle Rock. Toronto: McClelland and Stewart, 2006.

Too Much Happiness. Toronto: McClelland and Stewart, 2009.

New Selected Stories. London: Chatto and Windus, 2011.

Dear Life. Toronto: McClelland and Stewart, 2012.

Family Furnishings: Selected Stories, 1995–2014. Toronto: McClelland and Stewart, 2014.

2. CITED FIRST PUBLICATION OF STORIES IN PERIODICALS OR BOOKS (ALPHABETIZED)

Laidlaw, Alice. "At the Other Place." *Canadian Forum* (September 1955): 131–33.

———. "The Dimensions of a Shadow." *Folio* 4.2 (April 1950): n.p.

———. "Story for Sunday." *Folio* 5.1 (December 1950): n.p.

———. "The Widower." Folio 5.2 (April 1951): n.p.

Munro, Alice Laidlaw. "The Idyllic Summer." *Canadian Forum* (August 1954): 106–07, 109–10.

Munro, Alice. "Carried Away." *New Yorker* 21 Oct. 1991: 34–46, 48–51, 54–61.

———. "Changing Places." Writing Home: A PEN Canada Anthology. Ed. Constance Rooke. Toronto: McClelland & Stewart, 1997. 190–206.

———. "Dear Life." *New Yorker* 19 Sept. 2011: 40–42, 44–47.

———. "Dulse." *New Yorker* 21 July 1980: 30–39.

———. "The Edge of Town." *Queen's Quarterly* 62.3 (Autumn 1955): 368–80.

———. "The Ferguson Girls Must Never Marry." *Grand Street* 1.3 (Spring 1982): 27–64.

———. "Good-by Myra" ("Day of the Butterfly"). *Chatelaine* July 1956: 16–17, 55–58.

———. "Home." *New Canadian Stories: 74.* Eds. David Helwig and Joan Harcourt. Ottawa: Oberon, 1974. 133–53.

———. "Home." Revised. *New Statesman.* December 17, 2001–January 7, 2002: 84–93.

———. "Home: A Story." Revised. *Virginia Quarterly Review* 82.3 (Summer 2006): 108–28.

———. "Leaving Maverley." *New Yorker* 28 Nov. 2011: 64–71.

———. "The Peace of Utrecht." *Tamarack Review* 15 (Spring 1960): 5–21.

———. "Sunday Afternoon." *Canadian Forum* Sept. 1957: 127–30.

———. "The Time of Death." *Canadian Forum* June 1956: 63–66.

———. "The Trip to the Coast" ("A Trip to the Coast"). *Ten For Wednesday Night.* Ed. Robert Weaver. Toronto: McClelland and Stewart, 1961: 74–92.

———. "The View From Castle Rock." *New Yorker* 29 Aug. 2005: 64–77.

———. "Wenlock Edge." *New Yorker* 5 Dec. 2005: 80–91.

———. "What Do You Want to Know For?" *Writing Away.* Ed. Constance Rooke. Toronto: McClelland and Stewart, 1994. 203–20.

———. "Working For A Living." *Grand Street* 1.1 (1981): 9–37.

3. OTHER WORKS BY ALICE MUNRO

Munro, Alice. Advance proof of supplanted *Who Do You Think You Are?* (August 11, 1978). John and Myrna Metcalf Collection. Rare Books and Special Collections. McGill University Library. Item 6000.

———. "Author's Commentary." *Sixteen By Twelve: Short Stories by Canadian Writers.* Ed. John Metcalf. Toronto: Ryerson, 1970. 125–26.

———. "A Better Place Than Home." *The Newcomers: Inhabiting a New Land.* Ed. Charles E. Israel. Toronto: McClelland & Stewart, 1979. 113–24.

———. "Everything Here Is Touchable and Mysterious." *Weekend Magazine* [*Toronto Star*] 11 May 1974: 33.

———. "Good Woman in Ireland." *Brick* 72 (Winter 2003): 26–30.

———. Introduction. *The Moons of Jupiter.* By Munro. 1982. Toronto: Penguin, 1986. xiii–xvi.

———. Introduction. *Selected Stories.* By Munro. New York: Vintage, 1997. xiii–xxi.

———. "What is Real?" *The Canadian Forum* (September 1982): 5, 36.

———. Untitled poem [pseud. Anne Chamney]. *The Canadian Forum* Feb. 1967: 243.

———. "Wenlock Edge." Submitted typescript. July 16, 2005. *New Yorker* Files.

4. CITED INTERVIEWS WITH ALICE MUNRO

Freake, Douglas, et al. "Alice Munro." *What* 6 (1986): 8–10.

Gardiner, Jill Marjorie. Appendix Interview, June 1, 1973. "The Early Short Stories of Alice Munro." MA Thesis. University of New Brunswick, 1973. 169–82.

Gibson, Graeme. "Alice Munro." *Eleven Canadian Novelists.* Toronto: Anansi, 1972. 241–64.

Hancock, Geoff. "An Interview with Alice Munro." *Canadian Fiction Magazine* 43 (1982): 74–114.

Metcalf, John." A Conversation with Alice Munro." *Journal of Canadian Fiction* 1.4 (Fall 1972): 54–62.

Slopen, Beverly. "PW Interviews Alice Munro." *Publisher's Weekly* 22 Aug. 1986: 76–77.

Stainsby, Mari. "Alice Munro Talks to Mari Stainsby." *British Columbia Library Quarterly* 35.1 (1971): 27–30.

Struthers, J. R. (Tim). "The Real Material: An Interview with Alice Munro." *Probable Fictions*. Ed. Louis K. MacKendrick.Downsview, ON: ECW, 1983. 5–36.

Thacker, Robert. Telephone Interview. 29 Apr. 1987.

———. Interview. 6 Sept. 2013.

———. Interview. 12 May. 2014.

B. Secondary Sources

The Alice Munro Papers: First Accession. Eds. Apollonia Steele and Jean F. Tener. Calgary: U of Calgary P, 1986.

The Alice Munro Papers: Second Accession. Eds. Apollonia Steele and Jean F. Tener. Calgary: U of Calgary P, 1987.

Arnold, Marilyn. *Willa Cather's Short Fiction*. Athens: Ohio UP, 1984.

Atwood, Margaret. Introduction. *Carried Away: A Selection of Stories* by Alice Munro. New York: Knopf/Everyman's Library, 2006. ix–xx.

Auden, W. H. "A. E. Housman." *Collected Poems*. Ed. Edward Mendelson. New York: Modern Library, 2007. 182.

Aubrey, Kim. "How to Write Like Alice Munro." *Writer's Chronicle* 38.1 (2005): 12–15.

Bailey, Nancy I. "The Masculine Image in *Lives of Girls and Women*." *Canadian Literature* 80 (1979): 113–18, 120.

Bennet, Donna and Russell Morton Brown. "Open Secret: Telling Time in Alice Munro's Fiction"; "Open Secrets? Alice Munro and the Mystery Story." *Open Letter* 11.9 (Fall 2003) and 12.1 (Winter 2004): 185–209.

Beran, Carol L. "Images of Women's Power in Contemporary Canadian Fiction by Women." *Studies in Canadian Literature* 15.2 (1990): 55–76.

Besner, Neil K. *Introducing Alice Munro's* Lives of Girls and Women. Toronto: ECW, 1990.

Blodgett, E. D. *Alice Munro*. Boston: Twayne, 1988.

———. "Prisms and Arcs: Structures in Hébert and Munro." *Figures in a Ground: Canadian Essays on Modern Literature Collected in Honor of Sheila Watson*. Eds. Diane Bessai and David Jackel. Saskatoon, SK: Western Producer Prairie, 1978. 99–121, 333–34.

Bloom, Harold. Ed. *Alice Munro*. New York: Bloom's Modern Critical Views/ Infobase, 2009.

———. *The Anxiety of Influence: A Theory of Poetry*. New York: Oxford UP, 1973.

Brooks, Cleanth, and Robert Penn Warren. "Interpretation." In *Understanding Fiction*. 2nd ed. New York: Appleton-Century Crofts, 1959.

Brown, Marion Marsh, and Ruth Crone. *Only One Point of the Compass: Willa Cather in the Northeast*. Danbury, CT: Archer Editions Press, 1980.

Bucholt, Maggie. "Rhyming Actiom in Alice Munro's Stories." *Writer's Chronicle* 39.6 (May/Summer 2007): 46–54.

Buss, Helen M. *Mapping Our Selves: Canadian Women's Autobiography in English*. Montreal: McGill-Queen's UP, 1993.

Byatt, A. S. "Justice for Willa Cather." Rev. of *Willa Cather and the Politics of Criticism*. By Joan Acocella. *New York Review of Books* 30 Nov. 2000: 51–53.

Cam, Heather. "Learning From the Teacher: Alice Munro's Reworking of Eudora Welty's 'June Recital.'" *Span* 25 (1987): 16–30.

Canitz, A. E. Christa. Rev. of *The Other Country* by James Carscallen and *The Tumble of Reason* by Ajay Heble. *University of Toronto Quarterly* 65 (1995–96): 247–50.

Carrington, Ildikó de Papp. *Controlling the Uncontrollable: The Fiction of Alice Munro*. DeKalb: Northern Illinois UP, 1989.

———. "'Don't Tell (on) Daddy': Narrative Complexity in Alice Munro's 'The Love of a Good Woman.'" *Studies in Short Fiction* 34 (1997): 159–70.

———. "Other Rooms, Other Texts, Other Selves: Alice Munro's 'Sunday Afternoon' and 'Hired Girl.'" *Journal of the Short Story in English* 30 (1998): 2–8.

———. "Recasting the Orpheus Myth: Alice Munro's 'The Children Stay' and Jean Arouilh's Eurydice." In *The Rest of the Story*. 191–203.

———. "Talking Dirty: Alice Munro's 'Open Secrets' and John Steinbeck's *Of Mice and Men*." *Studies in Short Fiction* 31 (1994): 595–606.

———. "What's in a Title?: Alice Munro's 'Carried Away.'" *Studies in Short Fiction* 30 (1993): 555–64.

———. "Where are You, Mother?: Alice Munro's 'Save the Reaper.'" *Canadian Literature* 173 (2002): 34–51.

Carscallen, James. "Alice Munro." *Profiles in Canadian Literature* 2. Ed. Jeffrey M. Heath. Toronto: Dundurn, 1980. 73–80.

———. *The Other Country: Patterns in the Writing of Alice Munro*. Toronto: ECW, 1993.

———. "The Shining House: A Group of Stories." *The Art of Alice Munro: Saying the Unsayable*. Ed. Judith Miller. Waterloo: U of Waterloo P, 1984. 85–101.

———. "Three Jokers: The Shape of Alice Munro's Stories." *Centre and Labyrinth: Essays in Honour of Northrop Frye.* Ed. Eleanor Cook, et al. Toronto: U of Toronto P, 1983. 128–46.

Cather, Willa. *April Twilights (1903).* Ed. Bernice Slote. Rev. ed. Lincoln: U of Nebraska P, 1968.

———. "Before Breakfast." *The Old Beauty and Others.* 1948. New York: Vintage, 1976. 141–66.

———. *A Lost Lady.* 1923. New York: Vintage, 1972.

———. *My Ántonia.* 1918. Boston: Houghton Mifflin, 1978.

———. "Miss Jewett." *Not Under Forty.* 1936. Lincoln: U Nebraska P, 1988. 76–95.

———. *My Mortal Enemy.* 1926. New York: Vintage, 1961.

———. "Old Mrs. Harris." *Obscure Destinies.* 1932. New York: Vintage, 1974. 75–190.

———. "Paul's Case." *Willa Cather's Collected Short Fiction, 1892–1912.* Ed. Virginia Faulkner. Introduction. Mildred R. Bennett. Rev. ed. Lincoln: U of Nebraska P, 1970. 243–61.

———. Preface. *Country of the Pointed Firs and Other Stories.* By Sarah Orne Jewett. Ed. Willa Cather. 1925. New York: Anchor, 1989. 6–12.

———. Rev. of *A Shropshire Lad* by A. E. Housman. *Lincoln Courier. The World and the Parish: Willa Cather's Articles and Reviews, 1893–1902.* 2 vols. Ed. William M. Curtin. Lincoln: U of Nebraska P, 1970. 2: 706–09.

———. *The Professor's House.* 1925. New York: Vintage, 1973.

———. *The Song of the Lark.* 1915. New York: Penguin, 1999.

Charman, Caitlin J. "There's Got to Be Some Wrenching and Slashing: Horror amid Retrospection in Alice Munro's 'Fits.'" *Canadian Literature* 191 (2006): 13–30.

Clark, Miriam Marty. "Allegories of Reading in Alice Munro's 'Carried Away.'" *Contemporary Literature* 37 (1996): 49–61.

Condé, Mary, and Héliane Ventura, eds. *Open Letter.* Special issue on Alice Munro. 11.9 (Fall 2003) and 12.1 (Winter 2004).

Conron, Brandon. "Munro's Wonderland." *Canadian Literature* 78 (1978): 109–12, 114–18, 120–23.

Cox, Ailsa. *Alice Munro.* Horndon, Tavistock, Devon: Northcote House, 2004.

Dahlie, Hallvard. "Alice Munro and Her Works." *Canadian Writers and Their Works.* Ed. Robert Lecker, Jack David, and Ellen Quigley. Toronto: ECW, 1985. 213–54.

———. "The Fiction of Alice Munro." *Ploughshares* 4.3 (Summer 1978): 56–71.

———. "Unconsummated Relationships: Isolation and Rejection in Alice Munro's Stories." *World Literature Written in English* 11 (April 1972): 43–48.

Davey, Frank. "Canadian Canons." *Critical Inquiry* 16 (Spring 1990): 672–81.

Davies, Robertson. "Dark Hamlet with the Features of Horatio: Canada's Myths and Realities." In *Voices of Canada: An Introduction to Canadian Culture*. Ed. Judith Webster. Burlington, Vermont: Association for Canadian Studies in the United States, 1977. 42–46.

Dawson, Anthony B. "Coming of Age in Canada." *Mosaic* 11.3 (Spring 1978): 47–49, 53, 55–59, 61.

Ditsky, John. "The Figure in the Linoleum: The Fiction of Alice Munro." *The Hollins Critic* 22 (1985): 1–10.

Duffy, Dennis. "'A Dark Sort of Mirror': 'The Love of a Good Woman' as Pauline Poetic." *The Rest of the Story: Critical Essays on Alice Munro*. Ed. Robert Thacker. Toronto: ECW, 1999. 169–90.

———. "Too Little Geography; Too Much History: Writing the Balance in 'Meneseteung.'" *National Plots: Historical Fiction and Changing Ideas of Canada*. Ed. Andrea Cabajsky and Brett Josef Grubisic. Waterloo, ON: Wilfrid Laurier UP, 2010. 197–213.

Duncan, Isla. *Alice Munro's Narrative Art*. New York: Palgrave Macmillan, 2011.

Eagleton, Terry. *Literary Theory: An Introduction*. Minneapolis: U of Minnesota P, 1983.

Eakin, Paul John. *Fictions in Autobiography: Studies in the Art of Self-Invention*. Princeton: Princeton UP, 1985.

Eureka Studies in Teaching Short Fiction. Special Issue on Alice Munro. 6.2 (Spring 2006).

Forceville, Charles. "Alice Munro's Layered Structures." *Shades of Empire in Colonial and Post-Colonial Literature*. Ed. C. C. Barfoot and Theo D'haen. Amsterdam: Editions Rodopi B. V., 1993. 301–10.

Foy, Nathalie. "'Darkness Collecting': Reading 'Vandals' as a Coda to *Open Secrets*." *The Rest of the Story: Critical Essays on Alice Munro*. Ed. Robert Thacker. Toronto: ECW, 1999. 147–68.

Franzen, Jonathan. "Alice's Wonderland." Rev. of *Runaway*, by Alice Munro. *New York Times Book Review* 14 Nov. 2004: 1, 14–16.

Gardiner, Jill. Marjorie. *The Early Short Stories of Alice Munro*. Diss. U of New Brunswick, 1973.

Gardiner, Judith Kegan. "On Female Identity and Writing by Women." *Critical Inquiry* (1981): 347–61.

Garson, Marjorie. "Alice Munro and Charlotte Brontë." *University of Toronto Quarterly* 69 (2000): 783–825.

———. "Synecdoche and the Munrovian Sublime: Parts and Wholes in *Lives of Girls and Women*." *English Studies in Canada* 20 (1994): 413–29.

"A Genius of Sour Grapes." Wingham *Advance-Times* 16 Dec. 1981. n. p.

Gerlach, John. "To Close or Not to Close: Alice Munro's 'The Love of a Good Woman.'" *JNT: Journal of Narrative Theory* 37 (2007): 146–58.

Gilbert, Paula Ruth. "All Roads Pass Through Jubilee: Gabrielle Roy's *La Route d'Altmount* and Alice Munro's *Lives of Girls and Women*." *Colby Quarterly* 29 (1993): 136–44.

Gilbert, Sandra M., and Susan Gubar. *The Madwoman in the Attic: The Woman Writer and the Nineteenth-Century Literary Imagination*. New Haven: Yale UP, 1979.

———. *Sexchanges*. New Haven: Yale UP, 1989. Vol. 2 of *No Man's Land: The Place of the Woman Writer in the Twentieth Century*. 1988–94.

———. *The War of the Words*. New Haven: Yale UP, 1988. Vol. 1 of *No Man's Land: The Place of the Woman Writer in the Twentieth Century*. 1988–94.

Gittings, Christopher E. "Constructing a Scots-Canadian Ground: Family History and Cultural Translation in Alice Munro." *Studies in Short Fiction* 34 (1997): 27–37.

Glover, Douglas. "The Mind of Alice Munro." *Canadian Notes and Queries* 79 (2010): 30–31.

Gold, Joseph. "Our Feelings Exactly: The Writing of Alice Munro." *The Art of Alice Munro: Saying the Unsayable*. Ed. Judith Miller. Waterloo: U of Waterloo P, 1984. 1–13.

Goldman, Marlene. "Penning in the Bodies: The Construction of Gendered Subjects in Alice Munro's 'Boys and Girls.'" *Studies in Canadian Literature* 15 (1990): 62–75.

Goodman, Charlotte. "Cinderella in the Classroom: (Mis) Reading Alice Munro's 'Red Dress—1946.'" *Reader* 30 (1993): 49–64.

Gunn, Janet Varner. *Autobiography: Towards a Poetics of Experience*. Philadelphia: U of Pennsylvania P, 1982.

Heble, Ajay. *The Tumble of Reason: Alice Munro's Discourse of Absence*. Toronto: U of Toronto P, 1994.

———. *The Tumble of Reason: Paradigmatic Reservoirs of Meaning in the Fiction of Alice Munro*. Diss. U Toronto, 1990. *DAI* 52 (1991): 3416A.

Heller, Deborah. *Daughters and Mothers in Alice Munro's Latest Stories*. Seattle: Workwoman's Press, 2009.

Henighan, Stephen. "The Sense of an Ending." *Times Literary Supplement* 27 October 2006: 21–22.

Hicks, Granville. "The Case Against Willa Cather." 1933. *Willa Cather and Her Critics*. Ed. James Schroeter. Ithaca: Cornell UP, 1967. 139–47.

Hooper, Brad. *The Fiction of Alice Munro*. Westport, CT: Praeger, 2008.

Houston, Pam. "A Hopeful Sign: The Making of Metonymic Meaning in Munro's 'Meneseteung.'" *Kenyon Review* 14.4 (1992): 79–92.

Howells, Coral Ann. *Alice Munro*. Manchester: Manchester UP, 1998.

———. "Intimate Dislocations: Buried History and Geography in Alice Munro's Sowesto Stories." *British Journal of Canadian Studies* 14 (1999): 7–16.

———. *Private and Fictional Words: Canadian Women Novelists of the 1970s and 1980s*. London and New York: Methuen, 1987.

———. "The Telling of Secrets/The Secrets of Telling: An Overview of Alice Munro's Enigma Variations from *Dance of the Happy Shades* to *Hateship, Friendship, Courtship, Loveship, Marriage*. *Open Letter* 11.9 (Fall 2003) and 12.1 (Winter 2004): 39–54.

Hoy, Helen. "Alice Munro: 'Unforgettable, Indigestible Messages." *Journal of Canadian Studies* 26 (1991): 5–21.

———. "'Dull, Simple, Amazing and Unfathomable': Paradox and Double Vision in Alice Munro's Fiction." *Studies in Canadian Fiction* 5 (1980): 100–115.

———. "'Rose and Janet': Alice Munro's Metafiction." *Canadian Literature* 121 (1989): 59–83.

Hunter, Adrian. "Story into History: Alice Munro's Minor Literature." *English* 53 (2004): 219–38.

———. "Taking Possession: Alice Munro's 'A Wilderness Station' and James Hogg's *Justified Sinner*." *Studies in Canadian Literature* 25.2 (2010): 114–28.

Hutcheon, Linda. *A Poetics of Postmodernism: Theory, History, Fiction*. London and New York: Routledge and Kegan Paul, 1988.

———. *The Politics of Postmodernism*. London and New York: Routledge, 1989.

———. *A Theory of Parody: The Teachings of Twentieth-Century Art Forms*. London and New York: Methuen, 1985.

The Inside of a Shell: Alice Munro's Dance of the Happy Shades. Ed. Vanessa Guigney. Newcastle upon Tyne: Cambridge Scholars P, 2015.

Irvine, Lorna. "Changing Is the Word I Want." In *Probable Fictions: Alice Munro's Narrative Acts*. Ed. Louis K. MacKendrick. Downsview, ON: ECW, 1983. 99–111.

———. "Questioning Authority: Alice Munro's Fiction." *CEA Critic* 50 (1987): 57–66.

———. *Sub/version: Canadian Fictions by Women*. Toronto: ECW Press, 1986.

Joyce, James. "Araby." *Dubliners*. 1914. Harmondsworth, England: Penguin, 1964. 27–53.

Kamboureli, Smaro. "The Body as Audience and Performance in the Writings of Alice Munro." *A Mazing Space: Writing Canadian Women Writing*. Ed. Shirley Neuman and Smaro Kamboureli. Edmonton: Longspoon/NeWest, 1986. 31–38.

Lamont, Linda. *Absurdity and Horror in Blaise and Munro*. Diss. U of Calgary, 1979.

Lecker, Robert. "The Canonization of Canadian Literature: An Inquiry into Values." *Critical Inquiry* 16 (Spring 1990): 656–71.

———. "Machines, Readers, Gardens: Alice Munro's 'Carried Away.'" *The Rest of the Story: Critical Essays on Alice Munro*. Ed. Robert Thacker. Toronto: ECW, 1999. 103–27.

———. "Response to Frank Davey." *Critical Inquiry* 16 (Spring 1990): 682–89.

Levene, Mark. "'It was about vanishing': A Glimpse of Alice Munro's Stories." *University of Toronto Quarterly* 68 (1999): 841–60.

Lewis, Edith. *Willa Cather Living: A Personal Record*. Foreward. Marilyn Arnold. 1953. Athens: Ohio UP, 1989.

Lilienfeld, Jane. "'Something I've been Meaning to Tell You': Alice Munro as Unlikely Heir to Virginia Woolf." *Virginia Woolf Out of Bounds*. Ed. Jessica Berman and Jane Goldman. New York: Pace UP, 2001. 92–96.

Literary History of Canada: Canadian Literature in English. Ed. W. H. New. 2nd ed. Vol. 4. Toronto: U of Toronto P, 1990.

Luft, Joanna. "Boxed In: Alice Munro's 'Wenlock Edge' and *Sir Gawain and the Green Knight*." *Studies in Canadian Literature* 35.1 (2010): 103–26.

Lynch, Gerald. *The One and the Many: English Canadian Short Story Cycles*. Toronto: U of Toronto P, 2001.

MacCulloch, Clare. *The Short Story in Canada: A Neglected Genre*. Guelph: Alive Press, 1973.

Macdonald, Rae McCarthy. "A Madman Loose in the World: The Vision of Alice Munro." *Modern Fiction Studies* 22 (1976): 365–74.

———. "Structure and Detail in *Lives of Girls and Women*." *Studies in Canadian Literature* 3 (1978): 199–200.

MacKendrick, Louis K., ed. *Probable Fictions: Alice Munro's Narrative Acts*. Downsview, ON: ECW, 1983.

MacKendrick, Louis K. *Some Other Reality: Alice Munro's* Something I've Been Meaning to Tell You. Toronto: ECW, 1993.

Marchand, Philip. "The Problem with Alice Munro." *Canadian Notes and Queries* 72 (2007): 10–15.

Martin, W. R. "Alice Munro and James Joyce." *Journal of Canadian Fiction* 24 ([1979]): 120–26.

———. *Alice Munro: Paradox and Parallel*. Edmonton: U of Alberta P, 1987.

———. "The Strange and the Familiar in Alice Munro." *Studies in Canadian Literature* 7 (1982): 214–26.

May, Charles E. "Why Does Alice Munro Write Short Stories?" *Wascana Review* 38.1 (2003): 16–28.

Mayberry, Katherine J. "'Every Last Thing ... Everlasting': Alice Munro and the Limits of Narrative." *Studies in Short Fiction* 29 (1992): 531–41.

Mazur, Carol and Cathy Moulder, eds. *Alice Munro: An Annotated Bibliography of Works and Criticism*. Lanham, MD: Scarecrow, 2007.

McCaig, JoAnn. "Alice Munro's Agency: The Virginia Barber Correspondence, 1976–83." *The Rest of the Story: Critical Essays on Alice Munro*. Ed. Robert Thacker. Toronto: ECW, 1999. 81–102.

———. *Reading In: Alice Munro's Archives*. Waterloo, ON: Wilfrid Laurier UP, 2002.

McCombs, Judith. "Searching Bluebeard's Chambers: Grimm, Gothic, and Bible Mysteries in Alice Munro's 'The Love of a Good Woman.'" *American Review of Canadian Studies* 30 (2000): 327–48.

McCarthy, Dermot. "The Woman Out Back: Alice Munro's 'Meneseteung.'" *Studies in Canadian Literature* 19 (1994): 1–19.

McGill, Robert. "'Daringly Out in the Public Eye': Alice Munro and the Ethics of Writing Back." *University of Toronto Quarterly* 76 (2007): 874–889.

———. "No Nation but Adaptation: 'The Bear Came Over the Mountain,' *Away From Her*, and What It Means to be Faithful." *Canadian Literature* 197 (2008): 98–111.

———. "Somewhere I've Been Meaning to Tell You: Alice Munro's Fiction of Distance." *Journal of Commonwealth Literature* 37 (2002): 9–29.

———. "Where Do You Think You Are? Alice Munro's Open Houses." *Mosaic* 35.4 (2002): 103–19.

McIntyre, Tim. "'The Way the Stars Really Do Come Out at Might': The Trick of Representation in Alice Munro's 'The Moons of Jupiter.'" *Canadian Literature* 200 (2009): 73–88.

Melsom, Ryan. "Roberta's Raspberry Bombe and Critical Indifference in Alice Munro's 'Labor Day Dinner.'" *Studies in Canadian Literature* 34 (2009): 142–59.

Mendelson, Edward. Editor's Preface. *Collected Poems* by W. H. Auden. New York: Modern Library, 2007. xxi–xxvii.

Messud, Claire. "Signs of Struggle." Rev. of *Cheating at Canasta*, by William Trevor. *New York Review of Books* 14 Feb. 2008: 20–22.

Miller, Judith Maclean, ed. *The Art of Alice Munro: Saying the Unsayable*. Waterloo: University of Waterloo Press, 1984.

———. "Deconstructing Silence: The Mystery of Alice Munro." *Antigonish Review* 129 (2002): 43–52.

———. "An Inner Bell that Rings: The Craft of Alice Munro." *Antigonish Review* 115 (1998): 157–76.

———. "On Looking into Rifts and Crannies: Alice Munro's *Friend of My Youth*." *Antigonish Review* 120 (2000): 205–26.

Miller, Karl. "The Passion of Alice Laidlaw." *Changing English* 14.1 (2007): 17–22.

Monaghan, David. "Confinement and Escape in Alice Munro's 'The Flats Road.'" *Studies in Short Fiction* 14 (1977): 165–68.

Morgenstern, Naomi. "The Baby or the Violin?: Ethics and Femininity in the Fiction of Alice Munro." *Literature Interpretation Theory* 14 (2003): 69–97.

Morris, Wright. *God's Country and My People*. 1968. Lincoln: U of Nebraska P, 1981.

———. *The Home Place*. 1948. Lincoln: U of Nebraska P, 1968.

Moss, John. *Sex and Violence in the Canadian Novel: The Ancestral Present*. Toronto: McClelland & Stewart, 1977.

Murphy, Georgeann. "The Art of Alice Munro: Memory, Identity, and the Aesthetics of Connection." *Canadian Women Writing Fiction*. Ed. Mickey Pearlman. Jackson: UP Mississippi, 1993. 12–27, 155–56.

New, W. H. "Every Now and Then: Voice and Language in Laurence's *The Stone Angel*." In *A Place to Stand On: Essays by and About Margaret Laurence*. Ed. George Woodcock. Edmonton: NeWest, 1983. 171–192.

———. "Pronouns and Prepositions: Alice Munro's Stories." *Open Letter* Ser. 3, No. 5 (Summer 1976): 40–49.

Nobel Prize Committee. Press Release. October 10, 2013. Accessed March 6, 2015. http://www.nobelprize.org/nobel_prizes/literature/laureates/2013/press.html

Nunes, Mark. "Postmodern 'Piercing': Alice Munro's Contingent Ontologies." *Studies in Short Fiction* 34 (1997): 11–26.

O'Brien, Sharon. "Becoming Noncanonical: The Case Against Willa Cather." *American Quarterly* 40 (1988): 110–26.

———. *Willa Cather: The Emerging Voice*. New York: Oxford UP, 1987.

O'Connor, Frank. *The Lonely Voice: A Study of the Short Story*. Cleveland: World, 1962.

Olney, James. "(Auto) biography." Rev. of *George Washington Williams*, by John Hope Franklin; *Lorelei Two*, by Clarissa M. Lorenz; *Terra Infirma*, by Rodger Kamenetz. *The Southern Review* 22 (1986): 428–41.

"Ordinary Outsiders: A Symposium on Alice Munro." *Virginia Quarterly Review* (Summer 2006): 80–128.

Osachoff, Margaret Gail. "'Treacheries of the Heart': Memoir, Confession, and Meditation in the Stories of Alice Munro." *Probable Fictions: Alice Munro's Narrative Acts*. Ed. Louis K. MacKendrick. Downsview, ON: ECW, 1983. 61–82.

Ozick, Cynthia. Letter to Ann Close. March 9, 1983. Alice Munro Papers. Third Accession. University of Calgary Archives. 396/87.3.1.3.

Packer, Miriam. "*Lives of Girls and Women*: A Creative Search for Completion." *Here and Now: A Critical Anthology*. Vol. 1 of *The Canadian Novel*. Ed. John Moss. Toronto: NC, 1978. 134–44.

Perreaux, Les. "Vindication for a Lifetime of Short Stories." *Globe and Mail* 9 Dec. 2013: A3.

Pfaus, B. *Alice Munro*. Ottawa: Golden Dog, 1984.

Prose, Francine. *Reading Like a Writer*. New York: HarperCollins, 2006.

Reading Alice Munro in Italy. Ed. Gianfranca Balestra, et al. Toronto: Frank Iacobucci Centre for Italian Canadian Studies, 2008.

Rasporich, Beverly J. *Dance of the Sexes: Art and Gender in the Fiction of Alice Munro.* Edmonton: U of Alberta P, 1990.

Redekop, Magdalene. "Alice Munro and the Scottish Nostalgic Grotesque." *The Rest of the Story: Critical Essays on Alice Munro.* Ed. Robert Thacker. Toronto: ECW, 1999. 21–43.

———. *Mothers and Other Clowns: The Stories of Alice Munro.* London: Routlege, 1992.

Reid, Verna. "The Small Town in Canadian Fiction." *English Quarterly* 6 (Summer 1973): 171–181.

Robson, Nora. *Wawanesh County: Parallels Between the World of Alice Munro and the White American South.* Diss. McGill U, 1978.

Rooke, Constance. "Fear of the Open Heart." *A Mazing Space: Writing Canadian Women Writing.* Eds. Shirley Neuman and Smaro Kamboureli. Edmonton: Longspoon/NeWest, 1986.

———. "Munro's Food." *Fear of the Open Heart: Essays on Contemporary Canadian Writing.* Toronto: Coach House, 1989. 41–53.

Ross, Catherine Sheldrick. *Alice Munro: A Double Life.* Toronto: ECW, 1992.

———. "'Too Many Things': Reading Alice Munro's 'The Love of a Good Woman.'" *University of Toronto Quarterly* 71 (2002): 785–811.

Scurr, Ruth. "The Darkness of Alice Munro." Rev. of *New Selected Stories*, by Alice Munro. *TLS* October 4, 2011. Online. March 23, 2014.

Schorer, Mark. "Technique as Discovery." 1948. *Myth and Method: Modern Theories of Fiction.* Ed. James E. Miller. Lincoln: U of Nebraska P, 1960. 86–108.

Sellwood, Jane. "'Certain Vague Hopes of Disaster': A Psychosemiotic Reading of Alice Munro's 'The Flood Boat' as the Flooding Text." *Studies in Canadian Literature* 17 (1992): 1–16.

Seyersted, Per. "'Who Do You Think You Are?: Alice Munro and the Place of Origin." *American Studies in Scandinavia* 24 (1992): 17–23.

Sheringham, Michael. "Making Up the Truth." Rev. of *Fictions in Autobiography*, by Paul John Eakin. *TLS* 10, Jan. 1986: 42.

Skaggs, Merrill Maguire. *After the World Broke in Two: The Later Novels of Willa Cather.* Charlottesville: UP of Virginia, 1990.

Smythe, Karen Elizabeth. *Figuring Grief: Gallant, Munro, and the Poetics of Elegy.* Kingston and Montreal: McGill-Queen's UP, 1992.

———. *Late Modern Works of Mourning: The Elegiac Fiction of Mavis Gallant and Alice Munro.* Diss. U of Toronto, 1990. *DAI* 51 (1991): 3416A.

———. "Sad Stories: The Ethics of Epiphany in Munrovian Elegy." *University of Toronto Quarterly* 60 (1991): 493–506.

Spengemann, William C. *Forms of Autobiography: Episodes in the History of a Literary Genre.* New Haven: Yale UP, 1980.

Strayed, Cheryl. "Munro Country." *Missouri Review* 32.2 (2009). September 18, 2010. http://www.missourireview.com/archives/bbarticle/munro-country/

Stelzig, Eugene L. "Poetry and/or Truth: An Essay on the Confessional Imagination." *University of Toronto Quarterly* 54 (1984): 17–37.

Stich, K. P. "The Cather Connection in Alice Munro's 'Dulse,'" *Modern Language Studies* 22. 4 (Fall 1989): 102–111.

———. "Letting Go with the Mind: Dionysus and Medusa in Alice Munro's 'Meneseteung.'" *Canadian Literature* 169 (2001): 106–25.

———. "Munro's Grail Quest: The Progress of Logos." *Studies in Canadian Literature* 32.1 (2007): 120–40.

Struthers, J. R. (Tim). "Alice Munro and the American South." *Canadian Review of American Studies* 6 (1975): 196–204.

———. "Alice Munro's Fictive Imagination." *The Art of Alice Munro: Saying the Unsayable*. Ed. Judith Miller. Waterloo: U of Waterloo P, 1984. 103–12.

———. "Reality and Ordering: The Growth of a Young Artist in *Lives of Girls and Women*." *Essays on Canadian Writing* 3 (Fall 1975): 32–46.

———. "Some Highly Subversive Activities: A Brief Polemic and Checklist of Works on Alice Munro." *Studies in Canadian Literature* 6 (1981): 140–50.

Stubbs, Andrew. "Fictional Landscape: Mythology and the Dialectic in the Fiction of Alice Munro." *World Literature Written in English* 23 (1984): 53–62.

Sturgess, Charlotte. "Alice Munro's 'The Progress of Love': Secrets, Continuity and Closure." *Etudes Canadiennes* 29 (1990): 223–33.

Tausky, Thomas E. "Biocritical Essay." *The Alice Munro Papers: First Accession*. ix–xxiv.

———. "'What Happened to Marion?': Art and Reality in Lives of Girls and Women." *Studies in Canadian Literature* 11 (1986): 52–76.

Thacker, Robert. "Alice Munro: An Annotated Bibliography." *The Annotated Bibliography of Canada's Major Authors, Volume 5*. Ed. Robert Lecker and Jack David. Toronto: ECW Press, 1984. 354–414.

———. *Alice Munro: Writing Her Lives: A Biography*. A Douglas Gibson Book. Revised ed. Toronto: Emblem, 2011.

———. "Alice Munro and the Anxiety of American Influence." *Context North America: Canadian–U.S. Literary Relations*. Ed. Camille La Bossière. Ottawa: U of Ottawa P, 1994. 133–44.

———. "Alice Munro's Willa Cather." *Canadian Literature* 134 (1992): 42–57.

———. "Canadian Literature's 'America.'" *Essays on Canadian Writing* 71 (2000): 128–39.

———. "Conferring Munro." *Essays on Canadian Writing* 34 (1987): 162–69.

———. "Connection: Alice Munro and Ontario." *The American Review of Canadian Studies* 14 (1984): 213–26.

———. "Gazing Through the One-Way Mirror: English-Canadian Literature and the American Presence." *Colby Quarterly* 29 (1993): 74–87.

———. "Go Ask Alice: The Progress of Munro Criticism." *Journal of Canadian Studies* 26 (Summer 1991): 156–69.

———. "Mapping Munro: Reading the 'Clues.'" *Dominant Impressions: Essays on the Canadian Short Story*. Ed. Gerald Lynch and Angela Arnold Robbeson. Ottawa: U of Ottawa P, 1999. 127–35.

———. "'One Knows it Too Well to Know it Well': Willa Cather, A. E. Housman, and *A Shropshire Lad*." *Willa Cather and the Nineteenth Century*. Cather Studies 10. Ed. Anne L. Kaufman and Richard Millington. Lincoln: U of Nebraska P, 2015. 300–27.

———, ed. *The Rest of the Story: Critical Essays on Alice Munro*. Toronto: ECW, 1999.

———. Rev. of *Stephen Leacock: The Sage of Orillia*, by James Doyle; *k. d. lang: Carrying the Torch*, by William Robertson; *Alice Munro: A Double Life*, by Catherine Sheldrick Ross; and *Dorothy Livesay: Patterns in a Poetic Life*, by Peter Stevens. *Biography* 17 (1994): 66–68.

———. "'So Shocking a Verdict in Real Life': Autobiography in Alice Munro's Stories." *Reflections: Autobiography and Canadian Literature*. Ed. K. P. Stich. Ottawa: U of Ottawa P, 1988. 153–61.

———. "What's 'Material'?: The Progress of Munro Criticism, Part 2." *Journal of Canadian Studies* 33 (Summer 1998): 196–210.

Trilling, Lionel. "Willa Cather." 1937. *Willa Cather and Her Critics*. Ed. James Schroeter. Ithaca: Cornell UP, 1967. 148–55.

Ventura, Héliane. "Country Girls and City Girls in Alice Munro's 'The Progress of Love.'" *Etudes Canadiennes* 29 (1990): 223–33.

Wallace, Bronwen. "Women's Lives: Alice Munro." *The Human Elements*. Ed. David Helwig. Ottawa, ON: Oberon, 1978. 52–66.

Ware, Tracy. "'And They May Get It Wrong, After All': Reading Alice Munro's 'Meneseteung.'" *National Plots: Historical Fiction and Changing Ideas of Canada*. Eds. Andrea Cabajsky and Brett Josef Grubisic. Waterloo, ON: Wilfrid Laurier UP, 2010. 67–79.

———. Email. 2 December 1999.

Warkentin, Germaine, ed. *Stories from Ontario*. Toronto: Macmillan, 1974.

Wayne, Joyce. "Huron County Blues." *Books in Canada* October 1982: 9–12.

Weaver, John. "Society and Culture in Rural and Small-Town Ontario: Alice Munro's Testimony on the Last Forty Years." *Patterns of the Past: Interpreting Ontario's History*. Eds. Roger Hall, William Westfall and Laura Sefton MacDowell. Toronto: Dundurn, 1988. 381–402.

Welty, Eudora. *The Eye of the Story: Selected Essays and Reviews*. 1978. New York: Vintage, 1979.

———. "How I Write." *The Virginia Quarterly Review* 31 (Spring 1955): 240–51.

Woodcock, George. *Introducing Margaret Laurence's* The Stone Angel: *A Reader's Guide*. 1989. Toronto: General, 1990.

Woodress, James. *Willa Cather: A Literary Life*. Lincoln: U Nebraska P, 1987.

Yeats, W. B. "Among School Children." *Poems* (Revised). *The Collected Works of W. B. Yeats*. Ed. Richard J. Finneran. New York: Macmillan, 1989. 215–17.

York, Lorraine M. "'Gulfs and Connections': The Fiction of Alice Munro." *Essays on Canadian Writing* 35 (1987): 135–46.

———. "Joyless in Jubilee?" Rev. of *Alice Munro* by B. Pfaus. *Essays on Canadian Writing* 34 (Spring 1987): 157–61.

———. "'The Other Side of Dailiness': The Paradox of Photography in Alice Munro's Fiction." *Studies in Canadian Literature* 8 (1983): 49–60.

———. "'The Rival Bards': Alice Munro's *Lives of Girls and Women* and Victorian Poetry." *Canadian Literature* 112 (Spring 1987): 211–16.

Index

A

"A. E. Housman" (Auden), 7
Acocella, Joan, 12
Agee, James, 143
Alfred A. Knopf, Inc., 10, 16, 21, 228, 244, 262
Alice Munro (Blodgett), 17, 21, 93, 96, 103–9, 168, 248
Alice Munro (Cox), 255
Alice Munro (Howells), 249
Alice Munro (Pfaus), 247
Alice Munro: An Annotated Bibliography of Works and Criticism (Mazur and Moulder), 17, 244
"Alice Munro—The Art of the Short Story," 254
Alice Munro: A Double Life (Ross), 184
Alice Munro: Paradox and Parallel (Martin), 22, 92, 248
Alice Munro: Writing Her Lives (Thacker), 4, 8, 10, 19, 112–13, 198, 232, 244, 246, 263, 282n1
"Alice Munro and the American South" (Struthers), 67, 134, 272n4, 280n17
"Alice Munro and Critics: A Paradigm" (Thacker), 3, 274n2
"Alice Munro and the White American South" (Robson), 67
"Alice Munro's Fictive Imagination" (Struthers), 69, 84, 96

Alice Munro's Narrative Art (Duncan), 10, 199
Alice Munro Papers: First Accession, 280n8
Alice Munro Papers: Second Accession, 280n14
Allen Lane, 16
"Among School Children" (Yeats), 90, 276n14
Anderson, Sherwood, 143, 192
The Annotated Bibliography of Canada's Major Authors (Thacker), 17, 247, 274n3
Antigonish Review, 251
The Anxiety of Influence (Bloom), 135
April Twilights (1903) (Cather), 278n9
"Araby" (Joyce), 40
Arnold, Marilyn, 277n1
The Art of Alice Munro: Saying the Unsayable (Miller), 17, 65–71, 247, 249, 251, 273n2, 274n3
Association for Canadian Studies in the United States (ACSUS), 3
Atwood, Margaret, 3, 4, 65, 68, 96, 201–2, 241–42
Aubrey, Kim, 252
Auden, W. H., 7, 8–9
Away From Her (Polley), 254

B

"The Baby or the Violin" (Morgenstern), 283n3
Bailey, Nancy I., 246
Barber, Virginia, 3, 26, 151, 233, 235, 244, 253
Basso, Susanna, 255
"Becoming Noncanonical: The Case Against Willa Cather" (O'Brien), 122
"Before Breakfast" (Cather), 115–18, 123, 129, 130–31, 142
Bennett, Donna, 244
Beran, Carol, 148, 151
Besner, Neil, 176, 184–85, 248, 282n6
A Bird in the House (Laurence), 97
Blodgett, E. D., 17, 22, 92, 93, 96, 101, 103–9, 116, 134, 138, 168, 169, 244, 246, 248, 276n12, 276n19, 279n2, 279n3, 281n3
Bloom, Harold, 135–36, 255–56
"Bloom's Modern Critical Views," 256
"The Body as Audience in the Writings of Alice Munro" (Kamboureli), 276n11
Books & Company, 261
British Columbia, 2, 3, 9, 14, 80–81, 148, 193, 195, 208, 220, 226
Brönte, Charlotte, 253
Brooks, Cleanth, and Robert Penn Warren, 40
Brown, Marion Marsh, and Ruth Crone, 277n7
Brown, Russell Morton, 254–55
Browning, Robert, 134
Bucholt, Maggie, 252
Buss, Helen M., 151
Byatt, A. S., 12, 202

C

"Canada's Successful Writers Must Count on Blessings from the U. S. First" (Metcalf), 252
Canadian Broadcasting Corporation (CBC), 245
Canadian Forum, 278n9
Canadian Literature, 246
The Canadian Postmodern (Hutcheon), 93–94, 98–100
The Canadian Short Story (Gadpaille), 93–94, 96, 276n9
Canadian Writers and Their Works (Dahlie), 66
Canitz, A. E. Christa, 170, 282n6
Carrington, Ildikó de Papp, 17, 22, 94, 96, 101–9, 116, 134, 151, 169, 244, 248, 250, 276n12, 276n13, 276n14, 277n6, 279n2, 279n3, 279n6, 281n2, 281n3
Carscallen, James, 69–71, 160, 170, 171, 172, 177–81, 183, 190, 282n6
"The Cather Connection in Alice Munro's 'Dulse'" (Stich), 276n12
Cather, Willa, 6, 10–13, 90, 106, 113, 115–31, 134, 138–42, 169, 177, 202, 212, 227, 261, 274n3, 276n12, 280n15, 280n1
Charman, Caitlin J., 257
Cheever, John, 143
Chekhov, Anton, 134, 210, 225, 230, 256
Clinton, ON, 2, 3, 155, 222
Close, Ann, 16, 261
Cohen, Matt, 46
The Collected Poetry of W. H. Auden (Auden), 8
"Connection: A Woman's Place in the Writings of Emily Carr, Willa Cather, Margaret Laurence, and Alice Munro" (Thacker), 7
Conron, Brandon, 246
Contemporary Literature, 170
Controlling the Uncontrollable: The Fiction of Alice Munro (Carrington), 17, 94, 101–9, 248
Cox, Ailsa, 255, 282n1
Critical Inquiry, 91–92

D

Dahlie, Hallvard, 65–66, 246
Dance of the Sexes: Art and Gender in the Fiction of Alice Munro (Rasporich), 22, 94–95
D'Angelo, Peter, 154, 192, 280n8
"'Daringly Out in the Public Eye': Alice Munro and the Ethics of Writing Back (McGill), 254
Daughters and Mothers in Alice Munro's Later Stories (Heller), 255
Davey, Frank, 91–92, 95
Davies, Robertson, 45–46, 50
Dawson, Anthony B., 246
"Deconstructing Silence: The Mystery of Alice Munro" (Miller), 251–52
Deptford trilogy (Davies), 45
The Diviners (Laurence), 50
Dubliners (Joyce), 40
Duffy, Dennis, 146, 201, 257–58
Duncan, Chester, 9
Duncan, Isla, 10, 199, 282n1
Duncan, Sara Jeannette, 45

E

Eagleton, Terry, 136–37
Eakin, Paul John, 83–84
ECW Press, 112–14, 184, 275n6
Elliott, George, 46
Engel, Marian, 46
English-Canadian literature, 90–91
English-Canadian nationalism, 2
Essays on Canadian Writing, 112–13, 249
Eureka Studies in Teaching Short Fiction, 255
Evans, Walker, 142–43

F

Faulkner, William, 263
Figuring Grief: Gallant, Munro, and the Poetics of Elegy (Smythe), 175–76
"The Fiction of Alice Munro" (Dahlie), 246
The Fiction of Alice Munro (Hooper), 282n1
Fitzpatrick, Margaret Anne, 67
Folio, 9, 23
Forceville, Charles, 250
Foy, Natalie, 151, 250
Franzen, Jonathan, 241
Freake, Douglas, 33–34, 137, 148, 279n.7
Fremlin, Gerald, 2, 154–55
Frye, Northrop, 4, 95, 179, 273n4

G

Gadpaille, Michelle, 93, 96, 101, 109, 275n6, 276n9
Gallant, Mavis, 89–90, 96, 105, 111, 176
Gardiner, Jill, 13, 28, 35, 40, 51–52, 73, 82, 136, 186, 271n3, 272n9, 272n6
Gardiner, Judith Kegan, 126, 278n10
Garson, Marjorie, 250
"A Genius of Sour Grapes" (*Wingham Advance-Times*), 49
Gerlach, John, 257
Gibson, Douglas, 16, 228, 252, 282n2
Gibson, Graeme, 50, 203
Gilbert, Sandra and Susan Gubar, 135–36, 276n10
Giller Prize, 145
Gittings, Christopher E., 250
giving up writing, 243
Glover, Douglas, 252, 257–59
God's Country and My People (Morris), 142
Godard, Barbara, 67–68
Gold, Joseph, 66–67, 276n14
The Golden Apples (Welty), 138, 280n9
Governor-General's Award, 15, 21, 145
Grand Manan, NB, 11, 115–16, 118, 121, 123, 129–30, 141, 273n3
The Great Prairie Fact and Literary Imagination (Thacker), 7, 8
"Gulfs and Connections: The Fiction of Alice Munro" (York), 279n2
Gunn, Janet Varner, 81, 84

H

Hancock, Geoff, 46
"'Hanging Pictures Together': *Something I've Been Meaning to Tell You*" (Martin), 69–70
Hardwick, Elizabeth, 137
Harper's 228, 229, 244
Heble, Ajay, 170, 173, 176, 179, 183, 248, 282n6
"'Heirs of the Living Body': Alice Munro and the Question of a Female Aesthetic" (Godard), 67–68
Heller, Deborah, 151, 255
Hemingway, Ernest, 256
Hick, Granville, 227
Henighan, Stephen, 227–28
Hogg, James, 253
home place, 80, 117, 140, 161, 177, 189, 191–93, 195, 202–3, 208–9, 216, 222, 258, 282n1
The Home Place (Morris), 142, 273n2
Hooper, Brad, 282n1
Horwood, Harold, 68
"The House of Willa Cather" (Welty), 139
Housman, A. E., 6–7, 12
Houston, Pam, 146–47, 186, 205, 249
"How I Write" (Welty), 138–39, 157–58
"How to Write Like Alice Munro" (Aubrey), 252
Howells, Coral Ann, 89–90, 97–98, 101, 173, 248, 249, 250, 254, 282n1
Hoy, Helen, 245, 247, 281n3
Hunter, Adrian, 253–54
Huron County, ON, 2, 3, 5, 7, 14, 22, 76, 80, 146, 154, 158, 165, 177, 181, 189, 202–5, 208, 216, 222, 226, 230, 258, 263, 279n6
Hutcheon, Linda, 93, 96, 98–100, 101

I

The Imperialist (Duncan), 45
"An Inner Bell that Rings: The Craft of Alice Munro" (Miller), 251
Introducing Alice Munro's Lives of Girls and Women (Besner), 184–85, 248
"The Invisible Iceberg" (Tener), 68
Irish heritage, 4, 5, 180, 198, 212, 217–26, 279–80n8
Irvine, Lorna, 100, 272n3, 273n1

J

James, Henry, 253, 256
Jewett, Sarah Orne, 117, 177, 277n4
Journal of Canadian Fiction , 246
Journal of Canadian Studies, 113, 190, 248
Journal of Narrative Theory, 257
Joyce, James, 40, 68, 135, 256

K

Kafka, Franz, 256
Kamboureli, Smaro, 276n11
Kovalevsky, Sophia, 230
Kroetsch, Robert, 100–101

L

Laidlaw, Anne Chamney, 211–15, 263–64, 269–70
Laidlaw, Robert Eric, 211–15, 263–64, 269
Laidlaw, William, 219
Lamont-Stewart, Linda, 68–69
Laurence, Margaret, 50, 65, 97, 279n2
Leacock, Stephen, 45, 50
Lecker, Robert, 91–92, 95, 151, 250
"L'écriture du secret/Writing Secrets" (*Open Letter*), 254
"Leda and the Swan" (Yeats), 276n14
Levene, Mark, 251
Lewis, Edith, 115, 121, 127–28, 278n7, 277n1, 280n15
Lilienfeld, Jane, 253
Literary History of Canada, 274n1
literary influences, 113, 129, 133–43, 158, 278n1
The Lonely Voice (O'Connor), 272n2
Lorenz, Clarissa M., 130–31, 278n12

A Lost Lady (Cather), 117, 120–21, 126, 130–31, 141
Luft, Joanna, 253
Lynch, Gerald, 252

M

MacCulloch, Claire, 94
Macdonald, Rae McCarthy, 246, 273n4, 276n11
MacKendrick, Louis K. 17, 151, 172, 183–84, 186–88, 245, 283n2
Macmillan of Canada, 21, 228, 262
"A Madman Loose in the World: The Vision of Alice Munro" (Macdonald), 273n4, 276n11
Maitland River (Menesetung/Meneseteung), 12, 149, 190, 193, 203, 204, 205
Man Booker International Prize, 228, 244
Marchand, Philip, 228, 230, 256–57
Martin, W. R., 22, 69–70, 92, 116, 134, 246, 248, 273n1, 274n3, 279n2, 279n5
Maxwell, William, 113
Mayberry, Katherine J., 171, 245, 249, 281n3
Mazur, Carol and Cathy Moulder, 17, 244
McCaig, JoAnn, 151, 252–53
McClelland and Stewart, 228, 275n6
McClure's Magazine, 277n1, 277n4
McCombs, Judith, 201
McCullers, Carson, 134, 135
McGill, Robert, 254, 283n2
McGrath, Charles, 16, 231–33, 235, 242
McGraw-Hill Ryerson, 1, 228
McIntyre, Tim, 257
Melsom, Ryan, 257
Mendelson, Edward, 8
Messud, Claire, 243–44
metafictional techniques, 69, 84, 96, 100, 137, 148, 254, 258, 279n7, 282n2
Metcalf, John, 61, 81–82, 84, 134, 191, 207, 252, 273n23, 274n4
Micros, Marianne, 151

Miller, Judith, 17, 247, 251–52, 273n2
Miller, Karl, 250
"The Mind of Alice Munro" (Glover), 258
Modern Fiction Studies, 246
Monaghan, David, 246
Morgenstern, Naomi, 283n3
Montrealer, 245
Moodie, Susanna, 45
Morris, Wright, 8, 117, 135, 140, 142, 273n2
Mosaic, 246
Moss, John, 246
Mothers and Other Clowns: The Stories of Alice Munro (Redekop), 177, 181–83, 248
Munro, Alice Laidlaw
  Books (in publication order):
    Dance of the Happy Shades, 2, 10, 15, 21, 23, 25, 32–33, 35, 42–43, 51, 75, 76, 80, 84, 105, 135, 136, 159, 160, 164, 169, 172, 244, 245, 271n2, 271n6, 272n7, 272n8, 272n9, 274n11, 279n2
    stories "Boys and Girls," 14, 42, 75, 160; "Dance of the Happy Shades," 172; "Day of the Butterfly," 33–35, 43, 44, 175 (see "Good-by, Myra"); "Images," 42, 51, 70, 160, 163, 172, 175, 180, 191, 265, 271n2; "The Office," 81. 136, 274n4; "An Ounce of Cure," 36, 93; "The Peace of Utrecht," 10, 14, 42, 43, 53–64, 81, 153, 159, 160–61, 162, 164, 172, 191, 207; "Red Dress—1946," 14, 42, 75, 160, 191; "The Shining Houses," 75; "Thanks for the Ride," 29, 36–44, 51–52, 84, 172, 195–96, 272n5, 281n4; "The Time of Death," 35, 36, 107, 175; "A Trip to the Coast," 35; "Walker Brothers Cowboy," 42, 51, 102, 146, 160, 172, 175
    Lives of Girls and Women, 2, 42, 49, 50–51, 61, 67, 68, 75, 80, 82, 96–97, 98, 105, 108, 135, 157,

159, 160, 179, 184–85, 191, 243, 244, 245, 272n6, 273n4, 276n9, 276n14, 277n3, 279n2, 279n6

stories "Baptizing," 42, 172; "Changes and Ceremonies," 172; "Epilogue: The Photographer," 172; "The Flats Road," 51, 172; "Heirs of the Living Body," 51;

Something I've Been Meaning to Tell You: Thirteen Stories, 1, 43, 52, 61, 105, 150, 159, 160, 172, 175–76, 186–88, 279n2

stories "Material," 1, 2, 11, 12, 31, 43, 44, 70–71, 80, 87, 158, 160, 168, 169, 172–73, 175, 180–81, 184, 187–88, 193, 229, 254, 262, 267; "Memorial," 43, 175; "The Ottawa Valley," 12, 14, 43, 52–53, 58, 62, 84–86, 137, 148, 159, 160–62, 164, 172, 172, 183, 191, 208–9, 220–21, 270, 279n6; "Something I've Been Meaning to Tell You," 254; "Tell Me Yes or No," 175; "Winter Wind," 14, 159, 175, 191, 220

Who Do You Think You Are? / The Beggar Maid, 3, 9, 14, 15, 16, 21, 43, 50, 61, 67, 76, 80, 85, 98, 108, 136, 137, 154, 155, 156, 160, 185, 193, 206, 208, 209, 225, 243–44, 252, 276n9, 277n3, 279n2, 279n6, 280n8

stories "The Beggar Maid," 225, 231; "Privilege," 70; "Royal Beatings," 206, 231, 249; "Wild Swans," 108

The Moons of Jupiter, 3, 10, 15, 16, 17, 21, 50, 61, 66, 75, 84–85, 92, 106, 112, 116, 125, 142, 231, 247, 249, 262, 276n11, 277n5, 279n2, 279n3, 280n6

stories "Accident," 225; "Bardon Bus," 82–83, 112; "Chaddeleys and Flemings," 10, 12, 15, 62–64, 79–80, 85–87, 115–16, 119, 129, 134, 137, 141, 142, 154, 156–57, 164, 189, 191, 211, 216, 219, 231–32, 262, 276n11, 279n2, 280n16; "Dulse," 10–12, 81, 106–7, 113, 116–31, 134, 135, 141–42, 167–68, 170, 212, 215–16, 222, 261–62, 274n3, 277n5, 277n6, 278n8, 278n11; "Hard–Luck Stories," 249; "Labor Day Dinner," 257; "The Moons of Jupiter," 15, 47, 58, 81, 85, 96, 119, 148, 154, 164, 209, 249, 257, 262, 274n3; "The Turkey Season," 262

The Progress of Love, 4, 5, 13–14, 21, 73–77, 89, 97, 106, 133, 154, 170, 228, 232–33, 235, 251, 265, 267, 279n2

stories "Circle of Prayer," 74–75, 150, 170, 171, 194, 267; "Eskimo," 73-74, 76; "Fits," 107, 257; "Jesse and Maribeth," 75; "Lichen," 233; "Miles City, Montana," 77, 81, 193–94, 196, 225, 233; "Monsieur les Deux Chapeaux," 180; "The Moon in the Orange Street Skating Rink," 75, 233; "The Progress of Love," 74, 105, 113, 151, 153–54, 156–59, 165, 191, 195, 208, 211, 232–35, 242, 249, 277n2; "A Queer Streak," 75, 157; "White Dump," 4, 5, 198, 232–33, 235–42, 245

Friend of My Youth, 109, 111, 147, 151, 174, 250, 255, 279n2

stories "Friend of My Youth," 113, 146, 151, 153, 162–65, 208; "Goodness and Mercy," 92, 168–69; "Meneseteung," 12, 146–48, 150, 165, 172, 186, 204–5, 222, 226, 249, 257–59, 279n2, 283n3

Open Secrets, 111, 148, 151, 169, 250

stories "The Albanian Virgin," 111, 189, 208; "Carried Away," 111, 116–17, 147, 172, 196, 249, 250, 281n4; "Vandals," 249, 254; "A Wilderness Station," 148, 219, 253–54

Selected Stories, 111, 146, 173, 196, 221, 235

The Love of a Good Woman, 111, 145, 147, 150, 151–52, 154, 164, 173, 197, 250, 251 stories "The Children Stay," 146, 235, 249; "The Love of a Good Woman," 9, 42–43, 146, 154, 163, 197, 201–2, 205–7, 226, 235, 249, 254–55, 257; "My Mother's Dream," 152, 162, 235, 255, 283n3; "Rich as Stink," 164; "Save the Reaper," 249, 254

Hateship, Friendship, Loveship, Courtship, Marriage, 197

stories "The Bear Came Over the Mountain," 3, 15, 254; "Family Furnishings," 255; "Hateship, Friendship, Courtship, Loveship, Marriage," 15;

Runaway, 197, 241, 255, 270

stories "Chance," 15; Juliet Triptych, 197, 255; "Passion," 199; "Soon," 270

The View From Castle Rock (Rejected title *Power in the Blood*, 219), 5, 6, 15, 197–98, 219, 227, 232, 250, 264, 282n2

stories "Hired Girl," 148, 232; "Home" (1974), 10, 14, 101, 109, 113, 137, 148–50, 151–54, 159, 162, 164–65, 183, 191, 198, 208–9, 216, 219, 220, 232, 255, 270, 279n6 (revised) 197, 209; "The View From Castle Rock," 217–19, 221, 225; "What Do You Want to Know For?", 207; "Working for a Living," 10, 15, 186, 198, 205, 209–16, 219, 232, 264

Carried Away, 241, 244

Too Much Happiness, 5, 6, 198, 228–30, 262

stories "Face," 229; "Fiction," 229; "Too Much Happiness," 15, 228, 230; "Wenlock Edge," 6, 9; "Wood," 148, 198, 228, 262

New Selected Stories, 12

Dear Life, 6, 9, 13, 14, 22, 262, 263, 265, 267, 268–70

stories "Dear Life," 14, 263, 265, 267–70; "Dolly," 15; "The Eye," 14, 269; "Finale" (section), 6, 9, 13, 14, 22, 264, 267–70; "Leaving Maverley," 265–67; "Night," 14, 269; "Train," 9; "Voices," 14, 269

uncollected stories "At the Other Place," 25–27, 29, 31, 38; "A Better Place Than Home," 219, 222–26, 279–80n8; "Changing Places," 219; "Characters," 246; "The Dimensions of a Shadow," 23; :The Edge of Town," 28–29, 35, 38, 50–52, 61–62; "The Ferguson Girls Must Never Marry," 47; "Good–by, Myra" ("Day of the Butterfly"), 29–34, 36, 38, 43–44; "The Idyllic Summer," 25; "Story for Sunday," 9, 24–25, 27; "The Widower," 23

other published writings "Author's Commentary," 36; "1847: The Irish," 219, 222, 224, 226; "Everything Here is Touchable and Mysterious," 12, 145, 149–50, 177–78, 181, 185, 190, 203–4, 206; "Good Woman in Ireland," 217, 226; "What is Real?", 185, 206, 232

manuscript material "The Boy Murderer," 9; "Places at Home," 14, 142, 192–93, 222; "Suicide Corners," 154, 158; "Suicide Ladies," 155–56; "The War Hero," 9

Munro, James, 207

Munro, Jenny, 268

"Munro's Food" (Rooke), 276n11

My Ántonia (Cather), 7, 117, 121, 141, 280n16

My Mortal Enemy (Cather), 142

N

Narrative, 199

narrative pace, 48

narrative perspective, 24–25, 32, 43–44, 50, 76, 126

narrative techniques, 2, 23–24, 32, 39, 40–44, 48, 50, 83, 126

National Plots: Historical Fiction and Changing Ideas of Canada, 257
The Neglected Genre: The Short Story in Canada (MacCulloch), 94
New, William, 23, 246, 272n3
New York Review of Books, 243
New York Times Book Review, 241
New Yorker, 3, 6–7, 16–17, 21, 66, 92, 111, 116, 119, 123–25, 129, 145–47, 154, 157, 197, 201–2, 294, 210, 217, 218, 220, 228, 231, 233, 241, 244, 246, 252, 263, 265, 267, 270, 279n3
Nixon, Richard, 1
No Man's Land: The Place of the Woman Writer in the Twentieth Century (Gilbert and Gubar), 136, 141
Nobel Prize in Literature (2013), 2, 3, 6, 17, 198–99, 268, 283n2
Not Under Forty (Cather), 227
Nunes, Mark, 250–51

O

O. Henry Awards, 146
O Pioneers! (Cather), 7
Ober, Warren U., 151
O'Brien, Sharon, 141, 277n1, 277n4, 277n8, 278n8, 280n12, 280n15
O'Connor, Flannery, 134, 135
O'Connor, Frank, 272n2
The Old Beauty and Others (Cather), 115, 142
"Old Mrs. Harris" (Cather), 11, 277n2
Olney, James, 130–31, 278n12
Olsen Tillie, 142
"On Female Identity and Writing by Women" (Gardiner), 126, 278n10
"On Wenlock Edge the wood's in trouble" (Poem 31) (Housman), 6
"On your midnight pallet lying" (Poem 11) (Housman), 12
The One and the Many: English-Canadian Short Story Cycles (Lynch), 252
Only One Point of the Compass: Willa Cather in the Northeast (Brown and Crone), 278n7, 278n8

Ontario, 1, 2, 3–4, 7, 10, 14–15, 22, 36, 45–64, 76, 77, 79–81, 104, 142, 146, 148–49, 154, 189, 192–93, 197, 201–16, 222, 225, 226, 243, 250, 258, 263–65, 272n1, 273–74n2, 276n11, 279–80n8, 282n1
Open Letter, 246, 254
"Order From Chaos: Writing as Self Defense in the Fiction of Alice Munro and Clark Blaise" (Lamont-Stewart), 68–69
"Ordinary Outsiders: A Symposium on Alice Munro" (*Virginia Quarterly Review*), 255
Osachoff, Margaret Gail, 274n4
"'The Other Side of Daliness': The Paradox of Photography in Alice Munro's Fiction" (York), 280n17
Ozick, Cynthia, 228, 261–62
The Other Country: Patterns in the Writing of Alice Munro (Carscallen), 160, 171, 172, 177–81, 183, 190

P

Packer, Miriam, 246, 272–73n1, 273n4
Patterson, Freeman, 251
Perreaux, Les, 268
Pfaus, B., 247, 248, 272n1, 274n3
"Phillis, Or, The Progress of Love" (Swift), 233
"Place in Fiction" (Welty), 48–49
Ploughshares, 246
Polley, Sarah, 254
Porter, Katherine Anne, 143
A Portrait of an Artist as a Young Man (Joyce), 68, 135
"Postmodern 'Piercing': Alice Munro's Contingent Ontologies" (Nunes), 250–51
Preface to *Country of the Pointed Firs* by Sarah Orne Jewett (Cather), 140
Price, Reynolds, 134, 135

Private and Fictional Worlds: Canadian Women Novelists of the 1970s and 1980s (Howells), 89–90, 94, 97–98, 248
The Private Memoirs and Confessions of Justified Sinner (Hogg), 253–54
Prize Stories 1997, 146, 154
Probable Fictions (MacKendrick), 17, 21, 65, 151, 247, 249, 262, 272n5, 274n3
"The Problem with Alice Munro" (Marchand), 228, 256–57
The Professor's House (Cather), 11, 123
"'Projection' in Alice Munro's *Something I've Been Meaning to Tell You*" (Fitzpatrick), 67
Prose, Francine, 241

R

Rasporich, Beverly J., 22, 94–95, 101–3, 107, 109, 169, 182, 272n1, 275n4, 276n10, 276n11, 279n4
Reading Alice Munro in Italy, 254, 255
Reading Like a Writer (Prose), 241
Reaney, James, 46
Redekop, Magdalene, 93, 145, 151, 171, 177, 182–83, 186, 188, 233, 245, 248, 250, 251, 275n4, 282n5
Reid, Verna, 45
The Rest of the Story: Critical Essays on Alice Munro (Thacker), 112–13, 249, 255
"Rhyming Action in Alice Munro's Stories" (Bucholt), 252
"The Rival Bards: Alice Munro's *Lives of Girls and Women* and Victorian Poetry" (York), 277n14
Robson, Nora, 67, 68
Rooke, Constance, 276n11
Ross, Catherine Sheldrick, 113, 154–55
Roughing It in the Bush (Moodie), 45
Roy, Gabrielle, 68
Ryerson Press, 228

S

scholarship on Canadian subjects published in the United States, 275–76n7
Scurr, Ruth. 12
Schorer, Mark, 271n4
setting and character, 15, 24–25, 28–29, 33, 35–37, 48, 51–52, 56–62, 76, 116, 209, 271n4, 272n5, 272n7
Shawn, William, 231
"The Shining House: A Group of Stories" (Carscallen), 70
A Shropshire Lad (Housman), 6, 12
Sir Gawain and the Green Knight, 253
Skaggs, Merrill Maguire, 117
Sleepless Nights (Hardwick), 137
Slopen, Beverly, 276n13
Smythe, Karen, 170, 175–76, 179, 183
"Some Highly Subversive Activities" (Struthers), 273n4, 276n8
"Some Notes on River Country" (Welty), 205
Some Other Reality: Alice Munro's Something I've Been Meaning to Tell You (Mackendrick), 172, 183–84, 186–88, 248
The Song of the Lark (Cather), 7, 90, 107, 278n8
Spengemann, William, 81
Stainsby, Mari, 273n3
Stelzig, Eugene L. 81
Stich, Klaus P., 116, 134, 141, 253, 276n12, 280n1
Strayed, Cheryl, 252
Stories from Ontario (Warkinton), 272n1
Struthers. J. R. (Tim), 50, 61, 67, 69, 84, 96, 134, 246, 272n4, 272n5, 273n4, 276n8, 280n17
Studies in Canadian Literature, 246
Studies in Short Fiction, 246, 247
Surfacing (Atwood), 3
Sub/Version: Canadian Fictions by Women (Irvine), 100
Swift, Jonathan, 233
Survival: A Thematic Guide to Canadian Literature (Atwood), 3, 4

T

Tamarack Review, 1, 169
Tausky, Thomas, 81
Tener, Jean F., 68
Tennyson, Alfred, Lord, 134
Times Literary Supplement, 228
Today, 49
"'Treacheries of the Heart': Memoir, Confession, and Meditation in the Stories of Alice Munro' (Osachoff), 274n4
Trevor, William, 133, 134, 243
Trilling, Lionel, 227
The Tumble of Reason: Alice Munro's Discourse of Absence (Heble), 173–74, 176, 248

U

Ulysses (Joyce), 68
University of Calgary Archives (*Alice Munro Fonds*), 5, 7–8, 18, 66, 68, 112, 116, 136, 139, 151, 158–59, 168, 192–96, 210, 222, 253, 273n1
University of Manitoba, 3, 9, 18
University of Ottawa, 22, 113, 199
University of Toronto (Department of English), 282n5
University of Vermont, 261
University of Waterloo, 1, 2, 3, 10, 21, 65, 247, 262
University of Western Ontario, 1, 264

V

Ventura, Héliane, 255
"Vindication for a Lifetime of Short Stories" (Perreaux), 268
Virginia Quarterly Review 197, 255

W

W. W. Norton, 16
Ware, Tracy, 202, 257–58
Warkentin, Germaine, 272n1
Weaver, John, 151, 203, 250
Weaver, Robert, 195, 281n4
Weekend Magazine, 12
Welty, Eudora, 28, 48–49, 113, 129, 134, 135, 138–39, 145, 157, 205, 280n9, 280n1
"What is Style?" (Gallant), 89–90, 105
"Who Reads Alice Munro?" (Metcalf), 252
"The Wild Swans at Coole" (Yeats), 276n14
Willa Cather: The Emerging Voice (O'Brien), 277n4, 278n8, 280n12, 280n5
Willa Cather: A Literary Life (Woodress), 277n4, 280n10
Willa Cather and the Politics of Criticism (Acocella), 12
Willa Cather Living (Lewis), 277n1
Winesburg, Ohio (Anderson), 210
Wingham, ON, 1 81, 189, 263, 264, 265
Wingham *Advance-Times*, 49
Woodress, James, 277n4, 280n10
Woolf, Virginia, 98, 253
World Literature Written in English, 246
Writer's Chronicle, 252
Writing In: Alice Munro's Archives (McCaig), 253

Y

Yeats, William Butler, 90, 108, 134, 276n14
York, Lorraine, 134, 272n1, 277n14, 279n2

www.ingramcontent.com/pod-product-compliance
Lightning Source LLC
Chambersburg PA
CBHW070751230426
43665CB00017B/2331